Lab Manual for MCITP Guide to Microsoft® Windows Server® 2008, Server Administration (Exam #70-646)

Michael Palmer

COURSE TECHNOLOGY
CENGAGE Learning™

Australia • Brazil • Japan • Korea • Mexico • Singapore • Spain • United Kingdom • United States

COURSE TECHNOLOGY
CENGAGE Learning™

**Lab Manual for MCITP Guide to Microsoft®
Windows Server® 2008, Server Administration
(Exam #70-646)**
Michael Palmer

Vice President, Career and Professional Editorial:
Dave Garza

Executive Editor: Steve Helba

Acquisitions Editor: Nick Lombardi

Managing Editor: Marah Bellegarde

Senior Product Manager: Michelle Ruelos
Cannistraci

Editorial Assistant: Sarah Pickering

Vice President, Career and Professional
Marketing: Jennifer Ann Baker

Marketing Director: Deborah S. Yarnell

Senior Marketing Manager: Erin Coffin

Associate Marketing Manager: Shanna Gibbs

Production Director: Carolyn Miller

Production Manager: Andrew Crouth

Content Project Manager: Brooke Greenhouse

Art Director: Jack Pendleton

Cover photo or illustration: Shutterstock

Manufacturing Coordinator: Amy Rogers

Compositor: PreMediaGlobal

For product information and technology assistance, contact us at
Cengage Learning Customer & Sales Support, 1-800-354-9706

For permission to use material from this text or product,
submit all requests online at **cengage.com/permissions**
Further permissions questions can be emailed to
permissionrequest@cengage.com

Microsoft® is a registered trademark of the Microsoft Corporation.

Library of Congress Control Number: 2010923240

ISBN-13: 978-1-4239-0282-9

ISBN-10: 1-4239-0282-3

Course Technology
20 Channel Center Street
Boston, MA 02210
USA

Cengage Learning is a leading provider of customized learning solutions with
office locations around the globe, including Singapore, the United Kingdom,
Australia, Mexico, Brazil, and Japan. Locate your local office at:
international.cengage.com/region

Cengage Learning products are represented in Canada by Nelson Education, Ltd.

For your lifelong learning solutions, visit **course.cengage.com**
Visit our corporate website at **cengage.com.**

Some of the product names and company names used in this book have been
used for identification purposes only and may be trademarks or registered
trademarks of their respective manufacturers and sellers.

Microsoft and the Office logo are either registered trademarks or trademarks
of Microsoft Corporation in the United States and/or other countries. Course
Technology, a part of Cengage Learning, is an independent entity from the
Microsoft Corporation, and not affiliated with Microsoft in any manner.

Any fictional data related to persons or companies or URLs used throughout
this book is intended for instructional purposes only. At the time this book was
printed, any such data was fictional and not belonging to any real persons or
companies.

Course Technology and the Course Technology logo are registered trademarks
used under license.

Course Technology, a part of Cengage Learning, reserves the right to revise this
publication and make changes from time to time in its content without notice.

The programs in this book are for instructional purposes only. They have been
tested with care, but are not guaranteed for any particular intent beyond
educational purposes. The author and the publisher do not offer any warranties or
representations, nor do they accept any liabilities with respect to the programs.

Printed in the United States of America
1 2 3 4 5 6 7 12 11 10 09 10

Contents

INTRODUCTION   v

CHAPTER ONE   **Introduction to Windows Server 2008**   **1**
Lab 1.1 Determine System Information to Aid with Deployment Planning   2
Lab 1.2 Determine Windows Server 2008 Networking Capabilities for Deployment Planning   5
Lab 1.3 Access Administrative Tools   7
Lab 1.4 Turn on Network Discovery   10
Lab 1.5 Obtain a MAC Address   12

CHAPTER TWO   **Installing Windows Server 2008**   **15**
Lab 2.1 Determine Windows Server 2008 Features That Can Be Installed   16
Lab 2.2 Configure Windows Server 2008 Ease of Access Options   18
Lab 2.3 Activate a Server and Install Upgrades   21
Lab 2.4 Use the System Configuration Tool   24

CHAPTER THREE   **Configuring the Windows Server 2008 Environment**   **27**
Lab 3.1 Configure Windows Server 2008 Services   28
Lab 3.2 Configure Taskbar Options   31
Lab 3.3 Configure Driver Updates, Remove Unused Programs, and Check Installed Updates   33
Lab 3.4 Configure a Network Interface Card   36

CHAPTER FOUR   **Introduction to Active Directory and Account Management**   **41**
Lab 4.1 Examine Active Directory Objects   42
Lab 4.2 Explore Active Directory Management Tools   45
Lab 4.3 Configure an Active Directory Audit Policy   51
Lab 4.4 Manage a User Account's Security Issues   54

CHAPTER FIVE   **Configuring, Managing, and Troubleshooting Resource Access**   **59**
Lab 5.1 Install the File Services Role with the Windows Search Service   60
Lab 5.2 Use File Server Resource Manager   63
Lab 5.3 Manage Shared Drives, Folders, and Files   66
Lab 5.4 Install Subsystem for UNIX-based Applications   71

CHAPTER SIX   **Configuring Windows Server 2008 Printing**   **75**
Lab 6.1 Install the LPR Port Monitor for UNIX/Linux Printing   76
Lab 6.2 Install a Shared Printer Using the Print Management Tool   79
Lab 6.3 Create a Printer Filter and Manage Print Jobs with the Print Management Tool   82
Lab 6.4 Troubleshoot a Print Spooler Problem   85

CHAPTER SEVEN   **Configuring and Managing Data Storage**   **89**
Lab 7.1 View the Properties of a Disk   90
Lab 7.2 Shrink a Disk Volume and Rescan Disks   93
Lab 7.3 Install Storage Manager for SANs   96
Lab 7.4 Schedule a Backup and Configure Backup Performance   98

CHAPTER EIGHT   **Managing Windows Server 2008 Network Services**   **101**
Lab 8.1 Configure IPv6   102
Lab 8.2 Create a DNS Stub Zone, Forwarder, and Root Hint   106
Lab 8.3 Configure DNS Round Robin and Netmask Ordering, and Troubleshoot a DNS Problem   109
Lab 8.4 Troubleshoot a DHCP Server Problem   112

CHAPTER NINE   **Deploying IIS and Active Directory Certificate Services**   **117**
Lab 9.1 Manage IIS Application Pools   118
Lab 9.2 Install the Certification Authority Web Enrollment Role Service and Learn How to Modify Values
    for Web Enrollment Pages   121
Lab 9.3 Manage a CA Server and Configure CA Auditing   124
Lab 9.4 Configure a CRL Publication Interval   127

CHAPTER TEN   **Configuring Remote Access Services**   **129**
   Lab 10.1 Configure Network Address Translation (NAT)   130
   Lab 10.2 Troubleshoot a VPN Server Problem   132
   Lab 10.3 Configure a RADIUS Server   136
   Lab 10.4 Install the TS Gateway and TS Web Access Role Services   140

CHAPTER ELEVEN   **Windows Server 2008 Virtualization**   **143**
   Lab 11.1 Configure Virtual Machine Hardware   144
   Lab 11.2 Add a Virtual Hard Disk and Edit a Virtual Hard Disk   147
   Lab 11.3 Manage Hyper-V Settings   151
   Lab 11.4 Take a Snapshot of a Virtual Machine   155

CHAPTER TWELVE   **Application and Data Provisioning**   **159**
   Lab 12.1 Install the Windows Process Activation Service (WAS) Support Role Service   160
   Lab 12.2 Configure TS RemoteApp Settings   163
   Lab 12.3 Configure Programs That Can Be Run Through TS RemoteApp   166
   Lab 12.4 Enable Offline Files   168

CHAPTER THIRTEEN   **Securing Windows Server 2008**   **171**
   Lab 13.1 Configure Default Domain Security Policies   172
   Lab 13.2 Configure Registry Security   176
   Lab 13.3 Install Health Registration Authority and Host Credential Authorization   178
   Lab 13.4 Configure a Health Registration Authority Network Policy   183

CHAPTER FOURTEEN   **Server and Network Monitoring**   **187**
   Lab 14.1 Use Task Manager to Monitor a Server   188
   Lab 14.2 Use Resource Monitor   191
   Lab 14.3 Use Performance Monitor to Evaluate Paging File and Memory Performance   194
   Lab 14.4 Use Performance Monitor to Evaluate Disk Performance   197

CHAPTER FIFTEEN   **Managing System Reliability and Availability**   **201**
   Lab 15.1 Use the Enable Boot Logging Option   202
   Lab 15.2 Change the DSRM Password and Access DSRM   204
   Lab 15.3 Configure Shadow Copies   207
   Lab 15.4 Use Network and Sharing Center to Diagnose a Connection Problem   210

INDEX   213

Introduction

The purpose of *Lab Manual for MCITP Guide to Microsoft® Windows Server® 2008, Server Administration (Exam #70-646)* is to offer hands-on activities to help you prepare for the Microsoft Certified IT Professional (MCITP) Exam #70-646 Pro: Windows Server 2008, Server Administrator. The Lab Manual is designed to accompany the Course Technology book, *MCITP Guide to Microsoft® Windows Server® 2008, Server Administration (Exam #70-646)*. The Lab Manual provides hands-on activities not found in *MCITP Guide to Microsoft® Windows Server® 2008, Server Administration (Exam #70-646)*. The hands-on activities in the Lab Manual give readers even more in-depth preparation for Exam #70-646. The Lab Manual is also intended to provide further experience in server administration.

The chapters in the Lab Manual parallel the same chapters in *MCITP Guide to Microsoft® Windows Server® 2008, Server Administration (Exam #70-646)*. The most effective way to use these combined learning resources is to first read a chapter in *MCITP Guide to Microsoft® Windows Server® 2008, Server Administration (Exam #70-646)* and complete the hands-on activities in that chapter. Next, complete the hands-on activities for the same chapter in the Lab Manual.

The hands-on activities in the Lab Manual can be completed in a classroom, in a computer lab, and individually. Most of the activities can be completed on a virtual machine, such as in Microsoft Hyper-V, or on a physical computer that is not configured as a virtual machine. The hands-on activities are suitable for both "on-ground" and online learning environments.

Intended Audience

Lab Manual for MCITP Guide to Microsoft® Windows Server® 2008, Server Administration (Exam #70-646) is intended for people who want to prepare for Exam #70-646 and become a Windows Server 2008 administrator. The focus is to give new and experienced readers hands-on activities to help them learn in depth the core technologies and features of Windows Server 2008. No prior server operating system experience is required, but it is helpful to have some prior experience with a Windows operating system, such as Windows 7, Vista, or XP.

Features

This Lab Manual includes the following features to provide an optimal learning experience:

- *Certification Exam Objectives*—For each chapter, the relevant Exam #70-646 objectives are listed.
- *Lab Objectives*—The learning objectives and goals of each lab are stated at the beginning of the lab.
- *Materials Required*—Every lab includes information about the Windows Server 2008 software setup needed to complete the lab.
- *Estimated Completion Time*—Every lab contains an estimated completion time, to help students effectively organize their lab time.
- *Activity Background*—The Activity Background information provides important details for each lab and places the lab activity within the context of the learning objectives.
- *Step-by-Step Instructions*—The hands-on activities in each lab are presented through clear step-by-step instructions.
- *Figures*—All labs include screen captures to help reinforce the lab activity steps.
- *Review Questions*—Review questions that reinforce your understanding of the completed activity are provided at the end of each lab.

System Requirements

Hardware

- Listed in the Windows Server Catalog of Tested Products or has the Certified for Windows Server 2008 sticker
- 1 GHz CPU or faster for an x86 computer or 1.4 GHz CPU or faster for an x64 computer (2 GHz or faster is recommended)
- 512 MB RAM or more (for x86 and x64 computers), but 2 GB or more is recommended
- 15 GB or more disk space (for x86 and x64 computers)
- DVD-ROM drive
- Super VGA or higher resolution monitor
- Mouse or pointing device
- Keyboard
- Network interface card connected to the classroom, lab, or school network for on-ground students—or Internet access (plus a network interface card installed) for online students
- Printer (to practice setting up a network printer)

Software

Windows Server 2008 Standard or Enterprise Edition (included with the DVD in the book, *MCITP Guide to Microsoft® Windows Server® 2008, Server Administration (Exam #70-646)*.

Virtualization

Windows Server 2008 can be loaded into a virtual server or workstation environment, such as Microsoft Hyper-V, Microsoft Virtual PC 2007, Microsoft Virtual Server, or VMware Server or Workstation.

Lab Setup

Only one Windows Server 2008 Standard or Enterprise Edition installation is needed for the activities in the Lab Manual. The installation can be on a physical server or in a virtual machine on a virtual server. Specific lab setup requirements for Windows Server 2008 are listed in the Materials Required section of each lab. Before you start a chapter in this book, first complete the hands-on activities for the same chapter in the parent book, *MCITP Guide to Microsoft® Windows Server® 2008, Server Administration (Exam #70-646)*.

Acknowledgments

I want to thank Nick Lombardi the Acquisitions Editor for Course Technology/Cengage Learning for his interest in this book. I'm especially grateful to Senior Product Manager Michelle Ruelos Cannistraci for her tireless efforts in guiding this book through all stages to completion. My thanks also go to Jill Batistick and John Bosco for their thorough work as Development Editors. Thanks additionally go to Brooke Baker for managing the production phase of the book. John Bosco and his Green Pen Quality Assurance staff have played a key role by providing technical editing and quality assurance services.

Introduction to Windows Server 2008

Labs included in this chapter:

- Lab 1.1 Determine System Information to Aid with Deployment Planning
- Lab 1.2 Determine Windows Server 2008 Networking Capabilities for Deployment Planning
- Lab 1.3 Access Administrative Tools
- Lab 1.4 Turn on Network Discovery
- Lab 1.5 Obtain a MAC Address

Microsoft MCITP Exam #70-646 Objectives

Objective	Lab
Planning for Server Deployment	1.1, 1.2, 1.3, 1.4, 1.5
Planning for Server Management	1.3, 1.4, 1.5

Lab 1.1 Determine System Information to Aid with Deployment Planning

Objectives

- Open the System Information window
- Determine information about existing servers or clients that can be used for deployment planning

Materials Required

This lab requires the following:

- Windows Server 2008 Standard or Enterprise Edition (*Note*: If you don't have access to Windows Server 2008 pre-installed in a lab or other location because you wait to install Windows Server 2008 until the next chapter, you can also perform this activity using either Windows Vista or Windows 7 for practice.)

Estimated completion time: **20 minutes**

Activity Background

As you plan to deploy Windows Server 2008, it is useful to determine the types of computers (and their capabilities) that are already connected to the network. What hardware and operating systems are already installed? Are servers already running Windows Server 2008? What hardware and software resources are used on existing servers? What clients are connected to the network, such as Windows Vista and Windows 7?

The following activity introduces you to the System Information tool available in Windows Server 2008 (as well as in Windows 7 and Windows Vista). The System Information tool enables you to determine system information about a computer including hardware resources, components, and the software environment. This information can help you survey computer resources as a way to assist in planning for Windows Server 2008 deployment. For example, consider a network that already has a computer running Windows Server 2008, Standard Edition. You might use the System Information tool to verify the server operating system and its resources to help you decide whether to add an additional server or upgrade the current server to Windows Server 2008, Enterprise Edition. The tool can also help you decide whether to add new hardware. For this activity, you need access to an account on a computer running Windows Server 2008. If you don't have access to Windows Server 2008, you can also perform the activity using Windows Vista or Windows 7 to practice obtaining information about clients on a network (the steps are the same as for Windows Server 2008).

Throughout the activities in this book, you may occasionally see the User Account Control box with a message that Windows needs your permission to continue. Whenever you see this box, click Continue. Keep this in mind for all of the activities because any interaction with the User Account Control box is not included in the steps.

Activity

1. Log on to Windows Server 2008, Windows Vista, or Windows 7.
2. Click **Start**, point to **All Programs**, and click **Accessories**.
3. Click **System Tools**.
4. Click **System Information**.
5. The System Information window opens, displaying the System Summary specifics in the right pane, such as the OS Name (see Figure 1-1). Review the system information in the right pane.

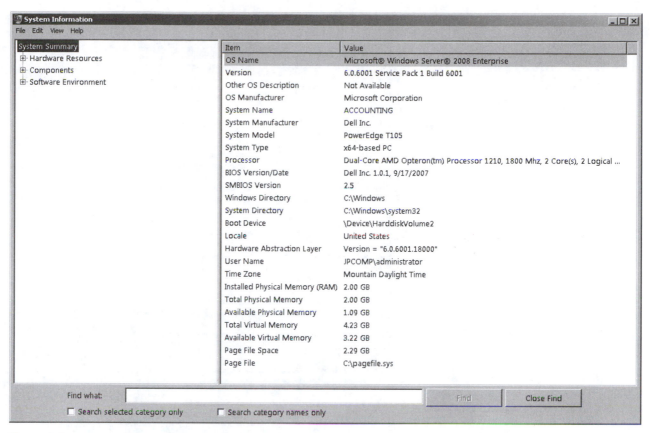

Figure 1-1   System Information window in Windows Server 2008

6. In the tree in the left pane, click the + plus sign in front of **Hardware Resources**.

7. In the tree in the left pane, click each of the following under Hardware Resources and view its associated information in the right pane:

   • **Conflict/Sharing** (see Figure 1-2)

   • **DMA**

   • **Forced Hardware**

   • **I/O**

   • **IRQs**

   • **Memory**

8. In the tree in the left pane, click the + plus sign in front of **Components**.

9. In the left pane, click each of the following under Components to view the corresponding information in the right pane:

   • **CD-ROM**

   • **Display**

   • **Printing**

   • **USB**

10. Under Components in the left pane, click the + plus sign in front of each of the following to view the hardware information that can be displayed for each category:

   • **Network**

   • **Ports**

   • **Storage**

11. In the left pane, click the + plus sign in front of **Software Environment**.

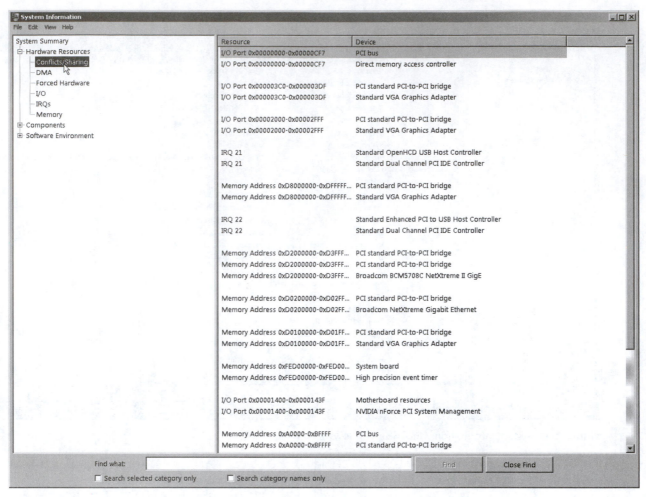

Figure 1-2   Viewing Conflict/Sharing information for the hardware resources

12. Under Software Environment in the left pane, click **Running Tasks** to view a list of tasks in the right pane that are running in Windows Server 2008.

13. In the left pane under Software Environment, click **Startup Programs** to view in the right pane the programs that start when you start Windows Server 2008.

14. Close the System Information window.

Review Questions

1. The _____ item for the System Summary in the System Information window enables you to determine the Windows Server 2008 edition that is installed.

2. Under which of the following categories in the System Information window would you find information about the network protocol in use?

    a. Hardware Resources → I/O

    b. System Summary

    c. Components → Network

    d. Software Environment → Environment Variables

3. You are planning to deploy a new Windows Server 2008 server that implements the same startup programs as on a Windows Server 2008 server that is already in service. What category of information within the System Information window enables you to determine the startup programs configured on the server that is already in operation?

   a. Components → Multimedia

   b. Hardware Resources → DMA

   c. System Summary

   d. Software Environment → Startup Programs

4. True or False? The System Information window provides information about how much physical memory, or RAM, is installed in a computer.

5. The _____ category in the System Information window enables you to determine the number of hard drives and CD/DVD drives that are connected to a computer.

Lab 1.2 Determine Windows Server 2008 Networking Capabilities for Deployment Planning

Objectives

- Understand general Windows Server 2008 networking capabilities
- Learn how to use the Windows Help and Support feature

Materials Required

This lab requires the following:

- Windows Server 2008 Standard or Enterprise Edition

Estimated completion time: **15 minutes**

Activity Background

Networking technology is always growing and changing to accommodate more options and to ensure stronger security. For example, multicasting is used more and more as the number of multimedia applications grows. Similarly, new wireless capabilities and security measures are being implemented for fast communications and enhanced security. And IPv6 is growing in use as more organizations recognize its advantages. In this activity, you access an overview of information about Windows Server 2008 networking capabilities that can help you plan how to deploy the operating system.

Activity

1. Click **Start** and click **Help and Support**.

2. If necessary, resize or maximize the Windows Help and Support window. Notice the topics about which you can find information.

3. Under Server Fundamentals, click **Networking** (see Figure 1-3).

4. Read the overviews for: TCP/IP, routing, remote access, network monitoring, and network access and security.

5. Close the Windows Help and Support window.

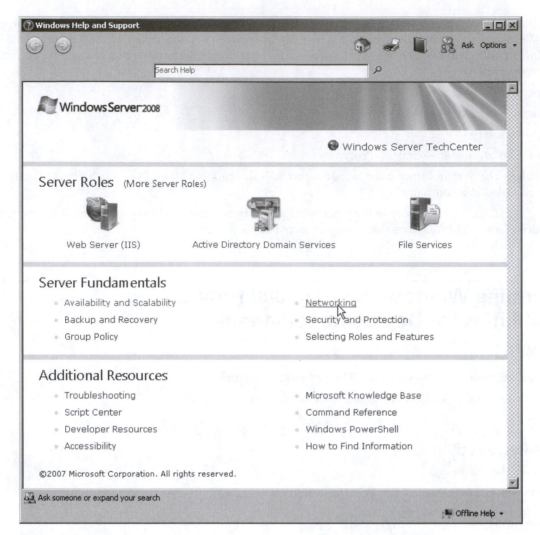

Figure 1-3   Windows Help and Support window

Review Questions

1. Windows Server 2008 supports TCP/IP with Internet Protocol versions _____ and _____.

2. Most network traffic from individual users is _____.

   a. unicast

   b. onecast

   c. multicast

   d. broadcast

3. In a deployment planning meeting, one of the managers in your company asks you whether Windows Server 2008 supports remote access solutions. Which of the following solutions do you mention? (Choose all that apply.)

   a. Dial-up remote access

   b. Routed remote access

   c. Telnet

   d. Virtual private networks

4. As you are planning deployment, you are considering wireless access. Which of the following security options does Windows Server 2008 support for both wireless and wired network connections?

    a. RFC 3522

    b. 802.1X

    c. Telnet

    d. TechNet

5. For essential network and Internet security, Windows Server 2008 offers _____ with Advanced Security.

Lab 1.3 Access Administrative Tools

Objectives

- Access the Administrative Tools menu
- Start administrative tools
- Use the Run option as an alternative for starting an administrative tool

Materials Required

This lab requires the following:

- Windows Server 2008 Standard or Enterprise Edition

Estimated completion time:	15 minutes

Activity Background

Windows Server 2008 offers a wide range of tools for the server administrator. For example, tools are provided to manage various Active Directory functions, Domain Name System (DNS), Dynamic Host Configuration Protocol (DHCP) Services, Hyper-V, and much more. To simplify access to the administrative tools, Microsoft has grouped many tools in one place—on the Administrative Tools menu. One of the most important tasks that you should learn when first deploying and administering a server is what is on the Administrative Tools menu and how to access the menu.

Another important lesson when first starting out is that many administrative functions can be accessed in more than one way. In this lab, you learn how to access the Administrative Tools menu in different ways. You also have an opportunity to survey the many tools on the Administrative Tools menu. An important factor to remember in this lab is that the tools on the menu can vary somewhat from server to server. This is because there is a base set of tools—such as Computer Management, Event Viewer, and Services—and additional tools that are added to the menu when you install new server roles, such as Active Directory Domain Services and Hyper-V. For this activity, log on using an account that has administrator privileges.

Activity

1. Click **Start** and point to **Administrative Tools** (see Figure 1-4; notice that there are tools for Active Directory, because Active Directory is installed on this particular server).

Figure 1-4   Opening the Administrative Tools menu

2. Survey the tools on the menu.

3. Click **Computer Management** on the menu. Notice that the Computer Management tool can be used to access the following:

- *System Tools*—such as Task Scheduler and Device Manager

- *Storage*—for managing disk storage

- *Services and Applications*—to manage server services, such as for printing, and for specific software applications

4. Close the Computer Management window.

5. Click **Start**, point to **All Programs**, and click **Administrative Tools**. Notice that the menu of tools now appears within the Start menu.

6. Click **Event Viewer**. The Event Viewer window enables you to view event logs so that you can track down specific events that have occurred on a server, such as a problem with an application or a security problem.

7. Close the Event Viewer window.

8. Click **Start** and click **Control Panel**.

9. If the Classic View is not displayed, click **Classic View** in the left portion of the Control Panel window.

10. Double-click **Administrative Tools** in the Control Panel window.

11. Double-click **Server Manager** in the right pane. Server Manager is one of the most powerful administrative tools because it unites many administrative capabilities into one tool. From Server Manager you can install server roles, install features, view the contents of event logs, configure the Windows Firewall, and accomplish many other administrative tasks.

12. Close the Server Manager window and the Administrative Tools window.

13. Besides the Administrative Tools menu, it is useful to know that you can start many administrative tools from the Start menu Run option. Click **Start** and click **Run**.

14. In the Open box within the Run dialog box, type **servermanager.msc** and click **OK** (see Figure 1-5) to open Server Manager.

15. Close the Server Manager window.

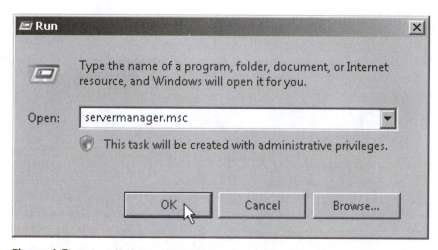

Figure 1-5   Using the Run option to open Server Manager

Review Questions

1. Which of the following are tools available from the Administrative Tools menu? (Choose all that apply.)

   a. Component Services

   b. Event Viewer

   c. Reliability and Performance Monitor

   d. Services

2. Which of the following are ways in which to open the Administrative Tools menu? (Choose all that apply.)

   a. Right-click the taskbar and click Administrative Tools.

   b. Click Start and click Administrative Tools.

   c. Click Computer and point to Administrative Tools in the left pane.

   d. Click Start, point to All Programs, and click Administrative Tools.

3. When you click Computer Management in the Administrative Tools menu _____.

   a. the Computer Management window opens

   b. the Computer Management menu is displayed

   c. you see options to shutdown the computer, lock the computer, log off, switch users, or start Task Manager

   d. Task Manager is started from which to manage services, tasks, and logged on users

4. True or False? The Administrative Tools menu contains the exact same list of tools on all Windows Server 2008 servers, regardless of what roles and features are installed.

5. True or False? When you have memory problems, the Administrative Tools menu contains the Memory Diagnostics Tool that enables you to test for memory problems.

Lab 1.4 Turn on Network Discovery

Objectives

- Turn on network discovery
- Learn where to enable file and printer sharing

Materials Required

This lab requires the following:

- Windows Server 2008 Standard or Enterprise Edition (*Note*: If you don't have access to Windows Server 2008 preinstalled in a lab or other location because you wait to install Windows Server 2008 until the next chapter, you can also perform this activity using Windows Vista or Windows 7 for practice.)

> Estimated completion time: **10 minutes**

Activity Background

Both peer-to-peer and server-based networking are primarily effective if network discovery and other network and resource sharing options are turned on in Windows Server 2008. Network discovery enables network computers and devices, such as printers, configured using TCP/IP to be visible to other computers and devices on the same network. Other network capabilities that can be turned on to complement network discovery are file sharing, public folder sharing, and printer sharing. Turning on these capabilities enables a Windows Server 2008 network to be well utilized. You learn more about sharing files and shared printers in Chapter 5, "Configuring, Managing, and Troubleshooting Resource Access," and Chapter 6, "Configuring Windows Server 2008 Printing."

In this activity, you use the Network and Sharing Center to ensure that network discovery is turned on. You also learn where to enable file sharing, public folder sharing, and printer sharing. If you don't have access to Windows Server 2008, you can also perform the activity using Windows Vista or Windows 7 to practice obtaining information about clients on a network (the steps are the same as for Windows Server 2008 and Windows Vista, but somewhat different for Windows 7). Log on using an account that has administrator privileges.

Activity

1. In Windows Server 2008 and Windows Vista, click **Start** and click **Network**. If you are using Windows 7, click **Start**, click **Computer**, and click **Network** in the tree in the left side of the Network window.

2. Click **Network and Sharing Center** near the top of the Network window.

3. In Windows Server 2008 or Windows Vista, look for the Sharing and Discovery section of the window. Click the down arrow for **Network discovery** (see Figure 1-6). In Windows 7, click **Change advanced sharing settings** in the left pane of the Network and Sharing Center window.

4. Ensure that the option button is selected for **Turn on network discovery**; if it is not, click it and then click **Apply**.

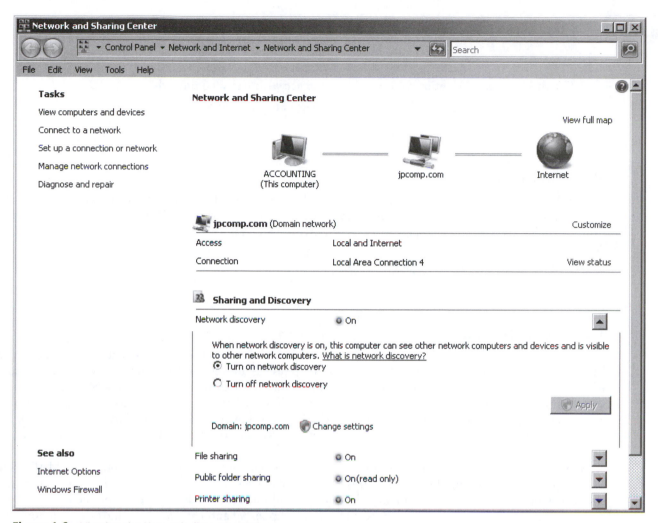

Figure 1-6 Viewing the Network discovery settings

5. Notice that you can also configure file sharing, public folder sharing, and printer sharing in the Network and Sharing Center window. (File and printer sharing are combined in Windows 7 and there are other Windows 7 options that can be configured, such as Media streaming. Also, additional options may be present in Windows Server 2008 and Windows Vista, depending on the upgrades that have been implemented.)

6. Close the Network and Sharing Center window in Windows Server 2008 or Windows Vista. If you are using Windows 7, close the Advanced sharing settings window.

7. Close the Network window, if it is still open.

Review Questions

1. You have just installed a server running Windows Server 2008 on a server-based network, but no users can see the server on the network to connect to it. Which of the following might be the problem in Windows Server 2008?

   a. IP sharing is not configured.

   b. Active Directory is not installed to support IPv6.

   c. UDP forwarding is disabled.

   d. Network discovery is turned off.

2. You can use the _____ tool to enable sharing a printer connected to Windows Server 2008.

3. The _____ tool enables you to turn on public folder sharing in Windows Server 2008.

Lab 1.5 Obtain a MAC Address

Objectives

- Use the Command Prompt window to execute network-based commands
- Obtain the MAC address of a computer connected to a network

Materials Required

This lab requires the following:

- Windows Server 2008 Standard or Enterprise Edition (*Note*: if you don't have access to Windows Server 2008 preinstalled in a lab or other location because you wait to install Windows Server 2008 until the next chapter, you can also perform this activity using Windows Vista or Windows 7 for practice.)

Estimated completion time: **10 minutes**

Activity Background

Network interfaces, including the network interface card (NIC) in a server or a client computer, are identified by both an IP address, such as 192.168.1.22, and a physical address or media access (MAC) address, such as 00-19-D2-4A-07-0B. The MAC address is programmed or "burned" into the NIC. Each NIC has a unique MAC address, just as each house in a town has a unique address. When one computer communicates with another computer on a network, it must know the MAC address of the computer with which it is communicating, as well as the IP address. A computer can use the Address Resolution Protocol (ARP) through network tools to determine another computer's MAC address.

As you work with servers and networks, it can be invaluable to know how to obtain the MAC address of another computer. Linking the MAC address with an IP address can be a great aid for using network trouble-shooting software, such as when you are identifying a malfunctioning NIC in a server or client computer. In this activity, you use the Command Prompt window and the *ipconfig* and *getmac* commands to learn how to obtain a MAC address. If you don't have access to Windows Server 2008, you can also perform this activity using Windows 7 or Windows Vista. You can log onto any type of account for this activity.

Activity

1. In Windows Server 2008, Windows Vista, or Windows 7 click **Start**, point to **All Programs**, and click **Accessories**.

2. Click **Command Prompt** under Accessories.

3. At the command prompt, type **ipconfig** and press **Enter** (see Figure 1-7).

4. The *ipconfig* utility enables you to determine the IP address of your computer, which is 192.168.0.72 in Figure 1-7. Find the IPv4 address for your computer in the Command Prompt window and record the address.

5. At the command prompt, type **getmac /s** plus your IPv4 address, such as *getmac /s 192.168.0.72* and press **Enter**.

6. The *getmac* command displays the MAC address of your computer's NIC under the Physical Address column. In Figure 1-8, the MAC address is 00-1E-C9-47-6B-09. (Note that if your computer has more than one NIC or is hosting a virtual connection, then more than one MAC address is displayed.)

7. Close the Command Prompt window.

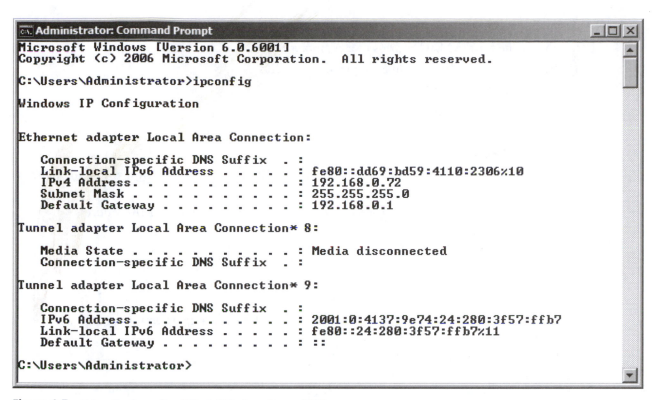

Figure 1-7   Using the *ipconfig* utility in Windows Server 2008

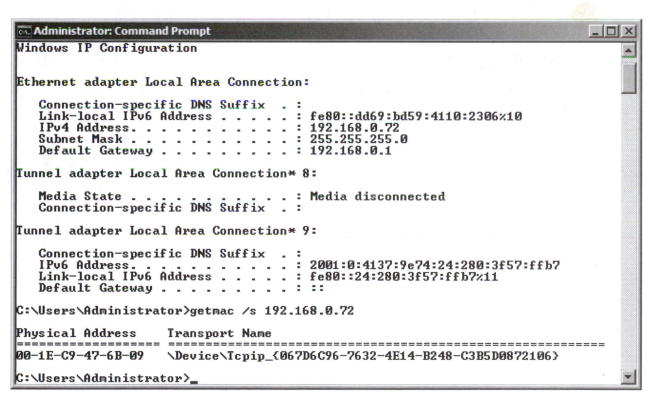

Figure 1-8   Using the *getmac* utility in Windows Server 2008

Review Questions

1. Another name for the MAC address of a computer is the _____ address.

2. The address 192.142.10.54 is an example of _____.

   a. a MAC address for a NIC

   b. a subnet mask address

   c. an IPv4 address

   d. a proxy address

3. Use the _____ command line tool to find IP address information for your Windows-based computer.

4. Which of the following protocols is used to determine another computer's MAC address?

   a. TCP

   b. ARP

   c. IP

   d. UDP

5. Use the _____ command to obtain the MAC address of a remote computer on a network.

INSTALLING WINDOWS SERVER 2008

Labs included in this chapter:

- Lab 2.1 Determine Windows Server 2008 Features That Can Be Installed
- Lab 2.2 Configure Windows Server 2008 Ease of Access Options
- Lab 2.3 Activate a Server and Install Upgrades
- Lab 2.4 Use the System Configuration Tool

Microsoft MCITP Exam #70-646 Objectives

Objective	Lab
Planning for Server Deployment	2.1, 2.2, 2.3, 2.4
Monitoring and Maintaining Servers	2.3, 2.4

Lab 2.1 Determine Windows Server 2008 Features That Can Be Installed

Objectives

- Use the Initial Configuration Tasks tool
- Determine what features can be installed in Windows Server 2008

Materials Required

This lab requires the following:

- Windows Server 2008 Standard or Enterprise Edition

Estimated completion time: **15 minutes**

Activity Background

Part of planning a Windows Server 2008 deployment is understanding the features that can be installed and deciding which are needed for a deployment. Before you bring a server live, it is important to plan what roles the server will play and which features to use for these roles. A server role represents a principal function of a server, such as establishing a file or print server. (You focus on installing roles in Chapter 3, "Configuring the Windows Server 2008 Environment" in *MCITP Guide to Microsoft Windows Server 2008, Server Administration [Exam #70-646]*.) Features are functions used to enhance or extend the capabilities of a server or the server environment, such as BitLocker drive encryption or the ability to set up a failover cluster of servers for redundancy.

In the following activity, you use the Initial Configuration Tasks tool to survey the Windows Server 2008 features that can be installed. The Initial Configuration Tasks tool displays each time you log on as Administrator, unless you check the box labeled *Do not show this window at logon* (not recommended until after you are comfortable with other management tools). Windows Server 2008 features can also be installed using Server Manager, which is a tool you learn to use in Chapter 3.

For all of the activities in this chapter, you'll need to log on to an account with administrator privileges. You can complete these activities using either Windows Server 2008 Standard or Enterprise Edition. Additionally, most of these activities can be completed on a virtual server or computer, such as in Hyper-V.

Throughout the activities in this book, you may occasionally see the User Account Control box with a message that Windows needs your permission to continue. Whenever you see this box, click Continue. Keep this in mind for all of the activities because any interaction with the User Account Control box is not included in the steps.

Activity

1. Log on and wait for the Initial Configuration Tasks window to be displayed. Maximize the window if necessary.

2. Scroll down to find the section titled "Customize This Server."

3. Click **Add Features**.

4. The Select Features window in the Add Features Wizard displays the features that can be installed (see Figure 2-1).

5. Notice that *.NET Framework 3.0 Features* is highlighted and that there is a description of this feature in the right side of the window. Read the description for .NET Framework 3.0. As you'll learn in Chapter 12, "Application and Data Provisioning," .NET Framework 3.0 is a feature that you are required to install when you install the application server role.

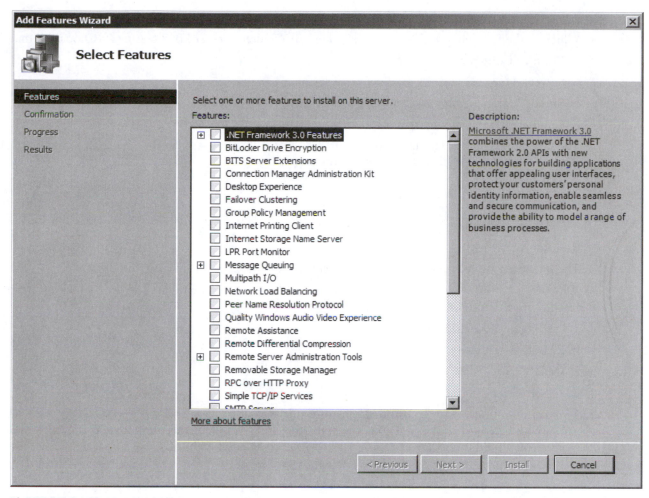

Figure 2-1 Select Features window

6. In the Features box, click each of the following and read the associated description to learn the purpose of that feature:
   - **BitLocker Drive Encryption**
   - **Failover Clustering**
   - **Internet Printing Client**
   - **LPR Port Monitor**
   - **Remote Assistance**
   - **Remote Server Administration Tools**
   - **SMTP Server**
   - **Wireless LAN Service**

7. Click any other features of interest to you and read their descriptions.

8. In the Select Features window, click **Cancel** to close the window.

9. Click **Yes** to verify that you want to close the wizard.

10. Minimize the Initial Configuration Tasks window.

Review Questions

1. Which of the following tools can be used to install Windows Server 2008 features? (Choose all that apply.)

   a. Features Configuration tool

   b. Server Manager

   c. Initial Configuration Tasks tool

   d. Computer Management tool

2. The LPR Port Monitor feature is commonly used to enable print services for _____ computers that are Windows Server 2008 clients. (Choose all that apply.)

   a. UNIX-based

   b. Pentium-based

   c. AMD processor-based

   d. Storage network

3. The BitLocker drive encryption feature protects data by _____ an entire disk volume.

4. When your server needs to transfer e-mail messages between different e-mail servers, which of the following features would you install to support this activity?

   a. Peer Name Resolution Protocol

   b. Remote Assistance

   c. SMTP Server

   d. Telnet Server

5. You are planning to set up applications on multiple file servers and the applications must have high availability because they are mission critical to your organization. To accommodate this need for high availability, you would install the _____ Windows Server 2008 feature.

Lab 2.2 Configure Windows Server 2008 Ease of Access Options

Objectives

- Understand the Ease of Access Center options for server deployment
- Start the Ease of Access Center tool
- Configure Ease of Access Center settings to enable direct accessibility

Materials Required

This lab requires the following:

- Windows Server 2008 Standard or Enterprise Edition

Estimated completion time: **20 minutes**

Activity Background

As you are planning a server deployment, it is important to take into account the needs of any server administrators or operators who have physical disabilities, visual impairment, hearing impairment, cognitive disabilities, or language disabilities. Windows Server 2008 offers the Ease of Access Center (which replaces Accessibility Options in Windows Server 2003) to help set up a server for direct accessibility for all employees. For example, some administrators or operators may have uncontrolled movements or suffer from arthritis. Others may be color blind or have legal blindness. Still others may need hearing assistance or have learning disabilities.

In this activity, you learn how to open the Ease of Access Center and configure options to help make a server more directly accessible.

Activity

1. Click **Start** and click **Control Panel**.

2. Click **Classic View** in the left side of the Control Panel window, if you are not already in the classic view, which displays icons or applets that you can select.

3. In the Control Panel window, double-click **Ease of Access Center** to display the Ease of Access Center window (see Figure 2-2). (Another way to open the Ease of Access Center is to press the Windows key on your keyboard and the letter u simultaneously.) Maximize the window, if necessary.

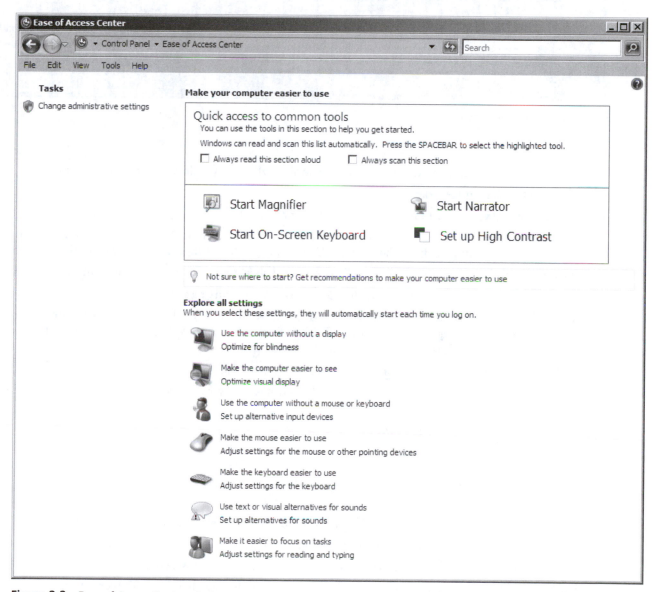

Figure 2-2   Ease of Access Center window

4. Click **Start Magnifier** in the Ease of Access Center window and move your cursor around to view how the magnifier tool can magnify a section of the screen.

5. If the **Magnifier** dialog box is not placed on top of the Ease of Access Center window so you can view it, click its button in the taskbar.

6. Review the options that can be configured in the Magnifier dialog box, such as the ability to set the scale factor (which is 2x by default).

7. Close the Magnifier dialog box, which should also close the magnifier.

8. If necessary, maximize the Ease of Access Center window and click **Start On-Screen Keyboard** to view the On-Screen Keyboard that you can navigate with a pointing device (see Figure 2-3).

Figure 2-3 On-Screen Keyboard

9. Use your pointing device to move the **On-Screen Keyboard** window around the desktop.

10. Close the On-Screen Keyboard window.

11. Click **Start Narrator** in the Ease of Access Center window.

12. In the Microsoft Narrator dialog box, notice the explanation that: "Narrator will read aloud what is on-screen as you navigate using the keyboard." Also notice the settings that you can configure for Narrator.

13. Click **Exit** in the Microsoft Narrator dialog box and click **Yes** to verify that you want to exit Narrator.

14. In the Ease of Access Center window, click **Set up High Contrast**.

15. In the Make the computer easier to use window, review the settings that you can configure for high contrast, such as configuring ALT + left Shift + PRINT SCREEN to toggle high contrast on or off. Also, notice that you can turn on Narrator and Magnifier from this window.

16. Click **Cancel** in the Make the computer easier to use window.

17. In the Ease of Access Center window, review the settings that you can configure as listed under Explore all settings.

18. Close the Ease of Access Center window.

Review Questions

1. How can you open the Ease of Access Center?

   a. Click Ease of Access Center in the Initial Configuration Tasks window.

   b. Click Add features in the Initial Configuration Tasks window.

   c. Click Start, point to Administrative Tools, and click Ease of Access Center.

   d. Click Start, click Control Panel, click Classic View, and double-click Ease of Access Center.

2. People who have impaired vision can make portions of the screen larger for viewing by using the _____.

3. One of the server administrators has severe arthritis in her left hand, but she can work the mouse without pain in her right hand. She can turn on the _____ to enable her to perform keyboard functions with the mouse.

4. Which of the following can be configured using the Ease of Access Center? (Choose all that apply.)

   a. Adjust settings for reading and typing.

   b. Adjust startup type for brightness and colors.

   c. Set up alternative key positions on the keyboard.

   d. Optimize for blindness.

5. True or False? The Ease of Access Center can be configured to audibly echo a user's keystrokes for users with a visual impairment.

Lab 2.3 Activate a Server and Install Upgrades

Objectives

- Activate a server after it is installed
- Use Windows Update to obtain current Windows Server 2008 updates

Materials Required

This lab requires the following:

- Windows Server 2008 Standard or Enterprise Edition and a connection to the Internet

Estimated completion time: **20–30 minutes**

Activity Background

After Windows Server 2008 is installed, it is important to activate the server operating system. Activation is an additional step beyond providing the product key to help verify that this copy of the operating system is legitimate. Activation also ensures that the product key is used with only one software license. There is a grace period of 60 days within which to activate Windows Server 2008. If you go beyond the grace period, there is a message that continues to display a warning that you have exceeded the grace period.

Also, in some cases, if you significantly upgrade or replace the server hardware—such as by replacing the CPU, adding CPUs, or changing the motherboard—Windows Server 2008 may display an activation warning and you'll have only a few days to reactivate the operating system.

In addition to activating the server, it is a good idea to manually check for any available operating system updates from Microsoft after you install a server. Installing updates in a timely fashion can help close security holes and fix potential problems before you encounter them. However, for some updates, such as a new service pack, consider waiting for several months after it is released so that others can find any flaws and Microsoft can fix them before you install the service pack.

In this activity, you learn how to activate your server and you install updates. Your server will need to have access to the Internet for the activity. Also, for some updates, you may have to reboot the computer.

Activity

1. Click **Start**, right-click **Computer**, and click **Properties** to open the System window (see Figure 2-4).

2. Click the link to **Activate Windows now** under the Windows activation section of the System window (in part of the link, you'll see the number of days left in which to activate Windows Server 2008).

3. In the Windows Activation window, click **Activate Windows online now**.

4. Enter the product key for your operating system and click **Next**.

5. In the Windows Activation window, you'll see the message "Activation was successful." Click **Close**.

6. Return to the System window. Under Windows activation, you'll see "Windows is activated."

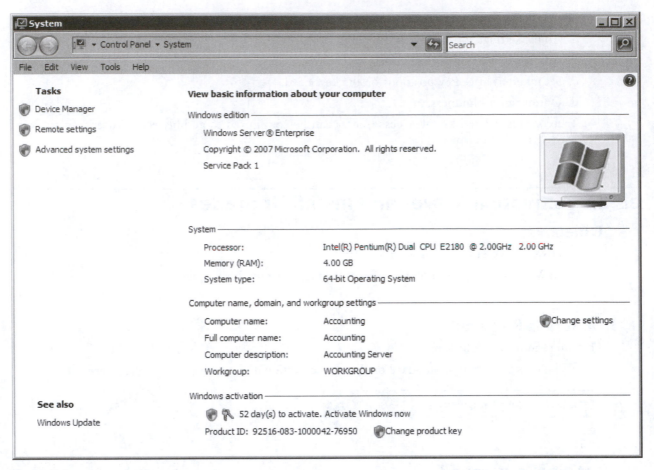

Figure 2-4   System window

7. In the left side of the System window near the bottom, click the link for **Windows Update**. (You can also open Windows Update from the Initial Configuration Tasks window, Server Manager, or Control Panel Classic view.)

8. In the Windows Update window, if automatic updating is not turned on click **Turn on now**. (Automatic updating should already be turned on from Activity 2-5 in *MCITP Guide to Microsoft Windows Server 2008, Server Administration [Exam #70-646].*) If you have to click Turn on now, Windows Server 2008 may commence obtaining updates and you may be able to skip Step 9. Also, Windows Update may determine that you need to install new Windows Update software before you can perform an actual update. If so, click **Install now** to install the new Windows Update software.)

9. If your server has not recently checked for updates, you'll see a box with a shield and a red x inside the shield with the message "Check for updates for your computer" (see Figure 2-5). If your server has previously checked for updates and obtained them, but has not installed them, you'll see a box with a gold shield and an exclamation point inside and the message "Install updates for your computer" (see Figure 2-6). Regardless of what you see, click **Check for updates** in the upper-left side of the Windows Update window.

10. The process of checking for updates may take several minutes.

11. Click the **Install updates** button in the Windows Update window. Some updates may require that you accept the license terms. If so, click **I accept the license terms** and click **Finish**.

12. After the updates are installed, you'll see "The updates were successfully installed." If you see the **Restart now** button, make sure that any work is saved and click the button.

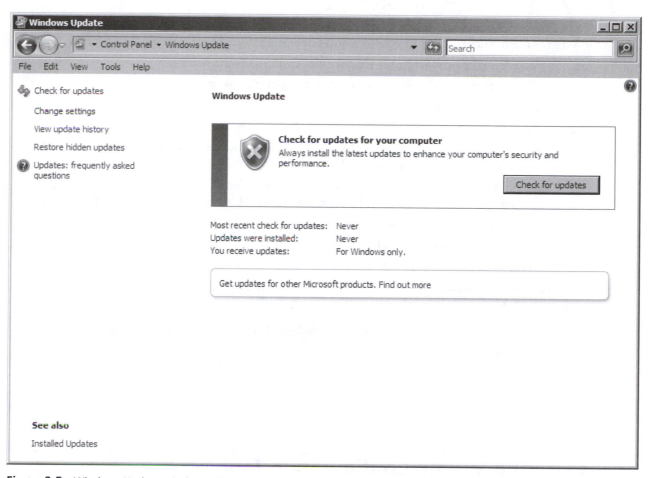

Figure 2-5   Windows Update window with a message to check for updates

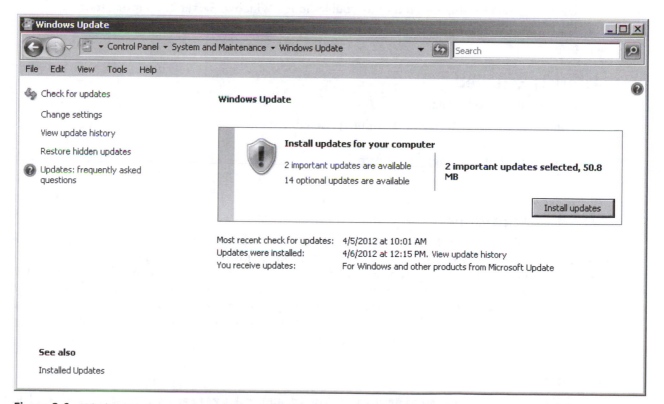

Figure 2-6   Windows Update window with a message that there are updates to install

Review Questions

1. What is the purpose of activating a Windows operating system? (Choose all that apply.)

   a. To make sure the product key is used with only one software license.

   b. To validate that this is a legitimate copy of the operating system.

   c. To initiate the software updates counter.

   d. To burn the Windows product key into the computer's BIOS.

2. True or False? If there are updates that have already been downloaded but not installed, you'll see a message about this when you open Windows Update.

3. You have been assigned to work on a server that was installed yesterday by another server administrator, but you're not sure if Windows Server 2008 has been activated. Which of the following enables you to find this out?

   a. Right-click the Start button and click Help.

   b. Right-click the taskbar and click Properties.

   c. Open the System window.

   d. Open the Activation tool from the Administrative Tools menu.

4. When you install Windows updates, be prepared to _____ the computer.

5. From which of the following can you start Windows Update? (Choose all that apply.)

   a. Server Manager

   b. Control Panel

   c. System window

   d. Initial Configuration Tasks window

Lab 2.4 Use the System Configuration Tool

Objectives

- Use the System Configuration tool to troubleshoot a Windows Server 2008 installation
- Use the System Information tool to troubleshoot a Windows Server 2008 installation

Materials Required

This lab requires the following:

- Windows Server 2008 Standard or Enterprise Edition

Estimated completion time: **15 minutes**

Activity Background

If there is a problem with a Windows Server 2008 installation, one tool that you can use to help is the System Configuration tool. This tool enables you, among other things, to boot into a diagnostic or selective startup mode from which to find and isolate a problem. You can also use it to determine what Windows Server 2008 services are employed at startup, to view startup programs, and to access system tools including the System window.

In this activity, you open the System Configuration tool and explore its capabilities. Also, from the System Configuration tool, you open the System Information tool and use it for troubleshooting a Windows Server 2008 installation.

Activity

1. Click **Start**, point to **Administrative Tools**, and click **System Configuration** (see Figure 2-7). (Another way to start this tool is to click **Start**, click **Run**, type **msconfig** in the Open box, and click **OK**.)

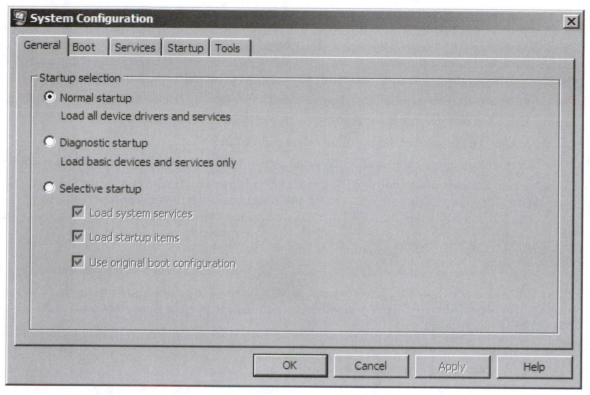

Figure 2-7   System Configuration tool

2. Ensure the **General** tab is selected.

3. Notice the three startup selections:

   - *Normal startup*—to start the server normally
   - *Diagnostic startup*—which launches essential services and drivers so that if one of these is corrupted, you can identify which one
   - *Selective startup*—which, in addition to starting essential services and drivers, enables you to specify other startup programs so you can determine if any of these are malfunctioning

4. Click the **Boot** tab.

5. Notice the available boot options:

   - *Safe boot*—which offers different safe boot options for diagnosing and fixing a server problem, including booting with minimal services with networking disabled, booting into the alternate shell (command prompt), booting into an interface from which to fix Active Directory, and booting with minimal services with networking enabled
   - *No GUI boot*—for booting without graphical services, such as windows
   - *Boot log*—for storing data about the boot process in a log to view later
   - *Base video*—for booting in a basic VGA video mode
   - *OS boot information*—which enables you to view drivers as they are being loaded during the boot process, in case there is a problem with a driver (such as for a disk drive)

6. Click the **Services** tab. The Services tab enables you to disable one or more services in case there is a problem with a service or it is corrupted. One approach is to click the Disable all button and then enable one service at a time until you find a service that is causing a problem. (Note that you will learn other, better tools for managing services. The System Configuration tool is primarily designed to identify a problem with a service.)

7. Use the scroll bar to view all of the services listed. Notice which services are running and which are stopped (in later chapters you'll learn about configuring services to automatically start at boot time).

8. Click the **Startup** tab. This tab lists programs that are automatically started when the server is booted. On a new installation, there are likely to be no programs listed or only a few. After you have installed many programs, consider revisiting the System Configuration tool. When programs are installed, they often add an element or feature that is listed under startup programs. If your server is slow to boot, consider disabling unneeded startup programs. You can always manually start such a program as needed after the server is booted.

9. Click the **Tools** tab. The Tools tab lists a range of tools that you can launch and use to fix a server problem.

10. Use the scroll bar to survey the tools that can be started from the Tools tab.

11. Click **System Information** on the Tools tab and click **Launch**.

12. In the System Information window, click the + plus sign in front of **Hardware Resources** in the left pane.

13. In the System Information window, click **Conflicts/Sharing** under Hardware Resources in the left pane. Scroll through the right pane to see if any resource conflicts are reported (refer to Figure 1-2 in Chapter 1). As you learned in Activity 1.1 in Chapter 1, you can click any of the options under Hardware Resources for system information, which can also help in troubleshooting a hardware problem encountered with a Windows Server 2008 installation.

14. In the System Information window, click the + plus sign in front of **Software Environment** in the left pane.

15. In the left pane under Software Environment, click **Windows Error Reporting** and check the right pane for any detected errors. This is another place to look to help in troubleshooting a Windows Server 2008 installation problem.

16. Close the **System Information** window.

17. Close the **System Configuration** window.

Review Questions

1. Under which heading in the System Information tool can you find information about hardware resource conflicts?

   a. Software Environment

   b. Hardware Resources

   c. Loaded Modules

   d. Input

2. You are troubleshooting a possible problem with a hard drive driver just after installing Windows Server 2008. Which of the following options on the Boot tab of the System Configuration tool can help you watch as hardware drivers are loaded during boot up?

   a. OS boot information

   b. No GUI boot

   c. Safe boot: Minimal

   d. Hard boot

3. True or False? The Services tab in the System Configuration tool only shows services that are started.

4. You've just installed a program that performs virus checking in Windows Server 2008. Since you installed the program, it now seems that it takes five times as long for the server to boot, which is not a good situation when you need to reboot quickly to return the server for live use. To determine if the virus checker has installed a program or service that starts when the server is booted check the _____ or the _____ tabs in the System Configuration tool.

5. Which of the following can you use to open the System Configuration tool?

   a. System Information tool

   b. Control Panel Hardware and Sound option

   c. Component Services tool

   d. Administrative Tools menu

CONFIGURING THE WINDOWS SERVER 2008 ENVIRONMENT

Labs included in this chapter:

- Lab 3.1 Configure Windows Server 2008 Services
- Lab 3.2 Configure Taskbar Options
- Lab 3.3 Configure Driver Updates, Remove Unused Programs, and Check Installed Updates
- Lab 3.4 Configure a Network Interface Card

Microsoft MCITP Exam #70-646 Objectives

Objective	Lab
Planning for Server Deployment	3.1, 3.4
Planning for Server Management	3.1, 3.2, 3.3, 3.4

Lab 3.1 Configure Windows Server 2008 Services

Objectives

- View services that can be configured in Windows Server 2008 and learn about their purpose
- Configure a service

Materials Required

This lab requires the following:

- Windows Server 2008 Standard or Enterprise Edition

Estimated completion time: **20 minutes**

Activity Background

After Windows Server 2008 is booted, many services start and run in the background. Services are programs that perform specific functions. For example, there is a service to enable printing, a service for Windows Firewall, a service for Windows Update, a service that enables users to log on to a server, and an array of other services.

Some services are configured to start automatically when the server is booted while others start through manual intervention by a server administrator. In some cases, the server administrator needs to stop a service because it is not needed or to restart a service that has stopped or is hung. If an attacker or malicious software work their way into a server, a first line of defense may be to stop a malicious service. As you are learning to configure a server, it is important to learn how to configure and manage services because they play a fundamental role in server deployment and a server's ability to fulfill its purpose.

In this activity, you learn how to view services and how to configure them. This activity gives you an introduction to services management. In later chapters, you learn how to troubleshoot server problems by troubleshooting server services. You'll work more with services throughout *MCITP Guide to Microsoft Windows Server 2008, Server Administration (Exam #70-646)*.

For all of the activities in this chapter, you'll need to log on to an account with Administrator privileges. Additionally, most of these activities can be completed on a virtual server or computer, such as in Hyper-V.

Throughout the activities in this book, you may occasionally see the User Account Control box with a message that Windows needs your permission to continue. Whenever you see this box, click Continue. Keep this in mind for all of the activities because any interaction with the User Account Control box is not included in the steps.

Activity

1. Click **Start**, point to **Administrative Tools**, and click **Services** (see Figure 3-1). (An alternative is to open Server Manager, click the + plus sign in front of Configuration in the left pane, and click **Services**.)

2. Scroll to view all of the services.

3. Click **Background Intelligent Transfer Service**.

4. Read the description for the Background Intelligent Transfer Service.

5. Notice that the Status column shows that Background Intelligent Transfer Service is Started, which means that the service is running. Also, the Startup Type column shows that the service is set to Automatic, which means that it starts automatically when the server is booted.

6. Click **Diagnostic Service Host** and read its description.

7. By default, Diagnostic Service Host service is not started automatically at boot up, which is reflected by no entry in the Status column. The Startup Type for this service is Manual, which means the server administrator must intervene and start it (or open a program that starts it).

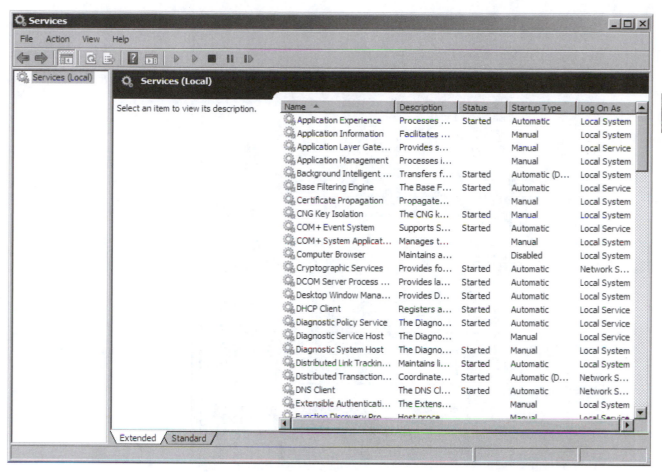

Figure 3-1   Services window

8. Find a service that has a Startup Type configured as Disabled. This Startup Type means that the service cannot be started unless the server administrator reconfigures it to Automatic or Manual.

9. Scroll to find the **Server** service and click it. Read the description for the Server service. This is a particularly important service because it enables file and printer sharing through the network.

10. Double-click **Extensible Authentication Protocol**, which is used for network authentication.

11. You see a **Properties** dialog box for this service, which enables you to configure the service (see Figure 3-2).

12. Click the **down arrow** for **Startup Type** and click **Automatic**. You have now configured this service to start automatically the next time the server is booted.

13. Assume that you need to have the Extensible Authentication Protocol service started now. For the Service status, notice that the service is currently Stopped. Click the **Start** button to start the service. Now notice that the Service status shows the service as Started.

14. Click the **Dependencies** tab. This tab shows the services that must also be running for the Extensible Authentication Service to run. The tab also shows any services that cannot run unless the Extensible Authentication Service is running, too.

15. Click **OK** in the Extensible Authentication Protocol Properties (Local Computer) dialog box.

16. In the Services window, notice that the Extensible Authentication Protocol service is now started and configured to start automatically.

17. Close the Services window.

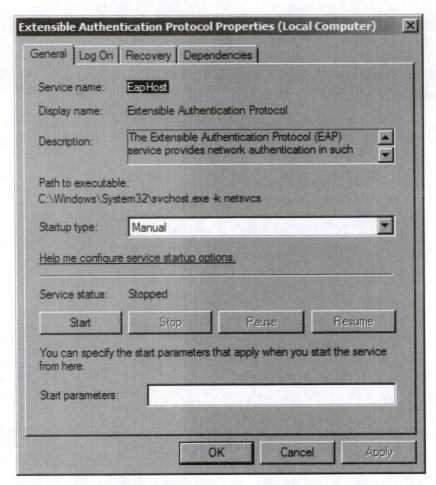

Figure 3-2 Extensible Authentication Protocol Properties (Local Computer) dialog box

Review Questions

1. When you connect a new printer to a computer running Windows Server 2008, the addition of the printer is not automatically recognized by the operating system. A possible problem might be that the Plug and Play service is _____.

2. While you are troubleshooting a problem using the System Configuration tool, you see a service you cannot identify. Which of the following tools enables you to view a description of a specific service?

   a. Server Manager under Features Summary

   b. Control Panel System applet

   c. Services tool on the Administrative Tools menu

   d. Command Prompt window by entering the name of the service and a question mark (?)

3. As the server administrator, you only want a particular service to start when you need to use it. To accomplish this, you can configure the service to start _____.

4. What is the function of the Diagnostic Service Host service?

   a. Enables diagnostics for detecting and solving problems with Windows components

   b. Enables a Microsoft technician to remotely access a Windows server to diagnose problems

   c. Starts Task Manager for finding problems

   d. Opens the Command Prompt troubleshooting window

5. True or False? One advantage of Windows Server 2008 is that no service depends on another service to be running.

Lab 3.2 Configure Taskbar Options

Objectives

- Configure the taskbar for customized administrator productivity
- Configure the Start menu for customized administrator productivity

Materials Required

This lab requires the following:

- Windows Server 2008 Standard or Enterprise Edition

Estimated completion time: **15 minutes**

Activity Background

You can be a more efficient server administrator when you configure your desktop for faster access to tools. One simple, but often omitted, step for easier management is to configure the taskbar. Configuring the taskbar enables you to put at your fingertips exactly the management features you need, which include:

- Taskbar presentation
- Start menu customizations
- Configuring the notification area or tray
- Configuring toolbars

In this activity, you learn how to configure all four taskbar capabilities.

Activity

1. Right-click an open area on the `taskbar` and click `Properties`. (An alternative is to click `Start`, click `Control Panel`, click `Classic View` (if necessary), and double-click `Taskbar` and `Start` menu.)

2. Four tabs are displayed in the Taskbar and Start Menu Properties dialog box: Taskbar, Start Menu, Notification Area, and Toolbars (see Figure 3-3).

3. Ensure that the `Taskbar` tab is selected.

4. Notice the options for customizing the behavior of the taskbar. For example, if your server has a relatively small monitor, you can increase the working area of the desktop by selecting *Auto-hide the taskbar*. This option makes the taskbar disappear unless you are pointing in the area of the taskbar.

5. Click `Auto-hide the taskbar` and click `Apply`. Notice that the taskbar disappears.

6. Move your pointer to the bottom of the display and notice that the taskbar reappears until you move the pointer away from it. Remove the `checkmark` from `Auto-hide the taskbar` and click `Apply` to undo your change.

7. Click the `Start Menu` tab in the Taskbar and Start Menu Properties dialog box.

8. Notice that Start menu is selected by default. If you select Classic Start menu, you can go back to the format of Start menus on earlier versions of Windows. Also notice that you can configure the Start menu to display recently opened files and recently opened programs, which can save you time if you frequently use certain files or programs.

9. Ensure `Start menu` is selected and then click the `Customize` button.

10. Use the `scroll bar` in the Customize Start Menu dialog box to see the options that you can select and notice which ones are configured by default. One way to help you quickly reach specific programs you use often is to select Favorites menu and configure links to frequently used programs, Web sites, or Web applications. Ensuring that Default Programs is selected is another way to configure quick access to frequently used programs, including third-party programs.

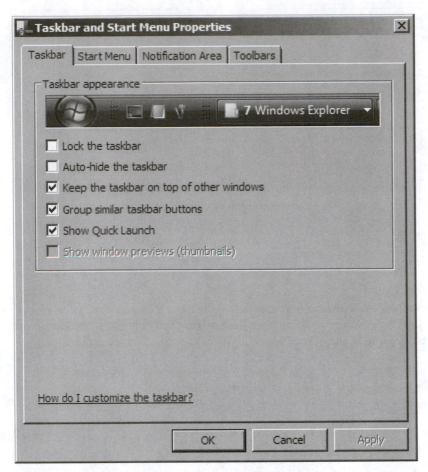

Figure 3-3 Taskbar and Start Menu Properties dialog box

11. On most systems, *Run command* is selected by default in the Customize Start Menu dialog box. This is because many server administrators like quick access to execute commands from the Start menu, such as the *msconfig* command you learned about in Lab 2.4. Another default selection is for the system administrative tools (Administrative Tools menu) to *Display on the All Programs menu and the Start menu*.

12. Click **OK** to close the Customize Start Menu dialog box.

13. Click the **Notification Area** tab in the Taskbar and Start Menu Properties dialog box.

14. On most systems *Hide inactive icons* is selected by default so that the notification area does not become cluttered. Notice you can also select whether to display the clock, volume control for speakers, and network icon to check the network connection status.

15. Click the **Toolbars** tab.

16. By default, the Quick Launch toolbar is selected, which is the toolbar just to the right of the Start button on the taskbar. The Quick Launch toolbar contains quick links to *Internet Explorer*, *Server Manager*, and *Show desktop*. Notice the additional toolbars you can add include Address, Links, and Desktop.

17. In the Toolbars tab, check the box for **Links** and click **Apply**. Notice the Links toolbar inserted just to the left of the notification area on the right side of the taskbar. You can customize the Links toolbar to contain frequently used links, such as to Microsoft Web-based documentation.

18. In the Toolbars tab, remove the checkmark for **Links** and click **Apply**.

19. In the Taskbar and Start Menu Properties dialog box, click **OK**.

Review Questions

1. Which of the following can you configure to display on the Start menu? (Choose all that apply.)

   a. Favorites menu

   b. Run command

   c. Recently opened files

   d. Recently opened programs

2. You use server applications that require extra space on the desktop to fully display. To gain a little extra space you can _____ the taskbar.

3. True or False? One limitation of configuring the taskbar is that the clock must always be displayed in the notification area.

4. Which of the following are toolbars that can be implemented on the taskbar? (Choose all that apply.)

   a. Command

   b. Desktop

   c. Quick Launch

   d. Status

5. The steps used to open the Taskbar and Start Menu Properties dialog box are to _____.

Lab 3.3 Configure Driver Updates, Remove Unused Programs, and Check Installed Updates

Objectives

- Configure Windows Server 2008 to use updated drivers when installing hardware
- Learn to remove unused programs
- Check to determine which updates are installed
- Learn how to remove an update

Materials Required

This lab requires the following:

- Windows Server 2008 Standard or Enterprise Edition

Estimated completion time: **20 minutes**

Activity Background

Whenever you install a new device in Windows Server 2008, it is important to ensure you use the latest device driver. A device driver is software that links a device's function with the operating system so that both can communicate and work together. For example, when you install a network adaptor or NIC, you also need to install driver software that enables the operating system to recognize the NIC and enable it to provide communications between the network, the NIC, and the operating system.

Computer device manufacturers often issue updates and fixes for specific device drivers as problems and security flaws are identified. Many devices come with a CD or DVD with driver software. However, the driver software on the CD or DVD is frequently outdated. You can configure the Windows Update program to determine if there is an updated driver when you install a device and then have Windows Update obtain the driver.

Also, as you manage a server, you may discover that there is software you no longer use or perhaps have never used. It is always advised to remove such software to help Windows Server 2008 run cleaner and faster, to recover disk space, and to close possible security holes created by the software. You can use the Programs and Features tool to uninstall programs.

Another important management task is to periodically check which updates have been installed on a server. This is particularly important when there are vital updates for security. A few years ago, many server managers failed to install a security update for Microsoft SQL Server and the result was that thousands of database servers were successfully attacked, compromising critical data. Whenever there is an update this important, plan to take the preemptive step to make sure the update is installed on your server.

In this activity, you configure Windows Update to find and apply the latest driver when you newly install a device. You also learn how to uninstall a program and how to determine what Windows updates have already been installed on a server.

Activity

1. Click **Start**, right-click **Computer**, and click **Properties** to open the System window.

2. Click **Advanced system settings** in the System window.

3. In the System Properties dialog box, click the **Hardware** tab (see Figure 3-4).

4. Click **Windows Update Driver Settings**.

5. In the Windows Update Driver Settings dialog box, there are three options:

   - Check for drivers automatically (recommended)

   - Ask me each time I connect a new device before checking for drivers

   - Never check for drivers when I connect a device

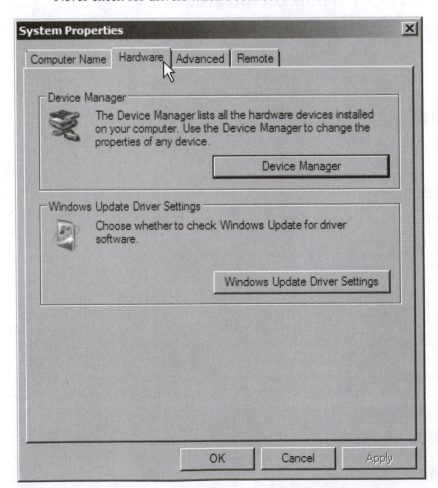

Figure 3-4   System Properties dialog box

Click **Check for drivers automatically (recommended)**, if it is not already selected.

6. Click **OK** in the Windows Update Driver Settings dialog box.

7. Click **OK** in the System Properties dialog box.

8. Close the System window.

9. Click **Start** and click **Control Panel**.

10. Click **Classic View**, if it is not already selected.

11. In the Control Panel window, double-click **Programs and Features**.

12. Under the Name column, review the programs that are already installed, if any. Note that you should periodically access the Programs and Features window to determine if there are any programs that you are not using and uninstall those programs. To uninstall a program, select the program and then click Uninstall/ Change or Uninstall (the Uninstall/Change button may not appear until you select a program in the list; also, if there are no Change options, you'll see only Uninstall). Always use this uninstall capability instead of just deleting the folder containing the program within the Program Files master folder. Using the uninstall capability helps ensure that all parts of the program are removed.

13. In the left portion of the Programs and Features window, click **View installed updates**.

14. In the Installed Updates window, you can view the updates that have already been installed for Windows Server 2008 and for other Microsoft programs, such as for Microsoft .NET Framework (see Figure 3-5). As you review the list of updates, you'll notice that many are for security. If you are not sure whether a particularly important security update has been installed, you can find out by opening this window. Also, there have been occasions when an update has not worked properly and it is important to remove the update to

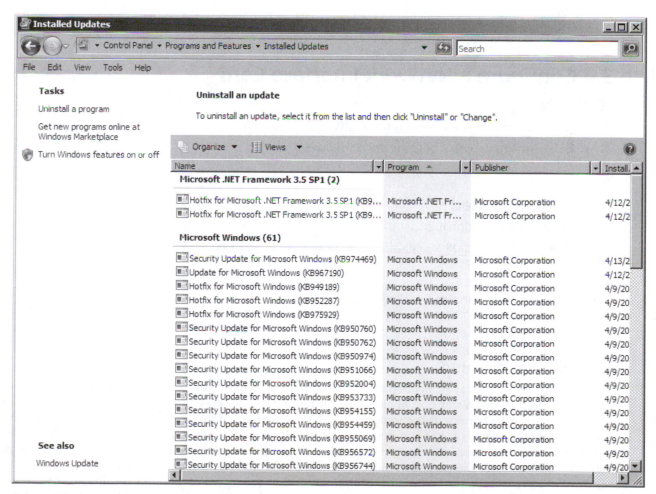

Figure 3-5 Installed Updates window

wait for another fix. You can remove an update by selecting it and clicking Uninstall (the Uninstall button may not appear until you first select an update).

15. Close the Installed Updates window.

Review Questions

1. A device driver is used to _____.

2. The safest way to remove a program is to use the _____ tool.

3. Which of the following are reasons to remove programs that are no longer used on a Windows Server 2008 server? (Choose all that apply.)

   a. Close security holes

   b. Enable Windows Server 2008 to run cleaner and faster

   c. Release the IRQs used by that program so they can be used by other programs

   d. Recover disk space

4. Microsoft has recently issued a critical update to ensure that a new virus cannot successfully attack Windows Server 2008. You can check to determine if your server has this update installed by checking the _____ window.

5. What tool enables you to tell Windows Server 2008 to use updated drivers when installing hardware?

   a. Device Controller

   b. Device Panel

   c. System Properties dialog box opened from the System window

   d. Device properties accessed from the Configuration option in Server Manager

Lab 3.4 Configure a Network Interface Card

Objectives

- Configure the network options for a NIC
- Learn how to update a NIC for the latest driver

Materials Required

This lab requires the following:

- Windows Server 2008 Standard or Enterprise Edition and a network interface card (NIC) installed in the computer

Estimated completion time: **15 minutes**

Activity Background

Most NICs have an array of properties that can be configured to take full advantage of a NIC's capabilities. For example, a NIC can transmit in either half or full duplex mode. Half duplex mode means that the NIC can transmit or receive, but not at the same time. Full duplex mode enables the NIC to transmit and receive at the same time, which equals faster communications. The duplex mode set on a NIC must match the duplex mode of the network device the NIC connects to, such as a network switch. Also, many NICs can transmit at different speeds (depending on the network's cable or wireless capabilities), such as at 10 Mbps, 100 Mbps, 1 Gbps, or faster. Typically you can configure the NIC to transmit at a given speed or to automatically detect the speed of the network. The specific features of a NIC are determined by the NIC's built-in capabilities and by the NIC driver.

An important NIC configuration option that is available in Windows Server 2008 is the ability to check for and install the latest NIC driver. After your NIC has been in use for awhile, it is likely that the NIC manufacturer has found and fixed problems with the NIC driver or improved the driver to offer more features. Consider periodically checking for an updated NIC driver so you can install it to take advantage of new features and updates, particularly security updates.

In this activity, you learn how to configure a NIC and update the NIC's driver.

Activity

1. Click **Start** and click **Control Panel**.

2. Ensure that **Classic View** is selected and then double-click **Network and Sharing Center**.

3. In the left portion of the Network and Sharing Center window, click **Manage network connections**.

4. Find your network connection, such as **Local Area Connection** (for a cable connection to the network) and right-click it.

5. Click **Properties**.

6. Click the **Configure** button.

7. The NIC's Properties dialog box is displayed (see Figure 3-6).

8. The specific tabs you see will depend on the NIC manufacturer and the NIC driver. Most NICs have the following tabs:

   - *General*—to provide general information about the NIC
   - *Advanced*—for configuring NIC options
   - *Driver*—for information about the driver and to obtain an updated driver

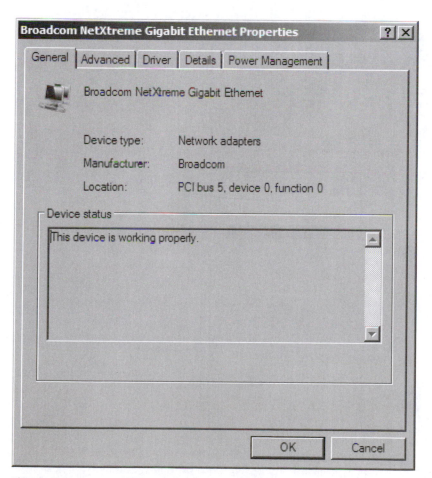

Figure 3-6   NIC Properties dialog box

- *Details*—for information about the NIC
- *Power Management*—to configure power management options, such as enabling the computer to turn off the NIC when the computer is in standby or hibernate mode

9. Ensure the **General** tab is selected. Under Device status, make sure that the NIC is working properly.

10. Click the **Advanced** tab (or your NIC's equivalent tab for configuring NIC options).

11. On the Advanced tab, click each of the properties that can be configured and determine the value or setting for that property.

12. Determine the speed and duplex mode in use or if the NIC is configured to automatically detect these settings. Typically you'll find options for speed or duplex or both combined (some NICs do not include these options or you may not see such options if you are working from a virtual server). Click the down arrow in the Value box to see the available settings that you can configure (see Figure 3-7 as an example).

13. Click the **Driver** tab.

14. Review the available buttons on the Driver tab, such as:

- *Driver Details*—View details such as the file name and location for the driver
- *Update Driver*—Obtain and install the latest driver for the NIC, such as by searching both your computer and the Internet for a newer driver
- *Roll Back Driver*—Go back to the previous driver version in case there is a problem after you update the NIC driver (this option may be grayed out or deactivated if there is no previous version to roll back to)
- *Disable*—Disable the driver so that it stops working (disabling the network connection), which can be useful when you need to work on the server and prevent users from accessing it until your work is finished; if you disable the driver, this button becomes the *Enable* button so you can restart the driver
- *Uninstall*—Remove the driver

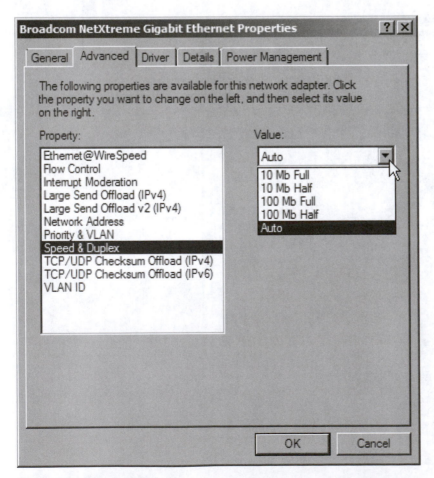

Figure 3-7 Advanced NIC options

15. Click **Driver Details** to view the current driver's folder location on the computer and the driver version.

16. Click **OK** in the Driver File Details box.

17. In the NIC Properties dialog box, click each tab that you have not yet viewed to see the information or options the remaining tabs offer.

18. Click **OK** in the NIC Properties dialog box.

19. Close the Network Connections window and close the Network and Sharing Center window.

Review Questions

1. Which of the following tools enables you to configure a NIC?

    a. Control Panel using the NIC Configuration applet

    b. Server Manager using the Configuration option

    c. NIC Module tool

    d. Network and Sharing Center

2. The manufacturer of the NIC in your server has issued a warning that network attackers have found a way to compromise the NIC's security. However, the manufacturer has developed a software patch to protect the NIC. To take advantage of the patch you should _____.

3. Users call to report they cannot connect to your company's server used for file sharing. You decide to determine if the NIC is working properly. Which of the follow steps can you take.

    a. Determine whether Server Manager will start, because Server Manager won't start when the NIC is not working

    b. Use the Component Service tool on the Administrative Tools menu

    c. Check the General tab in the NIC Properties dialog box

    d. Use the Check Status capability in the DCOM Config utility

4. The ability for a NIC to transmit and receive at the same time is called _____.

5. It is 6:00 A.M. and you have arrived at work early to install some new software on your law firm's server. You have verified that there are no users connected to the server over the network. Before you install the software, you want to take a step to ensure no one can access the server through the network while you are working. The precaution that you take is to _____.

INTRODUCTION TO ACTIVE DIRECTORY AND ACCOUNT MANAGEMENT

Labs included in this chapter:

- Lab 4.1 Examine Active Directory Objects
- Lab 4.2 Explore Active Directory Management Tools
- Lab 4.3 Configure an Active Directory Audit Policy
- Lab 4.4 Manage a User Account's Security Issues

Microsoft MCITP Exam #70-646 Objectives

Objective	Lab
Planning for Server Deployment	4.1, 4.3
Planning for Server Management	4.1, 4.2, 4.3, 4.4

Lab 4.1 Examine Active Directory Objects

Objectives

- Use the Active Directory Users and Computers tool
- Explore default Active Directory containers, accounts, and security groups

Materials Required

This lab requires the following:

- Windows Server 2008 Standard or Enterprise Edition with the Active Directory Domain Services role installed

Estimated completion time:	20 minutes

Activity Background

Active Directory contains many objects that are important to a Windows Server 2008 installation. Examples of objects that you will frequently manage include domains, OUs, domain controllers, users, and security groups. After Active Directory is installed, there are many objects created by default to help you get started. For example, there is a default Builtin folder that contains many pre-established security groups for easier management. Also, there is a Users folder that contains default user accounts, such as the Administrator account and more default security groups. As you plan a server's Active Directory deployment, you should become familiar with the default objects and containers, and strongly consider their implementation in your plan. Such planning can help ensure consistency with other Windows Server 2008 deployments so that it is easier to accomplish your management tasks and it is easier for new administrators to step in and be productive.

In this activity, you open the Active Directory Users and Computers MMC snap-in and use this tool to examine default user accounts, groups, OUs, and other container objects. You also learn how to add a client computer to Active Directory.

For all of the activities in this chapter, you'll need to log onto an account with Administrator privileges. Additionally, most of these activities can be completed on a virtual server or computer, such as in Hyper-V.

Throughout the activities in this book, you may occasionally see the User Account Control box with a message that Windows needs your permission to continue. Whenever you see this box, click Continue. Keep this in mind for all of the activities because any interaction with the User Account Control box is not included in the steps.

Activity

1. Click **Start**, type **mmc** in the Start Search box, and press **Enter**. (An alternative way to start the Active Directory Users and Computers tool instead of following Steps 1–5 is to open it from the Administrative Tools menu.)

2. In the console window, click the **File** menu, and click **Add/Remove Snap-in**.

3. In the Add or Remove Snap-ins window, click **Active Directory Users and Computers**.

4. Click the **Add >** button.

5. Click **OK** in the Add or Remove Snap-ins window.

6. In the tree in the left pane, click the **+** plus sign in front of **Active Directory Users and Computers**, if necessary, to display the items under it.

7. Click the **+** plus sign in front of the domain name, such as *jpcomp.com* to view the items under it (see Figure 4-1).

8. Click the **Builtin** folder in the tree.

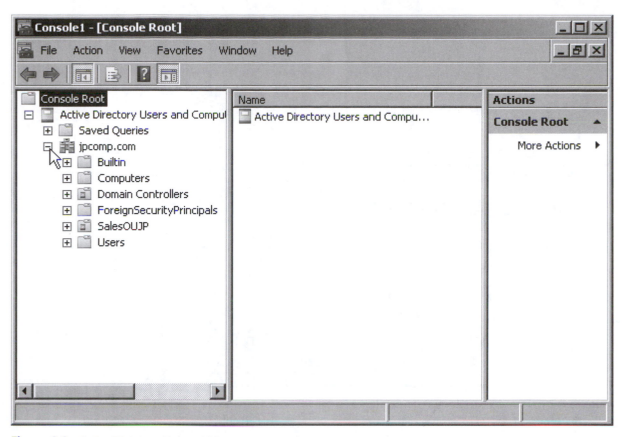

Figure 4-1   Active Directory Users and Computers snap-in

9. In the middle pane, review the listing of security groups. There are security groups that can be used in small, medium, and large organizations. Some examples of frequently used security groups are:

   - *Account Operators*—often used to delegate authority to create user accounts, such as to a user support department within an Information Technology division of a company
   - *Administrators*—a security group for local server administrators
   - *Backup Operators*—used to give specific accounts authority to back up the server
   - *Guests*—often used for temporary users, such as consultants
   - *Print Operators*—can be used to delegate printer management authority to specific accounts
   - *Server Operators*—used in many organizations for users who manage day-to-day server operations, including mounting CD/DVDs, performing backups, and rebooting servers
   - *Users*—a security group for general users

10. Right-click **Account Operators** in the middle pane and click **Properties**. Notice that the Account Operators group is a Builtin local security group, which is a domain local group because this server is a member of a domain. Also, the options to change the group scope and group type are deactivated. Click **Cancel**.

11. Right-click **Server Operators** in the middle pane and click **Properties**. Notice that the Server Operators group is also a Builtin local security group. Click **Cancel**.

12. Click **Computers** in the tree. When Active Directory is newly installed, there are no computers listed in the middle pane.

13. Click right-click **Computers**, point to **New**, and click **Computer**. In the New Object – Computer dialog box, you can add a computer to the domain by providing the computer's name in the Computer Name box (see Figure 4-2). However, note that you cannot add the name of the server that you are working from. Click **Cancel** in the New Object – Computer dialog box.

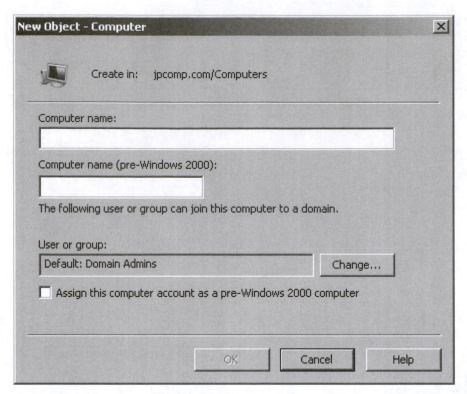

Figure 4-2   New Object – Computer dialog box

14. Click the **Domain Controllers** OU in the tree in the console window. In the middle pane, you should see the name of the server that you are working from.

15. Click the folder for **ForeignSecurityPrincipals** in the console tree. By default there are no computers listed in the middle pane. The ForeignSecurityPrincipals folder is used to hold the names of computers in trusted domains that are outside of the current forest. Listing the computers here gives those computers access to resources in the current domain.

16. Click the **Users** folder in the tree. This folder is provided as a general folder in which to hold users and security groups. Notice that the Administrator account is listed in the middle pane. There are also many security groups provided by default. Some examples of security groups include:

    - *DHCP Administrators*—users who manage the DHCP server
    - *DHCP Users*—all users who obtain IP addresses via the DHCP server
    - *DNSAdmins*—DNS server administrators
    - *Domain Admins*—administrators who manage domain functions
    - *Domain Users*—all users within a domain
    - *Enterprise Admins*—administrators in a medium or large enterprise of trees and domains, and might include, for example, those who manage Active Directory

17. Right-click **DHCP Administrators** in the middle pane and click **Properties**. Notice that this group is configured as a Domain local group (although you can change this designation). Click **Cancel** in the DHCP Administrators Properties dialog box.

18. Right-click **Domain Admins** and click **Properties**. Domain Admins is configured as a Global security group and the options to change Group scope and Group type are deactivated (because this group is not used for forest management and should not be a domain local group). Click **Cancel**.

19. Right-click two or three other security groups in the middle pane to view how they are configured.

20. Right-click the **Users** folder in the tree in the left pane and point to **New**. Notice the new objects you can create within this folder, such as Computer, Group, Printer, User, and Shared Folder. Click a blank area of the console to close the menus.

21. Right-click the **Domain Controllers** OU in the tree and notice there is an option on the menu to Delegate Control, which you might use to give management control to administrators of domain controllers and Active Directory within a domain. Note that you can delegate control of several Active Directory objects to match how responsibilities are allocated in your organization.

22. Close the console window.

23. Click **No** so that you do not save the console settings.

Review Questions

1. _____ is a default security group that can be used for those delegated authority to manage network printers through Windows Server 2008 Active Directory.

2. In which Active Directory container shown within the Active Directory Users and Computers tool should you add the names of computers that are members of a trusted domain that is a domain external to your Active Directory forest?

    a. Users folder

    b. Outsiders folder

    c. ForeignSecurityPrincipals OU

    d. DNS Users OU

3. You can open the Active Directory Users and Computers tool as a(n) _____ snap-in or from the _____ menu.

4. Your IT department has delegated authority over its DHCP and DNS servers to a small group of three administrators. Which of the following default security groups can be used to help assign them the proper security through Active Directory? (Choose all that apply.)

    a. DNSAdmins

    b. NetAdministrators

    c. Domain Users

    d. DHCP Administrators

5. There are four computers in the warehouse of your company that are used by multiple employees. You want to authorize these computers to the domain for better security. There is a(n) _____ folder in the Active Directory Users and Computers tool for this purpose.

Lab 4.2 Explore Active Directory Management Tools

Objectives

- Explore the Active Directory Domains and Trusts snap-in
- Explore the Active Directory Sites and Services snap-in
- Explore the ADSI Edit snap-in
- Explore the Group Policy Management snap-in

Materials Required

This lab requires the following:

- Windows Server 2008 Standard or Enterprise Edition with the Active Directory Domain Services role installed

Estimated completion time: **30 minutes**

Activity Background

For any Active Directory installation, it is important to become familiar with the tools used to manage Active Directory. There are many tools available for managing Active Directory, including a full range of MMC snap-ins. In this activity, you explore four important MMC snap-ins used for managing Active Directory elements:

- *Active Directory Domains and Trusts*—for managing domains and trusts, such as to set up trust relationships
- *Active Directory Sites and Services*—for creating sites to help manage replication services, among other things
- *ADSI Edit*—for providing low-level editing of Active Directory objects
- *Group Policy Management*—to configure group policy, such as on a local server or to apply throughout a domain

Activity

1. Click **Start**, type **mmc** in the Start Search box, and press **Enter**.

2. In the console window, click the **File** menu and click **Add/Remove Snap-in**.

3. In the Add or Remove Snap-ins window, click **Active Directory Domains and Trusts** under Available snap-ins. Click the **Add >** button.

4. Click **Active Directory Sites and Services** and click the **Add >** button.

5. Click **ADSI Edit** and click the **Add >** button.

6. Click **Group Policy Management** (which is the first of two different Group Policy Management selections listed under Available snap-ins). Click the **Add >** button. The Add or Remove Snap-ins window should now look similar to Figure 4-3.

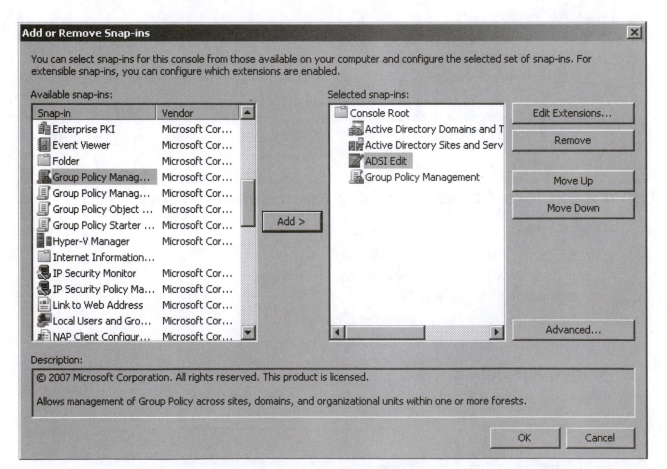

Figure 4-3   Add or Remove Snap-ins window

7. In the Add or Remove Snap-ins window, click **OK**.

8. In the tree in the left pane, click **Active Directory Domains and Trusts**.

9. In the middle pane, right-click the domain name. Note the following options on the menu:

   - *Manage*—used for general management functions, such as to create realms or external trusts

   - *Raise Domain Functional Level*—used to raise the domain functional level

   - *New Windows from Here*—used to open a new window showing only the domain

   - *Properties*—used to manage the domain description, establish trusts, and configure who manages the domain

   - *Help*—used to access help information

10. Click **Properties** on the menu.

11. Ensure the **General** tab is selected and note that you can enter a description of the domain.

12. Click the **Trusts** tab. You can use this tab to designate domains trusted by this domain and to designate domains that trust this domain (see Figure 4-4).

13. Click the **Managed By** tab, which you can use to designate a security group or specific users to manage this domain.

14. Click **Cancel** in the domain Properties dialog box.

15. In the console window, click **Active Directory Sites and Services** in the tree.

16. In the middle pane, right-click the **Sites** folder and notice the menu options (see Figure 4-5). Two particularly important options are Delegate Control, to configure who can create and manage sites, and New Site, which is used to create a new site. Click a blank area of the console to close the menu.

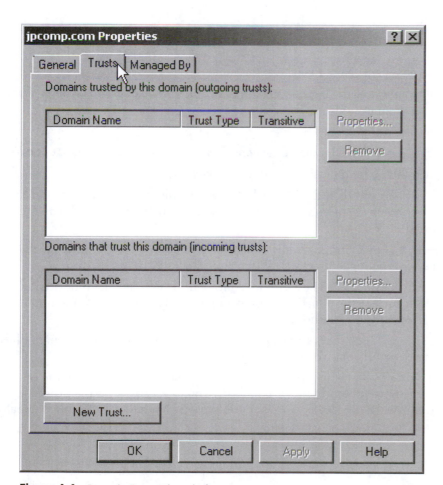

Figure 4-4   Domain Properties window

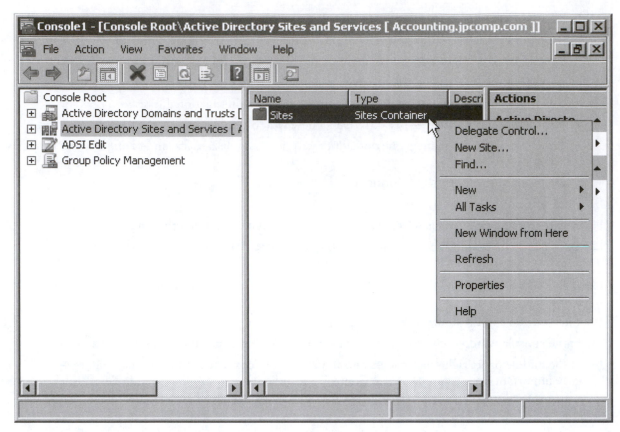

Figure 4-5   Menu options for sites

17. Double-click **Sites** in the middle pane. Note that there is a Subnets folder listed.

18. Right-click the **Subnets** folder and note the New Subnet option, which you can use to create multiple subnets for optimizing network communications.

19. Click a blank area of the console to close the menu.

20. Right-click **ADSI Edit** in the tree in the left pane of the console window and click **Connect to**.

21. In the Connection Settings window, leave the default settings and click **OK**.

22. Click **ADSI Edit** in the left pane and then double-click **Default naming context [*computer and domainname*]** in the middle pane (if your computer shows more than one *Default naming context* options, click the first one listed).

23. Right-click **DC=*domainname*,DC=com** in the middle pane (on some computers you might see *DC=local* depending on how the computer is configured) and click **Properties**.

24. Ensure the Attribute Editor tab is displayed. The attribute editor can be used to fine tune attributes for a specific Active Directory object, such as the domain in this example (see Figure 4-6). (Make sure you don't make any changes to the attributes.) Click **Cancel**.

25. Double-click **DC=*domainname*,DC=com** (or **local**) in the middle pane. Notice the domain objects in the middle pane. These are more objects that you can manage through ADSI Edit.

26. Click **CN=Builtin** and click **Action** in the menu bar of the console window. Review the options for configuring **CN=Builtin**, such as to move, delete, or rename it. You can also access the properties of this object and use the attribute editor (be absolutely sure you don't make changes). Click a blank area of the console to close the menu.

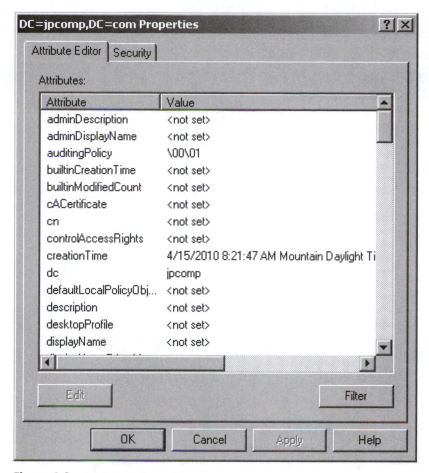

Figure 4-6   Attribute Editor tab

27. Click **Group Policy Management** in the tree in the left pane of the console window.

28. Double-click **Forest:** *domainname* in the middle pane.

29. Double-click **Domains** in the middle pane.

30. Double-click the domain name in the middle pane.

31. Right-click **Default Domain Policy** in the middle pane and click **Edit**.

32. The Group Policy Management Editor window opens, from which the user can configure specific group policies for the domain.

33. In the tree in the left pane under Computer Configuration, click **Policies**. Note the categories for which you can set policies for Computer Configuration (see Figure 4-7).

34. Leave the Group Policy Management Editor window open for the next lab, but close the original console window and click **No** so the settings are not saved.

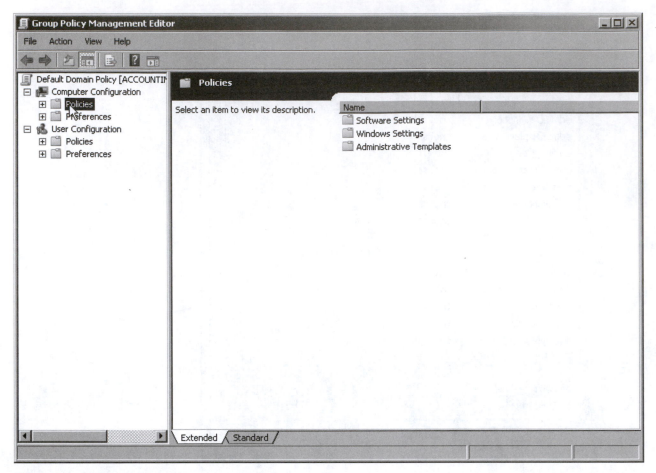

Figure 4-7   Group Policy Management Editor window

Review Questions

1. You can use the _____ snap-in to raise the domain functional level.

2. Which of the following MMC snap-ins enables you to configure the default domain policy?

    a. Active Directory Sites and Services

    b. Group Policy Management

    c. Active Directory Policy

    d. Domain Policy

3. To configure a realm trust, use the _____ snap-in.

4. When you configure sites, you can also configure which of the following?

    a. User profiles

    b. Account authentication

    c. Subnets

    d. Network trusts

5. The _____ snap-in enables you to configure domain attributes.

Lab 4.3 Configure an Active Directory Audit Policy

Objectives

- Configure auditing for directory services
- Audit the creation of user accounts and groups
- Audit the deletion of user accounts

Materials Required

This lab requires the following:

- Windows Server 2008 Standard or Enterprise Edition with the Active Directory Domain Services role installed

Estimated completion time: **20 minutes**

Activity Background

As you plan and implement your Windows Server 2008 deployment, consider the ability to audit activity related to Active Directory objects and general server activity. Auditing creates an audit trail of designated activities to help trace problems, pinpoint unauthorized access, and verify that procedures are correctly executed. For example, if you are managing an accounting server, your organization's external financial auditors may require the organization to audit the accounts of users such as the comptroller, accountants, and clerks. Some organizations audit the activities of server administrators to help protect the administrators and the organization. A company that has a research branch that develops cutting-edge products may audit specific files containing proprietary research information. Many organizations develop a written auditing policy and then have the server administrator implement that policy.

Before you can audit activities related to Active Directory, such as user account activity or changes made to Active Directory, it is first necessary to configure a domain-wide group policy to enable the auditing of directory service and object activities. After Active Directory auditing is enabled, you can create group policies to audit specific Active Directory and object activities. It is important to remember that audited activities are typically recorded in the Security log. (You learn how to view the Security log in Chapter 15, "Managing System Reliability and Availability" in *MCITP Guide to Microsoft Windows Server 2008, Server Administration [Exam #70-646].*) Also, keep in mind that auditing increases server overhead and can rapidly fill the Security log, making other security concerns harder to detect—so plan to audit only what is necessary.

In this activity, you use the Group Policy Management Editor window to enable Active Directory service auditing. Next, you use the Active Directory Users and Computers snap-in to configure auditing on Active Directory actions taken by the Administrators security group.

Activity

1. Make sure that the Group Policy Management Editor window is open.
2. In the right pane of the Group Policy Management Editor window, you should see the Windows Settings folder. Double-click **Windows Settings**.
3. In the right pane, double-click **Security Settings**.
4. In the right pane, double-click **Local Policies**.
5. In the right pane, double-click **Audit Policy**.
6. In the right pane, double-click **Audit directory service access** (see Figure 4-8).
7. In the Audit directory service access Properties dialog box, on the Security Policy Setting tab, click the box for **Define these policy settings** to select it.
8. Click each box for **Success** and **Failure**.
9. Click **OK** in the Audit directory service access Properties dialog box.

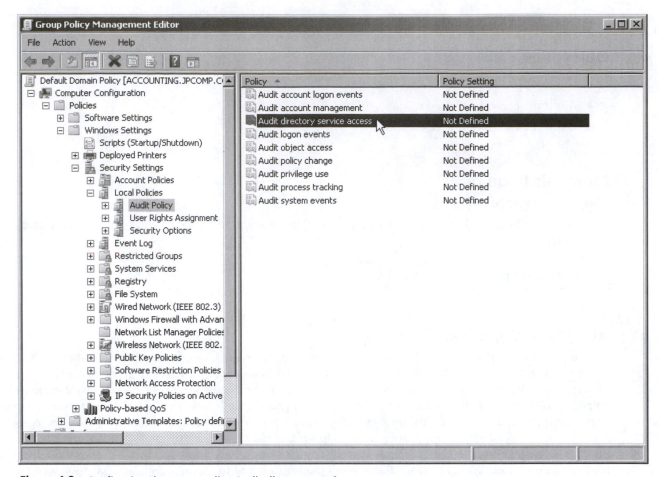

Figure 4-8   Configuring the group policy *Audit directory service access*

10. Next, assume that you want to audit objects, such as files that have their own access control lists (security settings). Double-click **Audit object access**.

11. In the Audit object access Properties dialog box, on the Security Policy Setting tab, click the box for **Define these policy settings**.

12. Click the boxes for **Success** and **Failure**.

13. Click **OK** in the Audit object access Properties dialog box.

14. Close the Group Policy Management Editor.

15. Now that you have enabled auditing for directory service access in Steps 6–9, you can set up to audit changes made in the domain by the Administrator account. Open the **Active Directory Users and Computers** console and expand the tree in the left pane to show the domain name.

16. Click the domain in the tree.

17. Click the **View** menu and click **Advanced Features** (only click it if there is no checkmark in front of this selection).

18. Right-click the domain name in the tree in the left pane and click **Properties**.

19. In the domain Properties dialog box, click the **Security** tab.

20. Click the **Advanced** button on the Security tab.

21. Click the **Auditing** tab.

22. In the Advanced Security Settings for *domainname* dialog box, click **Administrators (*domainname* Administrators)**, which is the Builtin Administrators security group you learned about in Step 9 of Lab 4.1.

23. Click the **Edit** button.

24. Use the `scroll bar` in the Auditing Entry for *domainname* dialog box to view all of the successful or failed events that you can select to audit for activities performed in the domain by the Administrators security group (see Figure 4-9).

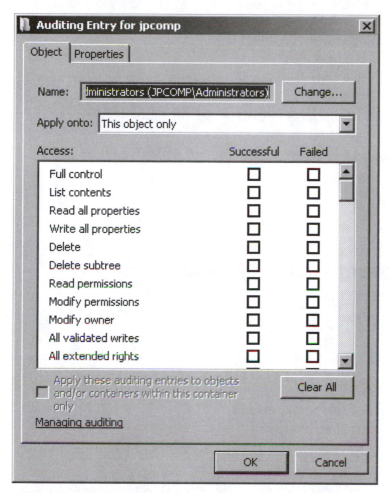

Figure 4-9   Auditing administrator activities performed on a domain

25. Click the **Successful** and **Failed** check boxes for **Create Group objects** to track the creation of security groups.

26. Click the **Successful** and **Failed** check boxes for **Create User objects** and for **Delete User objects** to track creating user accounts and deleting them.

27. Click **OK** in the Auditing Entry for *domainname* dialog box.

28. Click **OK** in the Advanced Security Settings for *domainname* dialog box.

29. Click **OK** in the *domainname* Properties dialog box.

30. Close the console window and click **No**, if necessary.

Review Questions

1. Auditing in Widows Server 2008 Active Directory can be based on which of the following? (Choose all that apply.)

   a. Type of action or activity

   b. Success of action or activity

   c. Failure of action or activity

   d. Active Directory object

2. Auditing is one component of a(n) _____ policy.

3. Where can you find the results of auditing?

    a. In the Audit OU

    b. In the Audit window

    c. In the ADSI Edit Auditing folder

    d. In the Security log

4. True or False? Before a server administrator configures auditing, it is good practice to have a written auditing policy already established by an organization.

5. Which MMC snap-in enables you to configure auditing to track when user accounts are created or deleted?

    a. Audit Editor

    b. Active Directory Users and Computers

    c. Active Directory Sites and Services

    d. Service tool on the Administrative Tools menu

Lab 4.4 Manage a User Account's Security Issues

Objectives

- Examine the security groups to which a user account belongs
- Create a user account
- Unlock a user account
- Reset a user account password

Materials Required

This lab requires the following:

- Windows Server 2008 Standard or Enterprise Edition with the Active Directory Domain Services role installed

Estimated completion time: **15 minutes**

Activity Background

At times it can be important to review what global (and in some cases, local) security groups an account belongs to because it is always important to ensure the right people have the right access to resources. For example, sometimes a user's job responsibilities change due to a promotion or company reorganization. A new person may come into a job, but her initial access to shared folders and printers may not be fully matched to her job assignments.

Another common account security issue is that a user temporarily locks an account after trying the wrong password or mistyping it too many times, when account lockout group policies are enforced on a network. This necessitates the administrator unlocking the account and possibly changing the password if the user has forgotten it.

For this activity, you learn how to examine the group memberships of an account, unlock an account, and quickly change an account password.

Activity

1. Open the **Active Directory Users and Computers** snap-in and expand the tree in the left pane to show the domain name and the folders and OUs under the domain.

2. Click the **Users** folder in the tree in the left pane.

3. Right-click the **Administrator** account in the middle pane and click **Properties**.

4. Click the **Member Of** tab to view the security groups to which the Administrator account belongs.

5. By default the Administrator account typically belongs to the following security groups:
   - Administrators
   - Domain Admins
   - Domain Users
   - Enterprise Admins
   - Group Policy Creator Owners
   - Schema Admins

6. Notice that you can use the Add or Remove buttons to add or remove a security group membership.

7. Click **Cancel** in the Administrator Properties dialog box.

8. Click the **Create a new user in the current container** button on the toolbar of the console.

9. In the New Object – User dialog box, enter a first name of **Megan** and a last name of **Cavalli** (and if you are sharing a server for this lab, enter your initials at the end of Cavalli).

10. Enter **mcavalli** (plus your initials at the end, if necessary) in the User logon name box and click **Next**.

11. In the New Object – User dialog box, enter a password of your choice and enter it again to confirm it. Note that the default password requirements are that the password must be six characters or longer and cannot contain the account name or portions of the user's full name. Also, be sure to include numbers, upper and lowercase letters, and characters such as $ or #. If you don't follow the default requirements, you'll see an error message in Step 13 and will have to return to this step.

12. For this activity, remove the checkmark from the **User must change password at next logon** box. Click **Next.**

13. Click **Finish** In the New Object – User dialog box.

14. The new account you created, **Megan Cavalli** should be highlighted in the middle pane of the console window. Click the **Action** menu and click **Properties**. (Alternatively, you could right-click the account and click Properties.)

15. In the Megan Cavalli Properties dialog box, click the **Member Of** tab. By default, the account should be a member of the Domain Users security group.

16. In the Megan Cavalli Properties dialog box, click the **Account** tab (see Figure 4-10). Notice the Unlock account option with a box in front of it in the middle of the Account tab. When a user has failed to enter the correct password too many times (when account lockout is enabled as a group policy), the account will be locked out and you will see on the Account tab the message: *Unlock account. This account is currently locked out on the Active Directory Domain Controller.* To unlock the account, you would check the box in front of this message.

17. Click **Cancel** in the Megan Cavalli Properties dialog box.

18. Sometimes when an account has been locked, it means that the user has forgotten his or her password. In the middle pane, the **Megan Cavalli** account should be highlighted; if not, click the account to highlight it.

19. Click the **Action** menu in the console window and click **Reset Password**. Type a new password in the **New password** text box and retype it in the **Confirm password** text box. Be sure to follow the default account password requirements mentioned in step 11. Also, ensure that the box is checked for **User must change password at next logon.** Checking this box when changing a user's password protects the server or account administrator so they do not have knowledge of the user's password after the user logs back on. It also follows practices supported by financial auditors for servers that handle accounting and money transactions.

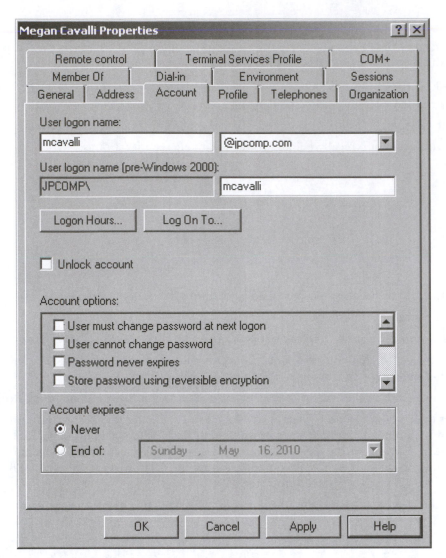

Figure 4-10   Account tab

20. In the Reset Password dialog box, notice there is also an option to Unlock the user's account. You could also unlock the account here to save steps.

21. Click **OK** in the Reset Password dialog box.

22. Click **OK** in the Active Directory Domain Services information box.

23. Close Active Directory Users and Computers and, if necessary, click **No** in the Microsoft Management Console box.

Review Questions

1. Your company has a new employee who needs access to the resource privileges available to the Research global security group. When you create this employee's new account using the Active Directory Users and Computers snap-in, how can you make this employee a member of the Research global security group? (Choose all that apply.)

   a. Go to the Member Of tab in that user's account properties.

   b. Go to the Profile tab in that user's account properties.

   c. Right-click that user's account and click Group Membership.

   d. Right-click that user's account, click Security, and click Group.

2. The _____ snap-in enables a server administrator to reset the password for an account.

3. Which of the following are security groups to which the Administrator account belongs by default?

   a. Enterprise Admins

   b. Group Policy Creator Owners

   c. Domain Guests

   d. Network Configuration Operators

4. After you reset a user's password, it is good practice to make sure the user must _____.

5. When a user fails to successfully log on too many times, that user's account can be _____.

4

CONFIGURING, MANAGING, AND TROUBLESHOOTING RESOURCE ACCESS

Labs included in this chapter:

- Lab 5.1 Install the File Services Role with the Windows Search Service

- Lab 5.2 Use File Server Resource Manager

- Lab 5.3 Manage Shared Drives, Folders, and Files

- Lab 5.4 Install Subsystem for UNIX-Based Applications

Microsoft MCITP Exam #70-646 Objectives

Objective	Lab
Planning for Server Deployment	5.1, 5.4
Planning for Server Management	5.2, 5.3
Monitoring and Maintaining Servers	5.2, 5.3

Lab 5.1 Install the File Services Role with the Windows Search Service

Objectives

- Install the File Services role
- Install Windows Search Service
- Install Distributed File System for sharing files

Materials Required

This lab requires the following:

- Windows Server 2008 Standard or Enterprise Edition with the Active Directory Domain Services role installed

Estimated completion time: **20 minutes**

Activity Background

The File Services role is one of the most frequent ways servers are used. On many networks, servers enable enterprises and individuals to store and share files in a centralized location. Through Windows Server 2008 and its NTFS file system, folders and files can be secured through file and share permissions to manage who can access folders and files and in what way. For example, some folders and files may be shared over the network, but only to let users read the contents of files without the authority to make changes. Permissions can also be fine-tuned to give certain access privileges to one set of users and different privileges to another.

The Windows Server 2008 File Services role can be installed with role services, such as Distributed File System (DFS) and the Windows Search Service. Another role service that you can install is the File Server Resource Manager.

In this activity, you install Windows Server 2008 File Services to include DFS, the Windows Search Service, and File Server Resource Manager. In Lab 5.2, you learn how to use File Server Resource Manager.

For all of the activities in this chapter, you'll need to log onto an account with Administrator privileges. Additionally, most of these activities can be completed on a virtual server or computer, such as in Hyper-V.

Throughout the activities in this book, you may occasionally see the User Account Control box with a message that Windows needs your permission to continue. Whenever you see this box, click Continue. Keep this in mind for all of the activities because any interaction with the User Account Control box is not included in the steps.

Activity

1. Click **Start**, point to **Administrative Tools**, and click **Server Manager** (or click the Server Manager icon in the taskbar).

2. Click **Add Roles**.

3. If you see the Before you Begin window, click **Next**.

4. Place a check in the check box for **File Services** and click **Next**.

5. Click **Next** in the File Services window.

6. In the Select Role Services dialog box, check the boxes for **File Server Resource Manager** and **Windows Search Service** (see Figure 5-1; note that you'll install DFS later in this activity). Click **Next**.

7. In the Configure Storage Usage Monitor window, click to select the check box or check boxes for **Local Disk**, such as *Local Disk (C:)*. This enables Windows Server 2008 File Services to monitor the amount

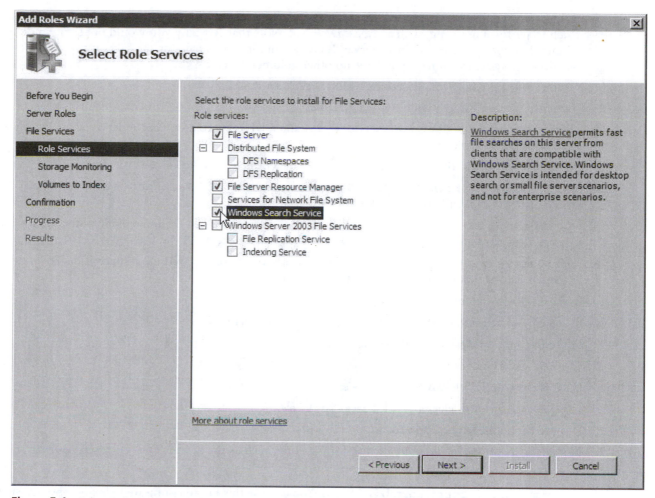

Figure 5-1   Select Role Services window

of disk space used on each volume and to provide reports on usage threshold, which is 85% by default. Notice that reports selected by default are *Files by Owner Report* and *Files by File Group Report*. Click the **Options** button to view all of the reports that can be selected including the following:

- *Large Files Report*—shows large files that are using disk space

- *Least Recently Accessed Files*—enables you to locate files that have not been recently used so that you can archive them

- *Most Recently Accessed Files*—enables you to locate files that are used often

- *Quota Usage Report*—indicates which disk quotas are close to filling (when disk quotas are configured)

- *Duplicate Files Report*—indicates files that can possibly be deleted because they are duplicates of other files

- *Files by Owner Report*—indicates how files are used by specific owners and identifies users who use a large amount of disk space

- *Files by File Group Report*—helps determine how files are used by groups and identifies groups that use a large amount of disk space

- *File Screen Audit Report*—indicates users or groups that do not follow file screening policies (you learn about file-screening polices in Lab 5.2)

8. Click **Cancel** in the Volume Monitoring Options dialog box.

9. Click **Next** in the Configure Storage Usage Monitoring window.

10. In the Set Report Options window, notice the default location to store reports about usage threshold, which is *systemdrive*:\StorageReports. Click **Next**.

11. In the Select Volumes to Index for Windows Search Service window, click the check boxes for volumes on which to perform indexing, such as *Local Disk (C:)*. Note that typically you would not set up indexing on a volume that contains the Windows Server 2008 system files. However, for the sake of practice in this activity, select the system volume if you have no other volumes. Click **Next**.

12. In the Confirm Installation Selections window, click **Install**.

13. In the Installation Results window, click **Close**.

14. Next, you practice installing a role service by installing DFS as a role service. In Server Manager, click **File Services** under Roles Summary.

15. Under File Services in the right pane of Server Manager, click **Add Role Services**.

16. Click the box for **Distributed File System**. The boxes for **DFS Namespaces** and **DFS Replication**, should also automatically have checkmarks. Click **Next**.

17. Enter a name for the namespace, such as the name of a server to hold DFS, the name of the organization, or a description of the file contents, such as *Research*. Click **Next**.

18. Select **Domain-based namespace** and click **Next**. (If Domain-based namespace is deactivated because Active Directory is not installed, select Stand-alone namespace instead.)

19. In the Configure Namespace window, click **Next**.

20. In the Confirm Installation Selections window, click **Install**.

21. In the Installation Results window, click **Close**.

22. Close Server Manager.

23. Click **Start** and click **Control Panel**.

24. If Classic view is not selected, click **Classic View**.

25. Double-click **Indexing Options**.

26. Notice the locations included by default for indexing, such as the Start Menu and Users folders.

27. Click the **Advanced** button.

28. Ensure the **Index Settings** tab is selected. You can use this tab to configure indexing options, such as to index encrypted files or to rebuild an index location.

29. Click the **File Types** tab. You can use this tab to index particular types of files.

30. Click **Cancel** in the Advanced Options dialog box.

31. Click **Close** in the Indexing Options dialog box.

32. Close Control Panel.

Review Questions

1. Which of the following tools enables you to manage indexing options for Windows Search Service?

   a. Folder Index tool on the Administrative Tools menu

   b. Indexing Options applet in Control Panel

   c. DFS Management tool

   d. Indexing OU in the Active Directory Users and Computers snap-in

2. When you install the File Services role, which of the following are storage management reports that you can select to use? (Choose all that apply.)

   a. Duplicate files report

   b. Large files report

   c. Smallest files report

   d. Files by owner report

3. File Services storage management reports are stored in the _____ folder by default.

4. Distributed File System is a(n)_____ service of the File Services role.

5. True or False? The Windows Search Service enables you to index by file types.

Lab 5.2 Use File Server Resource Manager

Objectives

- Use File Server Resource Manager to configure disk quotas and file screening management
- Configure and run storage management reports

Materials Required

This lab requires the following:

- Windows Server 2008 Standard or Enterprise Edition with File Server Resource Manager installed as in Lab 5.1

Estimated completion time: 30 minutes

Activity Background

When you implement the File Services role, also plan to manage how users store and use files on the server by using File Server Resource Manager. File Server Resource Manager brings several file-management capabilities under one roof, such as:

- Creating quotas to manage available disk space and limit how much users can store
- Creating file-screening rules to control what kinds of files users can store, such as blocking audio or e-mail files
- Managing and creating file storage reports

As you learned in Lab 5.1, File Server Resource Manager can be installed as a role service when you install the File Services role. The options to set disk quotas and to screen files that can be stored on a server are often put in place after an organization develops a formal plan for server storage management. Some organizations have a committee or management group that creates the server storage plan. File Server Resource Manager is another server management option you can take into account as you plan a server deployment and plan for server management.

For this activity, you open File Server Resource Manager and learn about the tools within. You first need to have performed Lab 5.1 to ensure File Server Resource Manager is installed.

Activity

1. On drive C: or another drive, create a folder named UserData plus your initials. (Click **Start**; click **Computer**; double-click the drive on which to create the folder, such as *Local Disk (C:)*; right-click in a blank area of the drive's window; point to **New**; click **Folder**; type the folder name, such as *UserDataJP* where *JP* represents your initials; and press **Enter**. Close the drive's window.)

2. Click **Start**, point to **Administrative Tools**, and click **File Server Resource Manager**.

3. In the left pane in the tree, click the + plus sign in front of **Quota Management** to view the items under it.

4. In the tree, click **Quota Templates**.

5. The middle pane displays existing quota templates that you can use to set quotas on user folders within a volume. Right-click **200 MB Limit Reports to User** and click **Create Quota from Template** (see Figure 5-2). Note that the 200 MB Limit Reports to Users quota template sets a 200 MB quota per each user and sends reports to a user as that user approaches the quota.

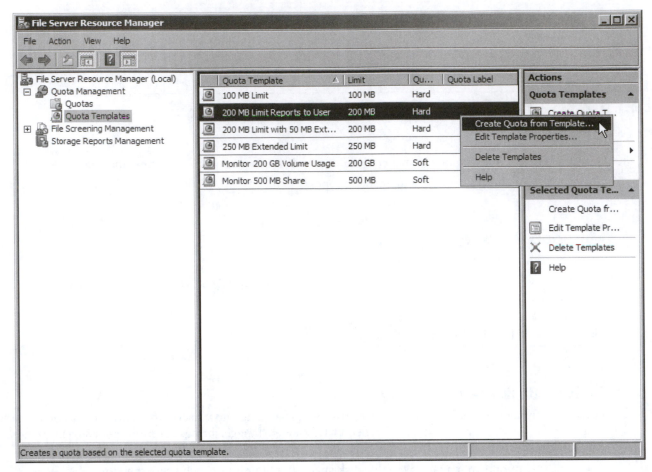

Figure 5-2   Using a quota template

6. In the Create Quota dialog box, specify the quota path, which is the path to the folder on which to set the quota. Click the **Browse** button and browse to the **UserData***initials* folder you created. Click the folder and click **OK** in the Browse For Folder dialog box.

7. In the Create Quota dialog box, leave the following selected by default:

   - **Create quota on path**

   - **Derive properties from the quota template (recommended)** with **200 MB Limit Reports to User** selected

   Also, review the contents of the Summary of quota properties box to see the properties that you are configuring. For example, there is a hard quota of 200 MB set per each user who stores files in this folder. A hard quota means that the quota is enforced (no new files can be stored) when a user has stored 200 MB of files, whereas a soft quota means that a user only receives a warning when he reaches 200 MB. When the user reaches 85% of the quota, he will receive a warning by e-mail. When the user reaches 95%, he receives another e-mail and an event log entry is made. When the user reaches 100% of the quota, he receives a third e-mail, an event log entry is made, and a report is generated for the system administrator (see Figure 5-3).

8. Click **Create** in the Create Quota dialog box.

9. In the tree, click the **+** plus sign in front of **File Screening Templates**.

10. In the tree, click **File Screen Templates** under File Screening Templates.

11. In the middle pane, there is a list of file screen templates that you can employ. Assume that you want to block users from placing audio and video files in the UserData*initials* folder. Right-click **Block Audio and Video Files** and click **Create File Screen from Template**.

12. Click the **Browse** button.

13. Browse to the **UserData***initials* folder and click the folder. Click **OK** in the Browse For Folder dialog box.

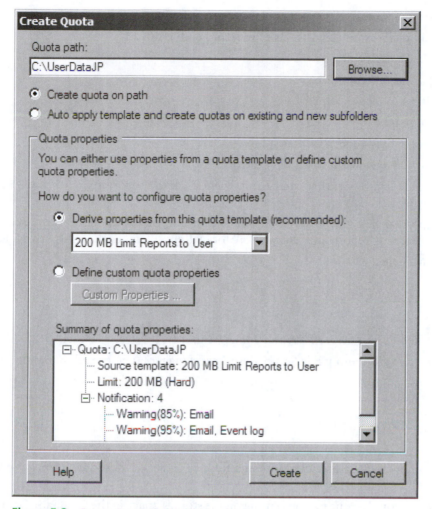

Figure 5-3   Create Quota dialog box

14. Ensure that **Derive properties from this file screen template (recommended)** is selected. Click the down arrow for this selection and notice that you can select to block the following types of files from being stored in the folder:

   • Audio and video files

   • Executable files

   • Image files

   • E-mail files

   You can also select to Monitor Executable and System Files instead of blocking files in this folder. Leave **Block Audio and Video Files** selected.

15. Examine the Summary of the screen properties box to view a summary of what you are selecting to block. Notice that the screen type is Active, which means that the audio and video files cannot be written to the folder. Another option is to use the Passive screen type, which means that such files can be written, but an e-mail warning will be sent to the user.

16. Click **Create** in the Create File Screen dialog box.

17. In the tree, right-click **Storage Reports Management** and click **Schedule a New Report Task**.

18. Click the **Add** button in the Storage Reports Task Properties dialog box.

19. Browse to the **UserData*initials*** folder and click the folder. Click **OK** in the Browse For Folder dialog box.

20. In the Select reports to generate box, review all of the reports that can be generated, and leave each one selected.

21. Click the **Schedule tab** in the Storage Reports Task Properties dialog box.

22. Click **Create Schedule** in the Storage Reports Task Properties dialog box.

23. In the Schedule dialog box, click **New**.

24. Set the **Schedule Task** parameter to **Monthly**.

25. Ensure the **Start time** is set to **9:00 AM**.

26. Click **OK** in the Schedule dialog box.

27. Click **OK** in the Storage Reports Task Properties dialog box.

28. Ensure that Storage Reports Management is selected in the tree.

29. In the middle pane, notice there is a report that can be run. Right-click the report and click **Run Report Task Now**.

30. In the Generate Storage Reports dialog box, ensure that **Generate reports in the background** is selected and click **OK**. (You can view reports in *systemdrive*:\StorageReports under the Interactive folder.)

31. Close File Server Resource Manager.

Review Questions

1. You can view reports generated by File Server Resource Manager in the _____ folder.

2. Which of the following can you screen using File Server Resource Manager? (Choose all that apply.)

   a. Spreadsheet files

   b. Image files

   c. Word files

   d. Executable files

3. To help you set up limits on how much a user can store in a folder, File Server Resource Manager provides _____ templates.

4. Some users have complained to you that one person is using up the storage space in the Company Documents folder. To quickly identify this user, which of the following storage reports do you run?

   a. Files by Owner

   b. Screening Audit

   c. Files by Computer Location

   d. Large Files by User

5. How often can you schedule to create storage reports? (Choose all that apply.)

   a. Once

   b. Weekly

   c. Monthly

   d. At system startup

Lab 5.3 Manage Shared Drives, Folders, and Files

Objectives

- Use the Shared Folders MMC snap-in to view, create, and manage file and folder shares
- Connect to a shared folder through the network
- View users connected to shared files
- Disconnect users of shared files and close shared files

Materials Required

This lab requires the following:

- Windows Server 2008 Standard or Enterprise Edition with network discovery turned on

Estimated completion time: **20 minutes**

Activity Background

Windows Server 2008 offers the Shared Folders tool for centrally managing shared folders to accomplish the following tasks:

- Share a folder or entire drive
- Configure shared folder permissions
- Stop a share
- Disconnect an account currently accessing a shared folder or drive
- Close an open file
- Diagnose folder or drive sharing problems

There are several ways to open the Shared Folders tool:

- As an MMC snap-in
- From the Administrative Tools Computer Management tool
- By using the *fsmgmt.msc* command from the Start menu Run dialog box, Start menu Start Search box, or Command Prompt window.

For this activity, you use the Shared Folders MMC snap-in to configure a shared folder and manage it.

Activity

1. Begin by creating a file and storing it in the UserData*initials* folder you created in Lab 5.2. Click **Start**, point to **All Programs**, click **Accessories**, and click **WordPad**.

2. In the Document - WordPad window, type the line: **This is a practice document.**

3. In the Document - WordPad window, click the **File** menu and click **Save As**.

4. In the Save As dialog box, enter **File** plus your initials, such as *FileJP* in the File name box. Click **Browse Folders** and browse to and open the UserData*initials* folder. Click **Save**.

5. In WordPad, click the **File** menu and click **Exit**.

6. Click **Start**, type **mmc** in the Start Search box, and press **Enter**.

7. In the console window, click the **File** menu, and click **Add/Remove Snap-in**.

8. In the Add or Remove Snap-ins window, click **Shared Folders**.

9. Click the **Add >** button.

10. In the Shared Folder dialog box, leave **Local computer (the computer this console is running on)** selected and leave **All** selected as well. Click **Finish**.

11. Click **OK** in the Add or Remove Snap-ins window.

12. In the Console1 - [Console Root] window, click **Shared Folders** in the tree in the left pane (see Figure 5-4). The three folders displayed in the middle pane of the console window are:

    - *Shares*—displays a list of the shared folders and disks, and enables you to create or stop shares
    - *Sessions*—lists user sessions connected to a shared folder or disk, and enables you to disconnect one or all sessions, if necessary
    - *Open Files*—displays shared files that are open, shows who is using them, and enables you to close a file, such as when a file is hung open even after a user has disconnected

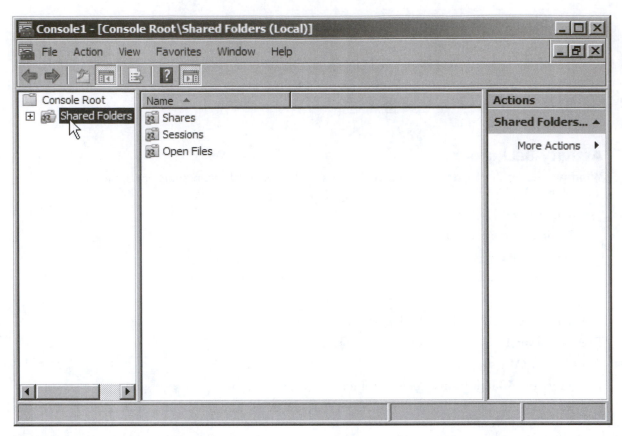

Figure 5-4   Shared Folders MMC snap-in

13. Double-click **Shares** in the middle pane of the console window. The middle pane now displays the shared folders and disks. The shares that are followed by the dollar sign ($) are hidden from normal view over the network. You are likely to see the following shares:

    - *ADMIN$*—an administrative share to the system root folder, which enables server administrators access through a network connection to the root folder hierarchy of folders

    - *C$*—a share for the root partition

    - *IPC$*—a share to enable network communication between programs, such as for programs that administrators use to remotely manage servers

    - *DFS namespace name*—the DFS namespace name you entered in Lab 5.1, such as *Research*

    Additional administrative shares you might see displayed after a server is configured include: PRINT$ for remote shared printer management and FAX$, which enables clients to use a shared fax machine.

14. Right-click **Shares** in the tree in the left pane and click **New Share**.

15. Click **Next** in the Create A Shared Folder Wizard.

16. In the Folder Path dialog box, click **Browse**.

17. In the Browse For Folder dialog box, browse to the **UserData***initials* folder and click that folder. Click **OK**.

18. In the Folder Path dialog box (see Figure 5-5), click **Next**.

19. In the Name, Description, and Settings dialog box, click **Next**.

20. In the Shared Folder Permissions dialog box, ensure that **All users have read-only access** is selected. Click **Finish**.

21. In the Sharing was Successful dialog box, click **Finish**.

22. In the console window for the Shared Folders MMC, notice that the share you created is now listed in the middle pane.

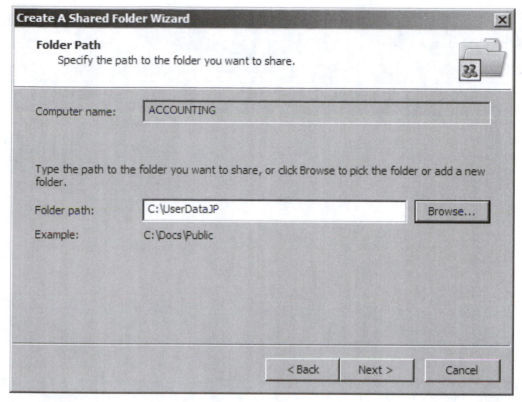

Figure 5-5   Folder Path dialog box

23. Next, remotely open the WordPad file you created earlier via the network. Click **Start** and click **Network**.

24. If you see the message, *Network discovery is turned off. Network computers and devices are not visible. Click to change....*, click the message and click **Turn on network discovery and file sharing**. Also, if you see the Network discovery and file sharing dialog box, select **Yes, turn on network discovery and file sharing for all public networks**.

25. In the Network window, double-click the name of your server. Double-click the **UserData***initials* folder. Right-click the **File***initials* file you created and click **Open**.

26. Minimize the WordPad and UserData*initials* windows.

27. In the console window for the Shared Folders MMC, click **Sessions** in the tree. In the middle pane, you'll see that your user account is connected to the computer share.

28. Right-click your account in the middle pane of the console window and notice there is a menu option for Close Session (see Figure 5-6), but do not click this option because you want to leave the session connected for the next step. Click the pointer in a blank area of the window to close the menu.

29. In the console window, click **Open Files** in the tree. You will likely see two connections. Depending on how it is connected, a single client may have two or more connections, such as a network connection for the computer and a connection for the user account.

30. In the console window, right-click a user and notice the menu option to Close Open File. This option is useful when a file is stuck open even though the user has disconnected. If other users report that they cannot access a shared file, try this technique to close the file and release a potential file lock. Often when a file is opened by a user it is locked so that other users cannot open and update it at the same time, which might result in conflicting updates or actions on the file.

31. Close the console window and click **Yes** to save the settings to Console1. In the Save As text box, enter Shared Folders plus your initials, such as *Shared FoldersJP* and click **Save**.

32. Close all other open windows.

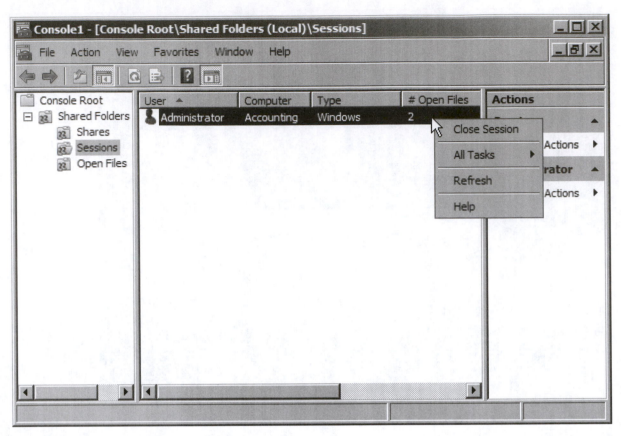

Figure 5-6   Sessions management options

Review Questions

1. Your organization has a shared file called FieldNotes that no one seems to be able to access after one of the managers opened the file earlier this afternoon. Which of the following do you suspect might be the problem?

   a. The file's share permissions are in the closed mode.

   b. There is still a file lock on the file.

   c. The file needs an owner.

   d. The non-managers shared special permission needs to be reset.

2. Use the _____ folder in the tree of the Shared Folders MMC snap-in to see what folder and drives are shared.

3. Which of the following shares is configured by default to enable administrators to use programs to remotely manage a server?

   a. ADM

   b. REMOTE

   c. IPC$

   d. DFS$

4. True or False? One shortcoming of the Shared Folders MMC snap-in is that you cannot monitor a shared DFS namespace.

5. Which of the following can you accomplish using the Shared Folders MMC snap-in?

   a. Create a shared folder

   b. Open a shared folder over the network

   c. Send a message to a user to ask him to disconnect from a share

   d. View shared files that are open

Lab 5.4 Install Subsystem for UNIX-based Applications

Objectives

- Install Subsystem for UNIX-based Applications
- Obtain and install Microsoft SDK for UNIX-based Applications

Materials Required

This lab requires the following:

- Windows Server 2008 Standard or Enterprise Edition and a connection to the Internet

Estimated completion time: **20 minutes**

Activity Background

Many organizations use Linux servers or workstations. Newer Linux operating systems are quickly replacing more traditional UNIX systems because Linux offers UNIX-like capabilities on a modern operating system engine—on lower-cost PC-based computers. As a server administrator, you are very likely to need the ability to configure Windows Server 2008 servers so that they can interoperate with Linux computers. Windows Server 2008 offers Subsystem for UNIX-based Applications for this purpose.

Subsystem for UNIX-based Applications enables UNIX/Linux applications to run on a Windows Server 2008 server, and enables executing UNIX/Linux scripts, running UNIX/Linux shells, and deploying UNIX/Linux editors. As a Windows Server 2008 administrator, you don't have to be an expert in UNIX/Linux to configure interoperability—but you should know how to install Subsystem for UNIX-based Applications so that others can deploy UNIX/Linux applications on a Windows Server 2008 server. When you plan and deploy a server, this Windows Server 2008 feature may be vital to your organization.

For this activity, you use Server Manager to install Subsystem for UNIX-based Applications. Check with your instructor about performing the download of UNIX/Linux tools in Step 13. If you do not have an Internet connection or permission to download the utilities and Software Development Kit (SDK), you can stop at Step 13 before clicking Download. Note that the utilities and SDK require about 100 MB of disk space.

Activity

1. Click **Start**, point to **Administrative Tools**, and click **Server Manager**, if Server Manager is not already open.

2. Scroll to the Features Summary section in Server Manager and click **Add Features**.

3. Click the box for **Subsystem for UNIX-based Applications** (see Figure 5-7).

4. Click **Next** in the Select Features dialog box.

5. Click **Install**.

6. In the Installation Results window, click **Close**.

7. Close **Server Manager**.

8. Click **Start** and point to **All Programs**.

9. Click **Subsystem for UNIX-based Applications**.

10. Click **Download Utilities for Subsystem for UNIX-based Applications**. (If you see the Internet Explorer box that refers to blocked Internet activity, click the Add button and follow any instructions to permit access to Microsoft's Web site. You may have to perform several authorizations.)

11. On the Microsoft Web site, click the **Continue** button. (Note that Internet Web sites change frequently and so some of the following steps may change.)

12. For this activity, click **No, I do not want to register. Take me to the download**. Click **Continue**.

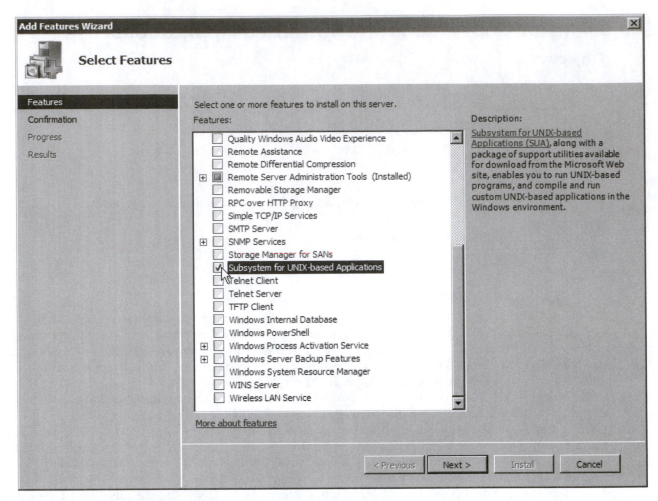

Figure 5-7 Installing Subsystem for UNIX-based Applications

13. Scroll to find the download that is appropriate for your computer. Look for X86 in the download name for 32-bit computers and AMD64 for AMD 64-bit computers or IA64 for Intel 64-bit computers, such as: *Utilities for SDK for UNIX-based Applications_AMD64.exe* or *Utilities for SDK for UNIX-based Applications_X86.exe.* Click the **Download** button next to the selection appropriate for your computer. (If you see a message that your security does not permit downloading the file, you'll have to configure Internet Explorer to enable downloads. To configure Internet Explorer, click the Tools menu, click Internet Options, click the Security tab, click the Custom Level button, and configure options to enable downloading files.)

14. For this activity click **Run**. It will take a few minutes to download the tools.

15. Click **Run** in the Internet Explorer - Security Warning dialog box to run the software on your server.

16. Click **Unzip**.

17. Click **OK** in the WinZip Self-Extractor box.

18. Minimize Internet Explorer, if necessary.

19. In the Utilities and SDK for UNIX-based Applications Setup Wizard, click **Next**.

20. In the Customer Information dialog box, enter your user name and click **Next**.

21. Review the End-User License Agreement, click **I accept the agreement**, and click **Next**.

22. In the Installation Options dialog box, leave **Standard Installation** selected and click **Next**.

23. Click **Next** in the Security Settings dialog box (leave the selection boxes blank).

24. In the Summary dialog box, click **Install**.

25. Click **Finish** when you see the Completing the Utilities and SDK for UNIX-based Applications Setup Wizard dialog box informing the user of a successful installation.

26. Click **Start**, point to **All Programs**, and click **Subsystem for UNIX-based Applications** to view some of the new utilities and other options (see Figure 5-8).

27. Close any open windows.

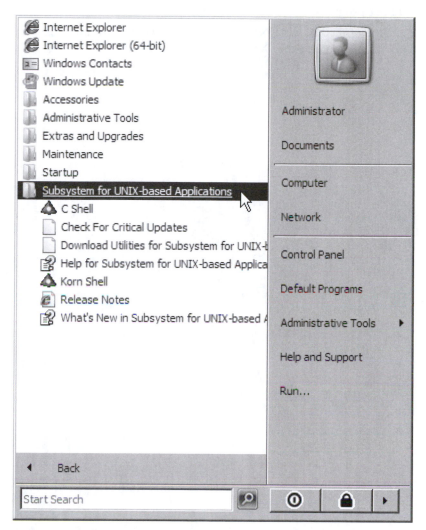

Figure 5-8   Subsystem for UNIX-based Applications options

Review Questions

1. As you are planning a Windows Server 2008 deployment, which of the following is important to know about Subsystem for UNIX-based Applications? (Choose all that apply.)

   a. It enables you to run UNIX/Linux scripts.

   b. It supports UNIX/Linux shells.

   c. It makes all pre-existing Windows programs capable of being compiled as UNIX/Linux programs with few modifications.

   d. It transforms Windows PowerShell into an environment for UNIX/Linux editors.

2. To obtain utilities for SDK for UNIX-based Applications, you must _____ them.

3. Subsystem for UNIX-based Applications is installed as a(n) _____?

   a. application from the Start menu Accessories folder

   b. server role

   c. server feature

   d. file services role service

4. True or False? To complete all of the steps for installing Subsystem for UNIX-based Applications, you must know how to compile a UNIX/Linux program.

5. True or False? When you use utilities for SDK for UNIX-based Applications, you must use the utilities appropriate for the processor in your computer, either X86, AMD64, or IA64.

CHAPTER SIX

CONFIGURING WINDOWS SERVER 2008 PRINTING

Labs included in this chapter:

- Lab 6.1 Install the LPR Port Monitor for UNIX/Linux Printing
- Lab 6.2 Install a Shared Printer Using the Print Management Tool
- Lab 6.3 Create a Printer Filter and Manage Print Jobs with the Print Management Tool
- Lab 6.4 Troubleshoot a Print Spooler Problem

Microsoft MCITP Exam #70-646 Objectives

Objective	Lab
Planning for Server Deployment	6.1, 6.2
Planning for Server Management	6.2, 6.3
Monitoring and Maintaining Servers	6.3, 6.4

Lab 6.1 Install the LPR Port Monitor for UNIX/Linux Printing

Objectives

- Install the UNIX/Linux printing capability
- Configure a UNIX/Linux printer port

Materials Required

This lab requires the following:

- Windows Server 2008 Standard or Enterprise Edition with the Print Services role installed with the Print Server and LPD Service role services
- Active Directory Domain Services role installed

Estimated completion time: **15 minutes**

Activity Background

In Lab 5.4 of Chapter 5, you installed Subsystem for UNIX-based Applications to enable Windows, Linux, and UNIX computers to interoperate on the same network. An additional element you can install is LPR (line printer) Port Monitor, which enables Windows computers to print documents on printers managed by UNIX or Linux computers. LPR Port Monitor is compatible with Windows XP, Vista, Windows 7, Server 2008, and Server 2008 R2, as well as Linux and UNIX computers.

LPR Port Monitor works by allowing a network computer to communicate with the Line Printer Daemon (LPD) service used for UNIX/Linux printing. LPD is a network printing system that uses TCP/IP communications. LPD is identified on a network by an IP address, such as an IP address for a Linux print server that manages one or more printers. LPD uses the LPD protocol for communications between a computer and a printer. You can read the official LPD protocol specifications at *www.ietf.org/rfc/rfc1179.txt*.

In this activity, you use Server Manager to install the LPR Port Monitor. Next, you use the Print Management tool to add a UNIX/Linux printer for management via Windows Server 2008. You will need to have the Print Services role installed with the Printer Server and LPD Service role services (which can be installed using Server Manager).

For all of the activities in this chapter, you'll need to log onto an account with Administrator privileges. Additionally, most of these activities can be completed on a virtual server or computer, such as in Hyper-V.

Throughout the activities in this book, you may occasionally see the User Account Control box with a message that Windows needs your permission to continue. Whenever you see this box, click Continue. Keep this in mind for all of the activities because any interaction with the User Account Control box is intentionally not included in the steps.

Activity

1. Click **Start**, point to **Administrative Tools**, and click **Server Manager** (or click the Server Manager icon in the taskbar).
2. In the Features Summary section, click **Add Features**.
3. In the Select Features window, click the box for **LPR Port Monitor** and click **Next**.
4. In the Confirm Installation Selections window, click **Install**.
5. In the Installation Results window, click **Close**.
6. Close any open windows in Server Manager and then close Server Manager.

   In the next steps you learn how to configure a printer port to use for printing to a UNIX/Linux printer, but you stop at the last step to enter an IP address because an actual printer is not required for this activity.

7. Click **Start**, point to **Administrative Tools**, and click **Print Management**.

8. Ensure that the items in the left pane in the tree under Print Servers are displayed. (If necessary, click the **+** plus sign in front of Print Servers. Also, if necessary click the **+** plus sign in front of the server name in the tree to view the items under it.)

9. Right-click your server name and click **Add Printer** (see Figure 6-1).

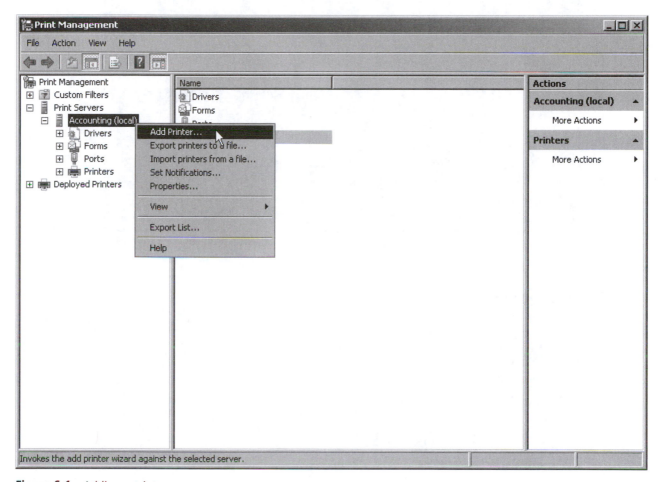

Figure 6-1   Adding a printer

10. In the Printer Installation dialog box, click **Create a new port and add a new printer**.

11. Click the down arrow for the box to the right of Create a new port and add a new printer and click **LPR port** (see Figure 6-2). Click **Next**.

12. In the Add LPR compatible printer dialog box, note that you can enter the IP address of the printer and also a name for the printer or print queue. Click **Cancel**.

13. Click **Cancel** in the Network Printer Installation Wizard dialog box.

14. Leave the Print Management window open for the next lab.

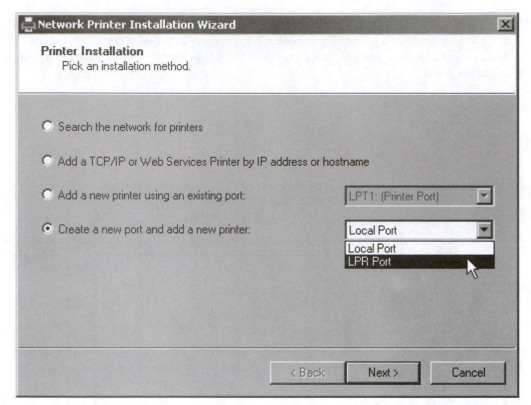

Figure 6-2   Creating a new port to add a UNIX/Linux printer

Review Questions

1. Which of the following options enables you to set up communications between Windows-based systems and UNIX/Linux printers?

   a. UNIX-based Print Application

   b. UNIX daemon

   c. Remote Print Management service

   d. LPR Port Monitor

2. The option mentioned in Question 1 is a _____.

   a. Server role installed through Server Manager

   b. Server feature installed through Server Manager

   c. Printer capability installed using the Control Panel Device Manager applet

   d. Printer capability installed using the Control Panel Add Hardware applet

3. When setting up to print to a UNIX/Linux printer via Windows Server 2008, which of the following do you need?

   a. Location of the printer

   b. Speed of the printer

   c. IP address of the printer

   d. MAC address of the printer

4. You can add a new UNIX/Linux printer through the _____ tool.

5. Communicating with a UNIX/Linux printer involves using the _____ service.

Lab 6.2 Install a Shared Printer Using the Print Management Tool

Objectives

- Install a shared printer through the Print Management tool
- Configure printer properties with the Print Management tool

Materials Required

This lab requires the following:

- Windows Server 2008 Standard or Enterprise Edition with the Print Services role installed with the Print Server role service
- Active Directory Domain Services role installed

Estimated completion time:	20 minutes

Activity Background

In Lab 6.1 you used the Print Management tool to configure a printer port for a UNIX/Linux printer. The Print Management tool is a comprehensive printing management tool that is installed when you install the Print Services role in Windows Server 2008. You can use this tool to set up a new local printer, network printer, or Internet printer. It provides one convenient place for configuring printer properties, managing print queues, checking the status of printers, and generally managing printers.

For this activity, you set up a shared printer and configure its properties. You don't need an actual printer connected to your server.

Activity

1. Ensure the Print Management window is open or, if it is not, click **Start**, point to **Administrative Tools**, and click **Print Management**.

2. Make sure that Print Servers is expanded in the tree. In the tree, right-click your server and click **Add Printer**.

3. In the Printer Installation dialog box, click **Add a new printer using an existing port** and click **Next**.

4. In the Printer Driver dialog box, ensure that **Install a new driver** is selected (see Figure 6-3) and click **Next**.

5. In the Printer Installation dialog box click **Canon** under Manufacturer and click **Canon iR8070 PCL**. Click **Next**.

6. In the Printer Name and Sharing Settings box, add your initials at the end of the printer name, such as *Canon iR8070 PCL JP*. Also, add you initials at the end of the share name. Notice that the box for **Share this printer** is checked. Click **Next**.

7. Review the information in the Printer Found dialog box and click **Next**.

8. In the Completing the Network Printer Installation Wizard dialog box, click **Finish**.

9. In the tree under your server's name, click **Printers**.

10. In the middle pane, right-click the printer you set up and click **Properties**.

11. Click the **General** tab, if necessary, and click **Printing Preferences**.

12. In the Printing Preferences dialog box, set the **Orientation** to **Landscape** and click **OK**.

13. Click the **Sharing** tab to verify the printer is shared (see Figure 6-4).

14. Click the **Ports** tab and click the box for **LPT2** to use line printer port 2.

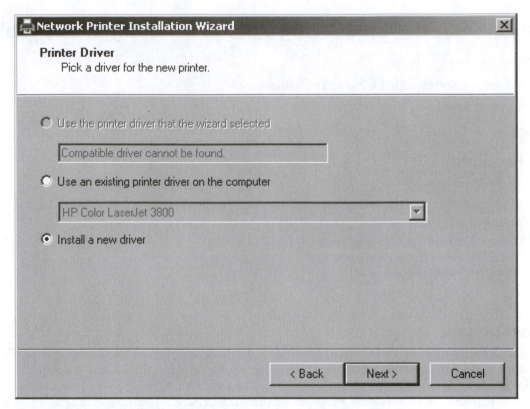

Figure 6-3   Printer Driver dialog box

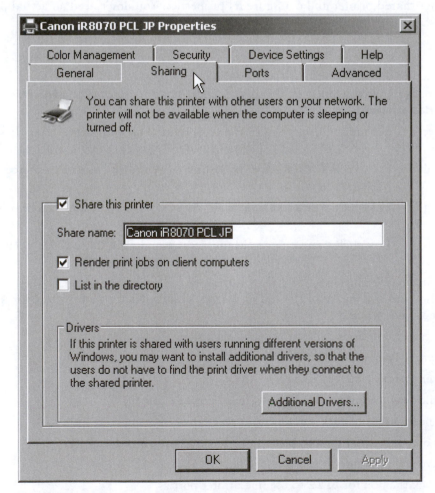

Figure 6-4   Sharing tab

15. Click the **Advanced** tab to review the default settings.

16. Click the **Security** tab.

17. Under Group or user names, review the groups and users configured by default. Click **Server Operators (domainname\Server Operators)** and click **Remove**.

18. On the Security tab, click each of the groups and users and verify their permissions.

19. Click the **Device Settings** tab and examine the device properties that can be configured. Notice that this printer has multiple drawers for holding paper. Under Installable Options, click the **down arrow** for **Stacker-A1** and click **On** to turn on the stacker.

20. Click the **Color Management** tab and notice there is a button for adjusting color management settings.

21. Click **OK** in the printer's Properties dialog box.

22. In the tree under the server name, click **Drivers**. In the middle pane, you'll see a listing of the drivers of all the printers connected to the server.

23. In the tree under the server name, click **Forms**. In the middle pane, review the many types of paper forms available to the printers connected to the server.

24. Click **Ports** in the tree. In the middle pane, review the ports for the server and notice which ports have a printer associated with them.

25. Click **Printers** in the tree. The middle pane lists the printers connected to the server. Leave the Print Management window open for the next activity.

Review Questions

1. True or False? When you configure a printer using the Print Management tool, printer sharing is not configured automatically.

2. You need to print over a hundred pages of spreadsheets using the landscape printing mode. Which tab in a printer's properties enables you to set up to use landscape printing?

   a. Advanced

   b. Paper

   c. General

   d. Device Settings

3. LPT3 when configured in a printer's properties is a(n) _____.

4. Which of the following are groups or users configured by default to have printer permissions? (Choose all that apply.)

   a. Domain Controllers

   b. Administrators

   c. Server Operators

   d. Guests

5. Your company needs to print 11×17 inch posters on a large printer. Where in the Print Management tool can you set up to print 11×17?

   a. Click Drivers in the tree.

   b. In the tree, right-click Print Servers and click Paper Size.

   c. Click the printer in the middle pane, click the Action menu, and click Paper Size.

   d. Click Forms in the tree.

Lab 6.3 Create a Printer Filter and Manage Print Jobs with the Print Management Tool

Objectives

- Create a printer filter through the Print Management tool
- Learn how to manage a print queue with the Print Management tool
- Learn how to manage print jobs with the Print Management tool

Materials Required

This lab requires the following:

- Windows Server 2008 Standard or Enterprise Edition with the Print Services role installed

Estimated completion time: **15 minutes**

Activity Background

The Print Management tool enables you to do more than install a printer and configure its properties. This tool also has features for managing print jobs and print queues on multiple printers and servers in one convenient place. Additionally, you can monitor the status of printers, so that you know when a printer is not available to users. Taking this a step further, you can set up printer filters to detect when printers are offline and have the printer filter send you an e-mail message to warn you about the problem, so you can quickly respond to bring the printers back online for users.

Consider an example in which the shipping department of a company uses three printers for printing shipping labels and forms. It is essential for all three printers to be functional and online to ensure products are sent in a timely fashion. The three printers can be configured and managed from a Windows Server 2008 print server via the Print Services role. Also, a printer filter can be configured to continuously monitor all three printers to be sure they have a ready status. If one or more printers goes to offline status, the printer filter sends an e-mail to alert the server administrator.

In this activity, you use the Print Management tool and the New Printer Filter Wizard to configure a printer filter. Additionally, you use the Print Management tool to learn how to manage a print queue and print jobs.

Activity

1. Be sure the Print Management window is open, or if it is not, click **Start**, point to **Administrative Tools**, and click **Print Management**.

2. In the tree in the left pane, right-click **Custom Filters** and click **Add New Printer Filter**.

3. In the Printer Filter Name and Description dialog box of the New Printer Filter Wizard, enter **Filter** plus your initials, such as *FilterJP*, for the filter name. Also, enter **Test filter** for the description. Click **Next**.

4. In the Define a printer filter dialog box, click the down arrow for the topmost **Field** box and click **Queue Status**.

5. Click the down arrow for the topmost **Condition** box and click **is exactly**.

6. Still in the Define a printer filter dialog box, click the topmost **Value** box and click **Offline** (see Figure 6-5).

7. In the Define a printer filter dialog box, click **Next**.

8. In the Set Notifications (Optional) dialog box notice that you can send an e-mail and run a script when a print queue of one of the printers managed by the server is offline. Click **Finish**.

9. Notice that your filter is now displayed under Custom Filters in the tree. You can click this filter at any time and the middle pane will list any print queues that are offline.

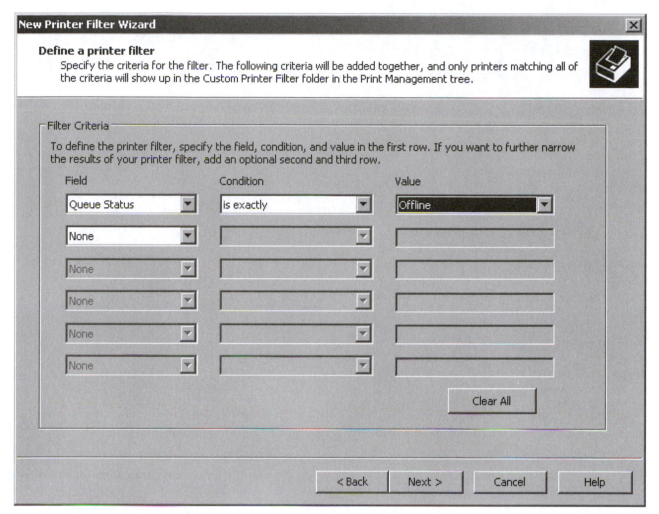

Figure 6-5   Configuring a printer filter

10. Under Custom Filters, click **All Printers (#)**. The middle pane lists the printers managed through the Print Management tool. Notice that the printer you created in Lab 6.2 is listed.

11. Right-click the printer you created, **Canon iR8070 PCL initials**. Notice the printer management options, such as Open Printer Queue, Pause Printing, Managing Sharing, Properties, Rename, and others (see Figure 6-6).

12. Click **Open Printer Queue** in the menu.

13. In the Canon iR8070 PCL *initials* window, click the **Printer** menu and review the options for managing the printer queue, such as Set As Default Printer, Pause Printing, Cancel All Documents, and others. Move your pointer to a blank area and click to close the menu.

14. Click the **Document** menu and view the options, which should be deactivated because you have no jobs in the print queue. For any print job, you can click it in the window, click the Document menu, and select to Pause, Resume, Restart, or Cancel the print job. You can also click to view the Properties of a print job. Move your pointer to a blank area and click to close the menu.

15. Close the Canon iR8070 PCL *initials* window.

16. In the tree of the Print Management window, click **All Drivers**. In the middle pane, you see the printer drivers for the printers that are installed. Notice the Driver Version column. You can use this column to help you determine if you have an older version of a driver by comparing the version number to that given on the Web site of the printer manufacturer.

17. In the tree, click **Printers Not Ready**. Printers with a not ready status would appear in the middle pane.

18. In the tree, click **Printers With Jobs**. Any printer currently active with print jobs would appear in the middle pane. Close the Print Management window.

Open Printer Queue...
Pause Printing
List in Directory
Deploy with Group Policy...
Set Printing Defaults...
Manage Sharing...
Print Test Page
Properties...
Delete
Rename
Help

Figure 6-6   Printer management options

Review Questions

1. Which of the following can you do with a printer filter? (Choose all that apply.)

    a. Install a printer

    b. Monitor a specific printer condition, such as an offline print queue

    c. Send an e-mail warning to a printer administrator about a monitored condition

    d. Determine the number of drawers in a printer and what paper is loaded in each drawer

2. When you create a printer filter you configure which of the following parameters for the filter criteria? (Choose all that apply.)

    a. Time

    b. Condition

    c. Value

    d. Field

3. Which of the following actions can you perform on a printer using the Print Management tool?

    a. Pause printing

    b. Manage printer sharing

    c. Rename a printer

    d. Delete a printer

4. To determine the version level of a specific printer's driver click _____ in the tree of the Print Management window.

5. When managing print jobs by opening a printer's print queue window, you can perform which of the following actions? (Choose all that apply.)

    a. Delete the printer

    b. Pause printing

    c. Cancel a specific print job

    d. Add new print jobs

Lab 6.4 Troubleshoot a Print Spooler Problem

Objectives

- Troubleshoot the Print Spooler service by determining on which services it depends
- Stop and start the Print Spooler service

Materials Required

This lab requires the following:

- Windows Server 2008 Standard or Enterprise Edition with the Print Services role installed

Estimated completion time: **10 minutes**

Activity Background

The Print Spooler service is central to the success of printing. Print files are accepted from the client and stored as spooler files on the print server. These files are automatically managed by the Print Spooler service. Occasionally, the Print Spooler service can hang or experience difficulties, causing the print queue to stop printing jobs listed in the queue. If you experience a situation in which print jobs won't print, you have verified that the printer has power, and the printer is properly connected, then suspect that the Print Spooler service may be hung.

The solution can be to stop and restart the Print Spooler service. When this action is necessary, it is important to remember that all of the print jobs in a print queue are lost and users must resubmit them. If you need to stop and restart the Print Spooler service, plan to let users know so that they can resubmit their print jobs.

For this activity, you check to determine what services are related to the Print Spooler service and then you stop and restart the Print Spooler service.

Activity

1. Click **Start**, point to **Administrative Tools**, and click **Server Manager**.
2. In the tree in the left pane, click the **+** plus sign in front of **Configuration** to display the elements under it.
3. In the tree under Configuration, click **Services**.
4. Click the **Standard** tab at the bottom of the middle pane, if it is not selected.
5. Scroll to find Print Spooler under the Name column in the middle pane (see Figure 6-7).
6. Check the Status column for Print Spooler and determine if the status is Started. Also, check to see if the Startup Type column indicates Automatic so that the service is automatically started when the computer is booted.
7. Double-click **Print Spooler** in the middle pane.
8. In the Print Spooler Properties (*servername*) dialog box, click the **Dependencies** tab (see Figure 6-8).
9. Notice that the Print Spooler service depends on the HTTP and Remote Procedure Call (RPC) services to be started.
10. Click **Cancel** in the Print Spooler Properties (*servername*) dialog box.
11. In the middle pane of Server Manager, scroll to find the HTTP service. You'll find it is not listed because this service is managed by the Windows Server 2008 operating system and is currently running.

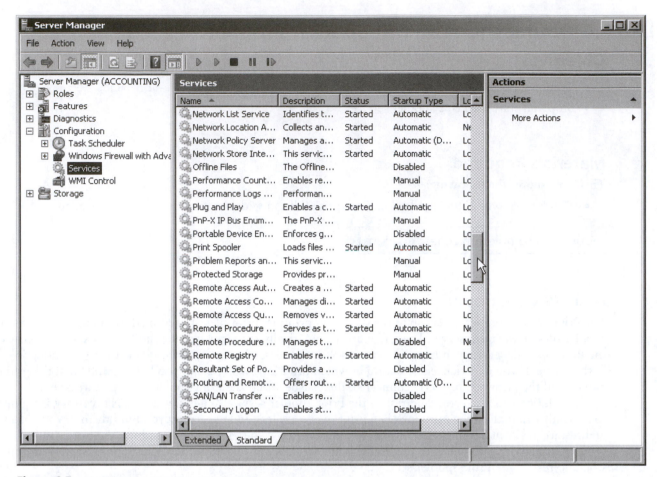

Figure 6-7   Checking the Print Spooler service in Server Manager

12. Scroll to find the Remote Procedure Call (RPC) service in the middle pane. Determine if this service has a Started status. (You may need to expand the Name column to distinguish this service from the Remote Procedure Call (RPC) Locator service. If needed, move your pointer to the separator line between the Name column and the Description column until you see a crosshair cursor and then drag the line to the right to expand the Name column.)

13. Double-click **Print Spooler** in the middle pane of Server Manager.

14. Even though the Print Spooler service may have a Started status, it may still be hung. You can correct the problem by stopping and restarting the service. In the Print Spooler Properties (*servername*) dialog box, click the **Stop** button. (If the Stop Other Services dialog box displays to ask if you want to stop the TCP/IP Print Server, click **Yes**.)

15. After the service is stopped, click the **Start** button to restart it.

16. Click **OK** in the Print Spooler Properties (*servername*) dialog box.

17. In Server Manager in the tree, click **Server Manager (*servername*).**

18. Close Server Manager.

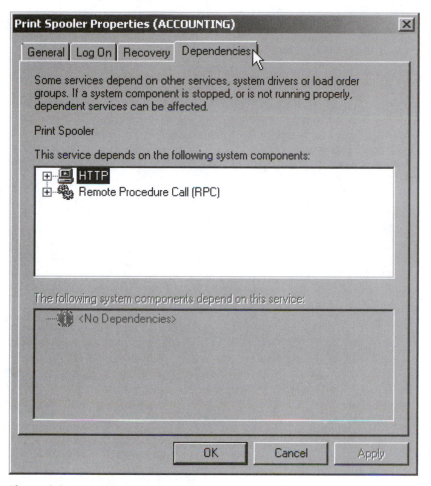

Figure 6-8   Dependencies tab

Review Questions

1. The Print Spooler service depends on which of the following services? (Choose all that apply.)

   a. File Replication

   b. Network List

   c. HTTP

   d. Remote Procedure Call (RPC)

2. True or False? You can use Server Manager to manage Windows Server 2008 services.

3. Which tab in the Print Spooler Properties dialog box enables you to start and stop the Print Spooler service?

   a. Dependencies

   b. Log On

   c. Services

   d. General

4. True or False? After you stop and restart the Print Spooler service, users will find their print jobs have resumed automatically without the need to resubmit them.

5. When you view Windows Server 2008 services, the _____ column shows whether or not a specific service is started.

CONFIGURING AND MANAGING DATA STORAGE

Labs included in this chapter:

- Lab 7.1 View the Properties of a Disk

- Lab 7.2 Shrink a Disk Volume and Rescan Disks

- Lab 7.3 Install Storage Manager for SANs

- Lab 7.4 Schedule a Backup and Configure Backup Performance

Microsoft MCITP Exam #70-646 Objectives

Objective	Lab
Planning for Server Management	7.2, 7.3
Planning for Business Continuity and High Availability	7.1, 7.2, 7.3, 7.4

Lab 7.1 View the Properties of a Disk

Objectives

- Understand a disk's properties and how they can be configured
- Learn from where to start disk maintenance tools
- Learn how to verify disk capacity allocation and if a disk is working

Materials Required

This lab requires the following:

- Windows Server 2008 Standard or Enterprise Edition

Estimated completion time: **15 minutes**

Activity Background

The Properties dialog box for a disk is a valuable tool for finding information about a disk and for launching disk maintenance tools. For example, one of the most fundamental but important pieces of information about a disk is the amount of unused disk space. As a server manager, you regularly need to watch the amount of unused disk space in order to make sure that you don't run out of disk space unexpectedly and to plan in advance for added disk storage.

The tabs available for a disk's properties include:

- *General*—shows information such as disk capacity, disk usage, and the file system
- *Tools*—provides tools for disk maintenance, such as the disk defragmenter
- *Hardware*—provides information about disk hardware and enables you to configure the hardware
- *Sharing*—used to configure disk sharing
- *Security*—used to configure disk security
- *Shadow Copies*—used to configure the shadow copy feature for backing up shared folders
- *Previous Versions*—enables users to access previous versions of files in a shared folder, for example, enabling a user to restore a file she has unintentionally deleted or overwritten
- *Quota*—used to configure disk quotas

In this activity, you use Server Manager to access and manage the properties of a disk.

For all of the activities in this chapter, you'll need to log on to an account with Administrator privileges. Additionally, most of these activities can be completed on a virtual server or computer, such as in Hyper-V.

Throughout the activities in this book, you may occasionally see the User Account Control box with a message that Windows needs your permission to continue. Whenever you see this box, click Continue. Keep this in mind for all of the activities because any interaction with the User Account Control box is intentionally not included in the steps.

Activity

1. Open Server Manager, if it is not open. Click **Start**, point to **Administrative Tools**, and click **Server Manager** (or click the Server Manager icon in the taskbar).

2. Click the + plus sign in front of **Storage** in the tree in the left pane.

3. In the tree, click **Disk Management**.

4. In the middle pane, right-click the **blue bar** over a drive letter, such as (C:) and click **Properties** (see Figure 7-1).

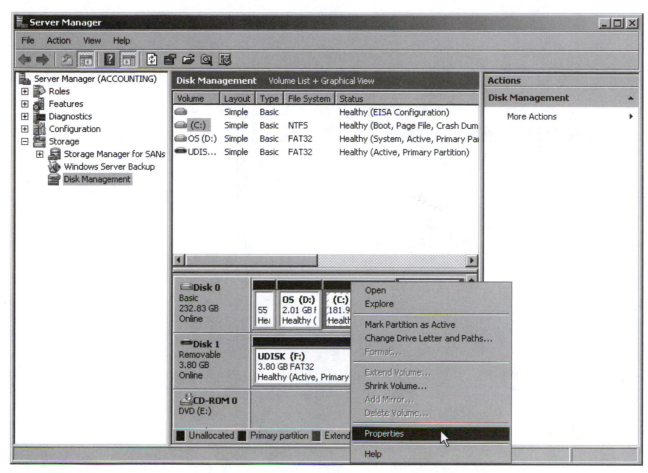

Figure 7-1   Accessing a hard drive's properties

5. Make sure the **General** tab is displayed. Notice the file system, used versus unused space, and capacity. Also, there are options to *Compress this drive to save disk space* and *Index this drive for faster searching*.

6. In the Local Disk (*driveletter:*) Properties dialog box, click the **Tools** tab and you see buttons for running the Disk Check, the Disk Defragmenter, and the Disk Backup tools.

7. Click the **Hardware** tab. This tab lists all of the drives connected to your computer, including hard, CD/DVD, and USB drives (see Figure 7-2).

8. On the Hardware tab, click a hard disk and click the **Properties** button.

9. In the Device Properties dialog box, make sure the **General** tab is displayed. Notice that you can verify the device is working on this tab. Click the **Policies** tab (if your disk has one) and notice that you can configure disk caching. Click the **Driver** tab to view the current driver and driver version. You can use this tab to install an updated driver. Close the Device Properties dialog box.

10. In the Local Disk (*driveletter:*) Properties dialog box, click the **Sharing** tab. By default the disk is not shared. You can configure sharing for the entire disk by clicking the Advanced Sharing button.

11. Click the **Security** tab and notice that you can configure security for the entire disk.

12. Click the **Shadow Copies** tab. This tab is used to enable automated backups of shared folders on this disk. Backing up shared folders permits users to restore specific folder and file contents, which can be invaluable when a file is modified but there is a need to go back to an earlier version. It's also useful because deleted or corrupted files can be instantly restored. You work with Shadow Copies in Chapter 15, "Managing System Reliability and Availability." Many organizations include Shadow Copies in their plan for Windows Server 2008 deployment.

13. In the Local Disk (*driveletter:*) Properties dialog box, click the **Previous Versions** tab. When the shadow copies capability is enabled, this tab lists the previous versions of backups that have been made of shared folders and files.

Figure 7-2   Hardware tab

14. Click the **Quota** tab. This tab enables you to configure disk quotas to help control the disk space allocated to users.

15. Close the Local Disk (*driveletter*:) Properties dialog box, but leave the Server Manager window open to Disk Management for the next activity.

Review Questions

1. You need to defragment a server disk. On which of the following tabs of that disk's Properties dialog box can you run the Disk Defragmenter?

   a. Tools tab

   b. Security tab

   c. Hardware tab

   d. General tab

2. True or False? Server users have recently called you to report that they cannot access shared files on one of the server's hard drives. You can verify that the hard drive is working properly by checking that drive's Properties dialog box.

3. Your hard drive manufacturer has issued a warning that an older disk driver can cause problems when writing to the disk. What tab in the disk's Properties dialog box enables you to determine the disk driver version number?

   a. Tools tab

   b. Previous Versions tab

   c. Hardware tab

   d. General tab

4. Automated backups of shared folders on a disk are called _____.

5. You've received a message from your database software that it cannot write a large record to the hard drive. You can check the amount of free disk space on the _____ tab in the Properties dialog box for the disk that houses the database.

Lab 7.2 Shrink a Disk Volume and Rescan Disks

Objectives

- Shrink a disk
- Rescan a disk

Materials Required

This lab requires the following:

- Windows Server 2008 Standard or Enterprise Edition with a formatted disk that has 200 MB of unused disk space that can be reallocated

Estimated completion time: **15 minutes**

Activity Background

There are times when you need to set up a new partition, but there is not quite enough free disk space available and there are no extra disks already installed in the server. One approach to solving the need for free disk space is to shrink a volume that has allocated, but unused space. In Lab 7.1, you learned how to determine the amount of unused space on a volume. When you verify you have enough unused space, you can shrink a volume to create unallocated disk space that can be partitioned for another purpose. Windows Server 2008 frees the space by rearranging files on the volume that you are shrinking and so that the volume does not have to be reformatted. Shrinking can be performed on a basic or dynamic volume. An important factor to remember is that some files, such as the paging file or files created for shadow copies, cannot be rearranged on the disk.

After you make a change to a disk, such as shrinking it or after adding a partition, your change sometimes does not display in the Disk Management tool. Instead of assuming there is a problem or rebooting to verify the change, you can simply use the rescan option in the Disk Management tool to detect and correctly redisplay your change. Keep the rescan option in mind to save you time and simplify disk management the next time you add or reconfigure disks.

In this activity, you shrink a disk and then you rescan it. Before you shrink the disk, check the disk's properties to verify that you have at least 12 GB of unused space. You'll use 200 MB of the unused space for this activity, but need to be sure you have plenty of remaining space for future activities.

Activity

1. Make sure that Server Manager is open with Disk Management displayed in the middle pane. If Disk Management is not displayed, refer to Steps 1–3 in Lab 7.1.

2. In the middle pane, right-click the `blue bar` over the drive letter that you plan to shrink, and click `Shrink Volume` (refer to Figure 7-1).

3. Wait for the Disk Management tool to query the volume to determine the available "shrink space."

4. In the Shrink *driveletter*: dialog box, enter **200** in the **Enter the amount of space to shrink in MB** box (see Figure 7-3).

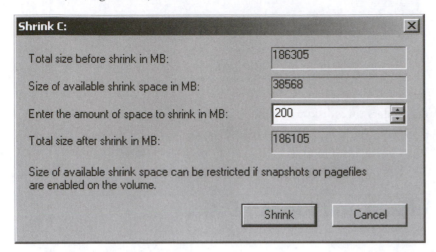

Figure 7-3 Specifying the amount of space to shrink

5. Click **Shrink**. After a few minutes, you'll see 200 MB of unallocated disk space displayed next to the drive you selected to shrink. The black bar over the unallocated space and the box underneath with the notation "unallocated" means that the space is not formatted.

6. For the sake of practice, or in case you don't see the newly unallocated disk space after a few minutes, click the **Action** menu in the menu bar of Server Manager.

7. Click **Rescan Disks** (see Figure 7-4).

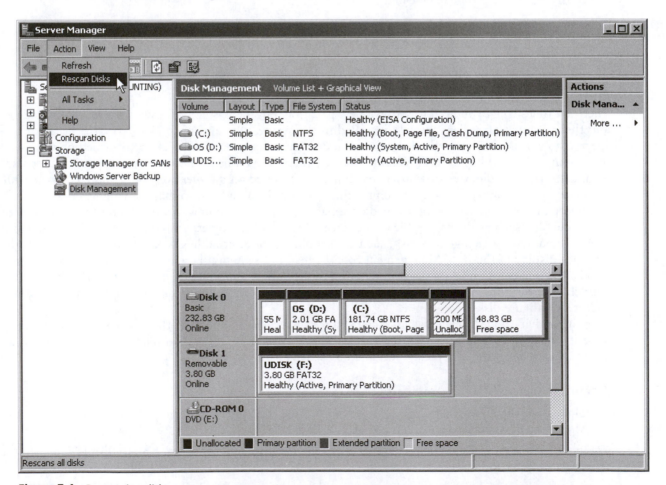

Figure 7-4 Rescanning disks

8. Right-click the **black bar** over the 200 MB space you created and click **Properties**.

9. Note that because this space is not formatted and allocated for a file system, only the Device Properties dialog box is displayed (see Figure 7-5). You don't see the full set of properties (as was the case in Lab 7.1 and Figure 7-2) because file properties, such as sharing and security, are not available for an unformatted disk.

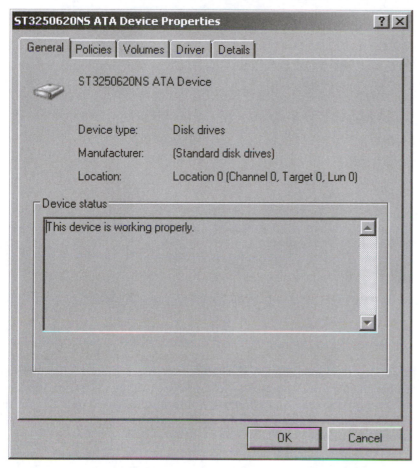

Figure 7-5   Device Properties dialog box

10. Click each of the tabs in the Device Properties dialog box to view their information.

11. Click **Cancel** in the Device Properties dialog box.

12. In the Server Manager window, click **Server Manager (Servername)** in the tree and leave Server Manager open for the next activity.

Review Questions

1. A common reason for shrinking a volume is to create a(n) _____?

2. True or False? When you shrink a volume, the newly created space is automatically formatted for the NTFS file system.

3. Two types of files that cannot be rearranged to shrink a disk are the _____ file and files used for _____.

4. From where can you initiate rescanning disks when you are using the Disk Management tool within Server Manager?

   a. File menu

   b. Action menu

   c. Options menu

   d. Manager menu

5. Which of the following must you specify when you shrink a volume? (Choose all that apply.)

   a. File system to be used for the new space

   b. Size of the Master Boot Record or Globally Unique Identifier Partition Table

   c. Location of the Master Boot Record or Globally Unique Identifier Partition Table

   d. Amount of space to shrink

Lab 7.3 Install Storage Manager for SANs

Objectives

- Understand the uses for Storage Manager for SANs
- Install Storage Manager for SANs

Materials Required

This lab requires the following:

- Windows Server 2008 Standard or Enterprise Edition

Estimated completion time: **15 minutes**

Activity Background

Storage Manager for Storage Area Networks (SANs) is a tool for managing iSCSI and Fiber Channel disk storage subsystems. A SAN is a group of information storage devices that compose a subnet. The storage devices are available to any server on the primary network and appear to the user as though they are attached to the server that the user is currently accessing. iSCSI is a popular high-speed technology used in SANs consisting of SCSI disk drives. iSCSI communicates via TCP/IP. Fiber Channel is a subnetwork technology used for SANs and employs gigabit high-speed data communications.

Using Storage Manager for SANs, you can accomplish tasks such as:

- View information about connected iSCSI and Fiber Channel disk storage subsystems
- Configure and manage logical unit numbers (LUNs) for SCSI drives
- Manage security for storage subsystems
- Plan future disk storage needs

The role of managing LUNs is especially important. A LUN is a number that identifies a physical SCSI drive or logical SCSI targets, such as SCSI volumes. Networks that use SANs can require the configuration of many LUNs for managed connections between servers and disk storage devices, which is especially true when SANs are configured for RAID.

To use Storage Manager for SANs, the SANs must employ Virtual Disk Service (VDS), which enables management of SAN disk volumes through one interface at a server.

As a server administrator, your first step is to understand how to install Storage Manager for SANs. In this activity, you use Server Manager to install Storage Manager for SANs.

Activity

1. Ensure that Server Manager is open with the main Server Manager display in the right pane. (If Server Manager is open, click Server Manager in the left pane, if necessary, to view the main Server Manager display in the right pane. If Server Manager is not open, click **Start**, point to **Administrative Tools**, and click **Server Manager**.)

2. In the right pane, scroll to the **Features Summary** section.

3. In the right pane under Features Summary, click **Add Features**.

4. In the Select Features window, click **Storage Manager for SANs** (see Figure 7-6).

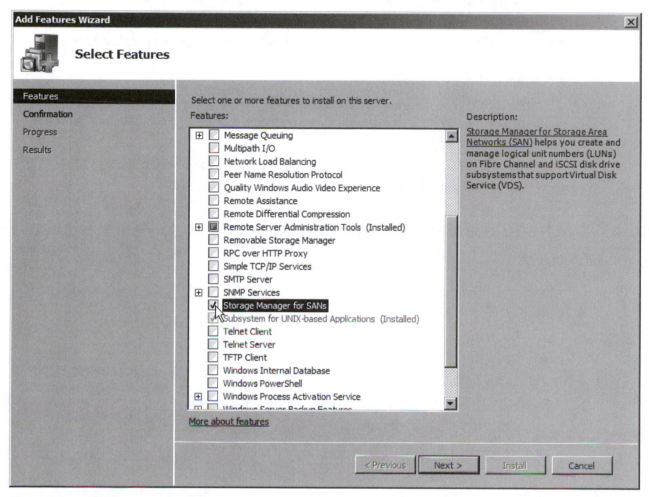

Figure 7-6 Installing Storage Manager for SANs

5. Click **Next** in the Select Features window.

6. Click **Install** in the Confirm Installation Selections window.

7. Click **Close** in the Installation Results window.

8. Click **Start**, point to **Administrative Tools**, and notice that Storage Manager for SANs is now listed. (If you have a VDS compatible SAN connected to your network, click Storage Manager for SANs, survey the options in the tree in the left pane, and then close the tool. If you open the tool without a VDS SAN connected, you'll see a message that the tool is unable to find VDS or a VDS hardware provider. Note that you can also start Storage Manager for SANs as an MMC snap-in.)

9. Close Server Manager.

Review Questions

1. iSCSI stands for _____.

2. The senior network administrator needs to be able to manage two SANs from the Windows Server 2008 server that you manage for your company. How do you install Storage Manager for SANs to enable the network administrator to manage the SANs?

    a. Use the Add Hardware applet in Control Panel.

    b. Install the Application Server Foundation role service in the Application Server role through Server Manager.

    c. Install the Storage Manager for SANs feature through Server Manager.

    d. Use the Action menu in the Disk Management tool.

3. Which of the following are tasks that can be performed using Storage Manager for SANs? (Choose all that apply.)

    a. Configure LUNs

    b. View information about disk storage subsystems connected via the network

    c. View data about current disk storage subsystems that can be used in planning for future storage needs

    d. Manage security for SANs

4. To use Storage Manager for SANs, the disk storage subsystems you purchase must employ _____.

5. After you install Storage Manager for SANs, this tool can be started from _____.

Lab 7.4 Schedule a Backup and Configure Backup Performance

Objectives

- Create a schedule for a regular backup
- Configure a backup performance option

Materials Required

This lab requires the following:

- Windows Server 2008 Standard or Enterprise Edition with the Windows Server Backup tool installed

Estimated completion time:	**15 minutes**

Activity Background

Many organizations use scheduling when they back up their servers. The Windows Server Backup tool contains a scheduling option to accommodate most organizations. Scheduling ensures that backups are done on a regular basis, as long as there is someone to insert the proper backup media prior to when the backup is scheduled to automatically begin. For example, a medical research lab backs up its servers through scheduling a back up every evening at 8:00 PM. This gives the individual researchers time to record and save their data before the servers are backed up.

    The Windows Server Backup tool also enables you to optimize backup performance using one of the following options:

- *Full backup*—which is a backup of the entire system
- *Incremental backup*—which only backs up files that are new or that have been updated
- *Custom backup*—which enables you to configure backups differently (full or incremental) for different volumes

    For this activity, you open the Windows Server Backup tool through Server Manager to schedule a backup and then you configure backup performance optimization through setting up a backup option. (Note: You can also open the Windows Server Backup tool as an MMC snap-in.) In Step 9, you cancel out of the Backup Schedule Wizard, because after that step it is necessary to select a destination for the backup, which requires a separate backup disk or volume and formatting that volume. So that you are not required to have a separate disk or to format a disk needlessly, you exit after configuring the backup schedule in Step 9. The Windows Server Backup tool should already be installed on the server. If it is not installed, you can install it as a feature via

Server Manager. (Open Server Manager, scroll to the Features section in the right pane, click Add Features, click Windows Server Backup Features, if necessary click Add Required Features to install PowerShell, and follow the steps to complete the installation.)

Activity

1. Be sure that Server Manager is open or open it if it is closed.

2. In the tree in the left pane, click the **+** plus sign in front of Storage.

3. In the tree, click `Windows Server Backup`.

4. In the Server Manager tool bar, click `Action` and click `Backup Schedule`.

5. In the Getting started window of the Backup Schedule Wizard, click `Next`.

6. In the Select backup configuration window, ensure that `Full Server (recommended)` is selected and click `Next`.

7. If you see the Windows Server Backup box with a message that one of the server volumes has an unsupported file system, click `OK`. This message is displayed, for example, if there is a FAT formatted volume.

8. In the Specify backup time window click `Once a day`, if it is not selected by default.

9. In the Select time of day box, select `7:00 PM` (see Figure 7-7). At this point, click `Cancel` to exit the Backup Schedule Wizard. (Note that the steps to continue with this process include specifying a backup destination, labeling the destination disk, reviewing your selections, and clicking Finish.)

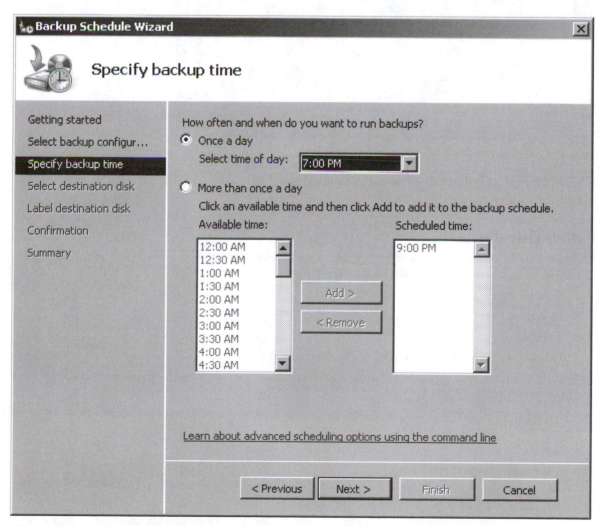

Figure 7-7   Specify backup time window

10. In the Server Manager tool bar, click the **Action** menu and click **Configure Performance Settings**.

11. In the Optimize Backup dialog box, select **Always perform a full backup**, if it isn't selected (see Figure 7-8).

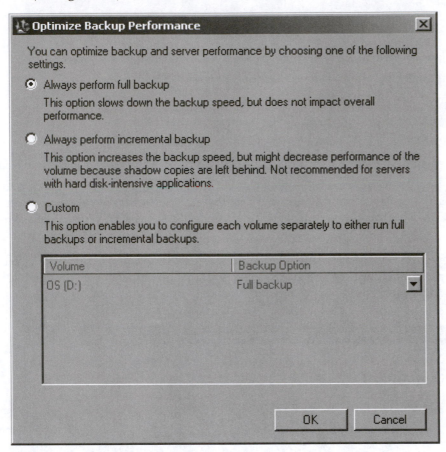

Figure 7-8   Optimize Backup Performance dialog box

12. Click **OK** in the Optimize Backup Performance dialog box.

13. Close Server Manager.

Review Questions

1. When you schedule a backup using the Windows Server Backup tool, which of the following are options that you can configure? (Choose all that apply.)

   a. To back up once a day

   b. To back up more than once a day

   c. To back up only large files

   d. To back up the memory contents of the computer

2. True or False? A backup schedule must initially be configured using the Backup Once option in the Windows Server Backup tool.

3. Which of the following backup performance optimization settings enables you to set up different backup approaches for different volumes?

   a. Full backup

   b. Full backup with specialization

   c. Custom backup

   d. Incremental backup with options

4. True or False? The Windows Server Backup tool can be opened from the Administrative Tools menu or as an MMC snap-in.

5. In a(n) _____ backup you back up only files that are new or have been recently updated.

MANAGING WINDOWS SERVER 2008 NETWORK SERVICES

Labs included in this chapter:

- Lab 8.1 Configure IPv6
- Lab 8.2 Create a DNS Stub Zone, Forwarder, and Root Hint
- Lab 8.3 Configure DNS Round Robin and Netmask Ordering, and Troubleshoot a DNS Problem
- Lab 8.4 Troubleshoot a DHCP Server Problem

Microsoft MCITP Exam #70-646 Objectives

Objective	Lab
Planning for Server Deployment	8.1, 8.2, 8.3
Planning for Business Continuity and High Availability	8.2, 8.3, 8.4

Lab 8.1 Configure IPv6

Objectives

- Learn to configure basic IPv6 properties
- Learn to configure advanced IPv6 properties

Materials Required

This lab requires the following:

- Windows Server 2008 Standard or Enterprise Edition

Estimated completion time: **15 minutes**

Activity Background

IPv6 was developed to address the limitations of IPv4, such as the depletion of IPv4 addresses and IPv4 security limitations. Although only a very small percentage of organizations currently use IPv6, its use is growing and many server administrators are developing plans for its implementation. IPv6 is now supported by all major operating systems, including Windows Server 2008. As you prepare for certification, it is also important for you to know about IPv6 and how to implement it.

To the server administrator, IPv6 offers the following advantages over IPv4:

- Better security, including mandatory use of IP security (IPsec)
- A 128-bit address structure, enabling 2^{128} IP addresses for IPv6 compared to 2^{32} IP addresses available for IPv4
- Automatic Private IP Addressing available on private and enterprise networks using DHCPv6 or a DNS server working in coordination with DHCPv6; or the ability of a host computer to automatically configure its own IPv6 address by building it from address prefixes offered by a local router
- A new flow label field to enable packet flow management by routers through Quality of Service (QoS) capabilities
- Use of sophisticated extension headers
- Use of Network Discovery (ND) protocol instead of Address Resolution Protocol (ARP) to discover physical addresses of network computers and routers as well as other information

Windows Server 2008 is fully compatible with IPv6. With Windows Server 2008 you can:

- Configure IPv6 in the Windows Server 2008 operating system
- Use IPv6 with Microsoft DNS
- Use IPv6 with Microsoft DHCP

You have already been using Windows Server 2008 with IPv4. In this activity, you configure IPv6 in Windows Server 2008 so that IPv6 can work alongside IPv4.

For all of the activities in this chapter, you need to log on to an account with Administrator privileges. Additionally, most of these activities can be completed on a virtual server or computer, such as in Hyper-V.

Throughout the activities in this book, you may occasionally see the User Account Control box with a message that Windows needs your permission to continue. Whenever you see this box, click Continue. Keep this in mind for all of the activities because any interaction with the User Account Control box is not included in the steps.

Activity

1. Click **Start** and click **Network**.
2. Click **Network and Sharing Center** in the top middle of the Network window.

3. In the Network and Sharing Center window, click **Manage network connections** on the left side of the window.

4. In the Network Connections window, right-click your network connection, such as *Local Area Connection*.

5. Click **Properties**.

6. In the Properties dialog box, click the box for **Internet Protocol Version 6 (TCP/IPv6)**, if it is not selected (see Figure 8-1).

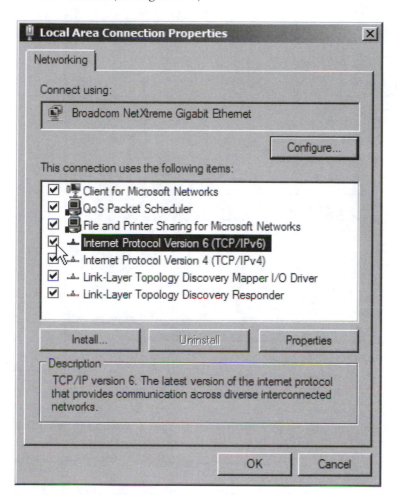

Figure 8-1   Enabling IPv6

7. Highlight **Internet Protocol Version 6 (TCP/IPv6)**, if necessary, and click **Properties**.

8. Review the contents of the Internet Protocol Version 6 (TCP/IPv6) Properties dialog box. Notice that there are two options for configuring the IPv6 address (see Figure 8-2):

   • *Obtain an IPv6 address automatically*—which is used to obtain an IPv6 address from a DHCP server or through automatic private IP addressing (when a DHCP server is not available the operating system assigns an IP address)

   • *Use the following IPv6 address*—which is used to assign a static (does not change) IPv6 address (notice that for this option you would enter the IPv6 address, the subnet prefix length, and the default gateway address)

9. In the Internet Protocol Version 6 (TCP/IPv6) Properties dialog box, click **Obtain an IPv6 address automatically**, if necessary. Normally you would assign a static IPv6 address to a server, but because you are not likely to have an IPv6 address easily available, we use Obtain an IPv6 address automatically for practice.

10. Click **Obtain DNS server address automatically**, if necessary.

11. Click the **Advanced** button in the Internet Protocol Version 6 (TCP/IPv6) Properties dialog box.

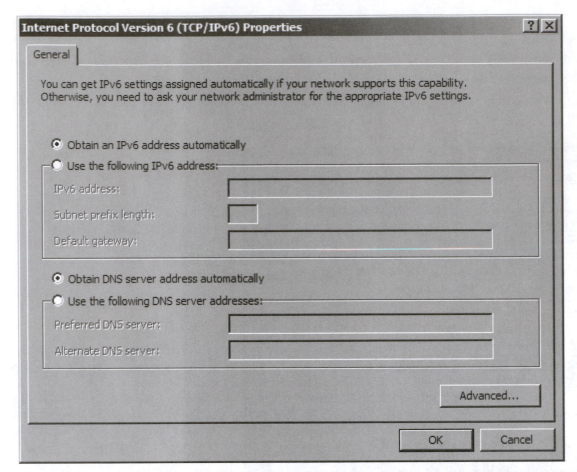

Figure 8-2 Internet Protocol Version 6 (TCP/IPv6) Properties dialog box

12. Click the **IP Settings** tab, if necessary, in the Advanced TCP/IP Settings dialog box. Note that when you have specified a static IP address by selecting the *Use the following IPv6 address* option in the Internet Protocol Version 6 (TCP/IPv6) Properties dialog box (refer to Step 8), you can use this tab to assign additional IPv6 addresses to a network interface. You also can use this tab to specify additional default gateways.

13. Click the **DNS** tab in the Advanced TCP/IP Settings dialog box. You employ this tab to specify a list of DNS servers to use in order of priority (when one DNS server cannot be reached or does not respond with information the next one on the list is contacted). You can specify an "in order of use" list of DNS servers only when *Use the following IPv6 address* is configured in the Internet Protocol Version 6 (TCP/IPv6) Properties dialog box. Also, notice the box for *Register this connection's addresses in DNS*. This option enables the IPv6 connection to use Dynamic DNS, which permits information in a DNS server to be automatically updated in coordination with a DHCP server.

14. Click **Cancel** in the Advanced TCP/IP Settings dialog box.

15. In the Internet Protocol Version 6 (TCP/IPv6) Properties dialog box, click **Obtain an IPv6 address automatically**, if necessary, and click **OK**.

16. Click **Close** in the Properties dialog box for the network connection.

17. Close the Network Connections window.

18. Close the Network and Sharing Center window and the Network window.

19. Click **Start**, point to **All Programs**, click **Accessories**, and click **Command Prompt**.

20. In the Command Prompt window, type **ipconfig** at the prompt and press **Enter**.

21. Look for the Link-local IPv6 Address listed just above the IPv4 Address (see Figure 8-3). The Link-local IPv6 Address is a unicast address assigned by the host through automatic private IP addressing

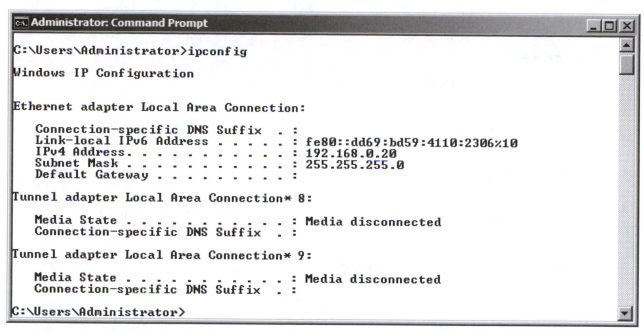

Figure 8-3   Viewing the Link-local IPv6 Address through *ipconfig*

when a DHCP server is not accessible to provide a leased IPv6 address. If your computer can access a DHCP server that leases IPv6 addresses, then you will see this address instead of a link-local address.

22. Close the Command Prompt window.

Review Questions

1. Which of the following are advantages of IPv6 over IPv4? (Choose all that apply.)

   a. Shorter IP addresses

   b. Use of extension headers

   c. IP addresses that do not use binary octets

   d. Better security

2. True or False? One problem with using IPv6 is that it does not support Quality of Service capabilities through routers.

3. When a computer is configured to *Obtain an IPv6 address automatically*, which of the following can occur? (Choose all that apply.)

   a. A static IPv6 address is assigned through a DNS server configured for automatic addressing.

   b. An IPv6 address is obtained from a DHCP server.

   c. An IPv6 address is assigned through automatic private IP addressing.

   d. A DNS server assigns a temporary IPv6 address intended to identify servers.

4. True or False? Multiple IPv6 addresses can be assigned to a server's network interface.

5. When you configure IPv6 in Windows Server 2008, use of Dynamic _____ is supported.

Lab 8.2 Create a DNS Stub Zone, Forwarder, and Root Hint

Objectives

- Configure a DNS stub zone
- Set Up a DNS root hint
- Configure a DNS forwarder

Materials Required

This lab requires the following:

- Windows Server 2008 Standard or Enterprise Edition, with the DNS Server and Active Directory Domain Services roles installed

Estimated completion time: **20 minutes**

Activity Background

In addition to their roles as authoritative/primary and secondary DNS request handlers, DNS servers also have supplementary roles. Three of these roles are to provide stub zones, to forward DNS queries, and to enable root hints.

A DNS stub zone contains only the essential information for DNS functions and is designed for quick resolution of DNS queries, such as between two or more namespaces—for example, when there is a parent holding company that owns five businesses, each with its own namespace. A DNS stub zone contains:

- *Start of Authority (SOA) name zone*—which is the first record in a zone; this record indicates if a server is authoritative for the current zone
- Name server (NS) records to identify authoritative servers
- A record for name servers that are authoritative

With DNS forwarding, DNS queries are resolved faster, especially when local DNS servers do not have the matching IP addresses. In this situation, one DNS server can be configured to forward the query to an offsite or remote DNS server that does have the IP address in its zones of authority. For instance, when there are multiple sites in an enterprise or when there is Internet connectivity, it is common to designate one DNS server to forward name resolution requests to a specific remote DNS server.

A root hint is a resource record that allows a DNS server to quickly locate an authoritative DNS server on the Internet (also called an Internet root server). Internet root servers are managed by the Internet Assigned Numbers Authority (IANA). When a DNS server receives a query for a domain it does not recognize, it can use the root hint to find that domain on the Internet. At the time the DNS Server role is installed in Windows Server 2008, a default list of root hints is loaded into DNS from the file, \Windows\System32\dns\CACHE.DNS.

In this activity, you create a DNS stub zone, create a forwarder, and view the root hints already set up by default. Ensure that the DNS Server role is installed as in Chapter 8, "Managing Windows Server 2008 Network Services" in *MCITP Guide to Microsoft Windows Server 2008, Server Administration (Exam #70-646)* before you begin.

Activity

1. Click **Start**, point to **Administrative Tools**, and click **DNS** to open the DNS Manager console for managing DNS servers. (You can also open the tool as an MMC snap-in.)

2. Click the DNS server under DNS in the tree in the left pane to select it, right-click the DNS server in the tree, and click **New Zone**.

3. In the Welcome to the New Zone Wizard window, click **Next**.

4. Click **Stub zone** in the Zone Type window (see Figure 8-4). Also, check **Store the Zone in Active Directory (available only if DNS server is a writeable domain controller)**, if necessary. Click **Next**.

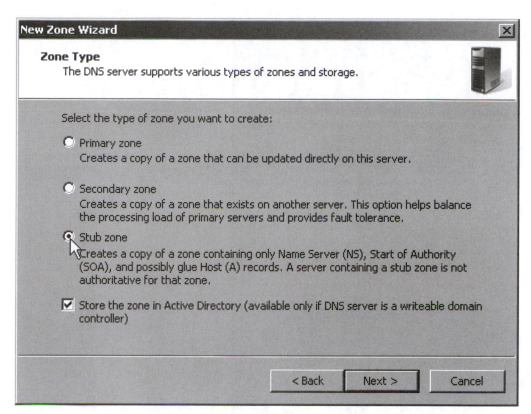

Figure 8-4   Configuring a stub zone

5. In the Active Directory Zone Replication Scope window, click **To all DNS servers in this domain:** **domainname**, if necessary. Click **Next**.

6. If you see the Forward or Reverse Lookup Zone window, click **Forward lookup zone**, if necessary, and click **Next**.

7. In the Zone Name window and in the Zone Name box, enter your domain name, such as *jpcomp.com* and click **Next**.

8. In the Master DNS Servers window, enter the IPv4 address or name of your authoritative DNS server and press **Enter**. (You can also enter the IPv4 address of your DNS server for practice, but you will likely see the DNS message box noted in Step 9.) Click **Next**.

9. In the Completing the New Zone Wizard window, click **Finish**. (If you see the DNS box with the message "The zone cannot be created. The zone already exists," click **OK** in the DNS box and then click **Cancel** in the New Zone Wizard.)

10. In the DNS Manager window, right-click the DNS server in the tree and click **Properties**.

11. Click the **Forwarders** tab in the *servername* Properties dialog box (see Figure 8-5).

12. Click the **Edit** button in the Forwarders tab.

13. In the Edit Forwarders box, enter the IP address of your DNS server for practice and press **Enter**. Click **OK** in the Edit Forwarders dialog box.

14. On the Forwarders tab in the *servername* Properties dialog box, you should see the IP Address and Server FQDN (fully qualified domain name) for the forwarder. In the *servername* Properties dialog box, click the **Root Hints** tab. Note that there are several root hints already set up under Name servers (see Figure 8-6). This listing of root hints is loaded from the \Windows\System32\dns\CACHE.DNS file. Also, in Figure 8-6, note that you can configure a new root hint by using the Add button.

15. Click **OK** in the *servername* Properties dialog box.

16. Leave the DNS Manager window open for the next activity.

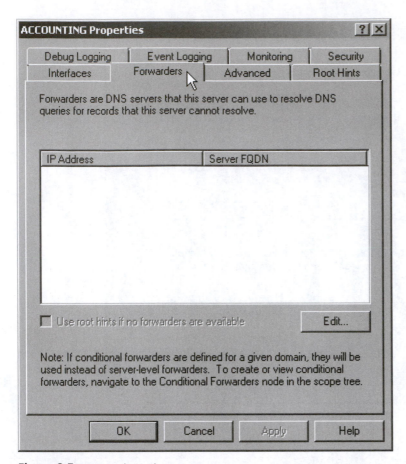

Figure 8-5 Forwarders tab

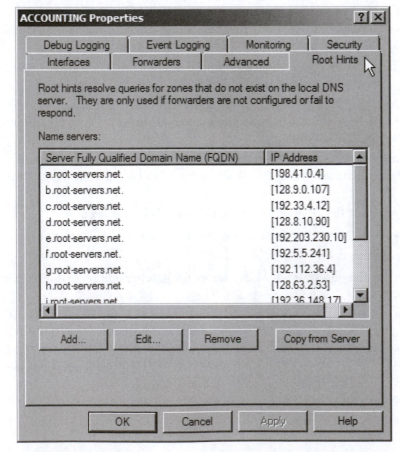

Figure 8-6 Root Hints tab

Review Questions

1. Which of the following is contained in a DNS stub zone? (Choose all that apply.)

   a. Name server records

   b. Start of Authority records

   c. List of failed queries

   d. DNS release records

2. Use the _____ Wizard to configure a DNS stub zone.

3. A DNS root hint is particularly useful for locating a(n) _____ on the Internet.

4. From where do you configure a DNS root hint?

   a. Properties dialog box for a DNS server

   b. Action menu Export List in DNS Manager

   c. DNS applet in Control Panel

   d. Alternate Services option in the DNS Manager window

5. The college you work for has a main campus location and three large branch sites. Each branch site has three or more DNS servers that continually need to send DNS queries to the DNS servers on the main campus. You want to designate one DNS server at each branch site to send DNS queries to the main campus. Which of the following should you configure at each branch site?

   a. A global hint

   b. A master DNS table

   c. A DNS forwarder

   d. A remote DNS locator

Lab 8.3 Configure DNS Round Robin and Netmask Ordering, and Troubleshoot a DNS Problem

Objectives

- Configure DNS round robin
- Enable netmask ordering
- Troubleshoot a DNS server problem

Materials Required

This lab requires the following:

- Windows Server 2008 Standard or Enterprise Edition, with the DNS Server and Active Directory Domain Services roles installed

Estimated completion time: **15 minutes**

Activity Background

On some medium and large networks, organizations have multiple servers that perform identical functions. For example, a college might use three servers for registering students for classes, and an online sporting goods sales organization might have five Web servers all used to take customer orders for products. When such organizations configure network services, it is important to implement load-balancing techniques to prevent one or two servers from doing all of the work while the remaining servers are idle.

One way to ensure load balancing in the preceding examples is to enable DNS round robin. In the college example, when Student1 queries DNS for a server, that student would be directed to RegistrationServer(1). Student2 would be directed to RegistrationServer(2) and Student3 would be directed to RegistrationServer(3). Then, Student4 would be directed to RegistrationServer(1), and so on.

A second way to achieve load balancing is to place each server on a separate subnet. To balance the load between subnets, you can configure netmask ordering. For example, consider an organization that uses two servers for its inventory system. InventoryServer(1) can be placed on subnet 178.54.1 and InventoryServer(2) can be placed on subnet 178.54.2. Netmask ordering then is used to equally distribute network traffic between each subnet, which results in balancing the load experienced by each server.

Finally, there may be times when problems develop in resolving computer names and IP addresses. To troubleshoot this issue, you can try to determine if the DNS server is stuck in a paused state or if it is stopped.

In this activity, you enable DNS round robin and netmask ordering. You also check to determine if a DNS server is paused or stopped.

Activity

1. Open the DNS Manager console, if it is not already open.

2. Right-click the DNS server in the tree in the left pane and click **Properties**.

3. In the *servername* Properties dialog box, click the **Advanced** tab.

4. On the Advanced tab, make sure the boxes are checked for the following (see Figure 8-7):

   - **Enable round robin**

   - **Enable netmask ordering**

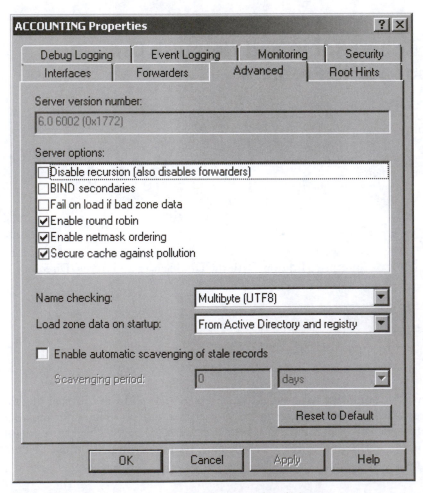

Figure 8-7   Configuring round robin and netmask ordering

Note that the *Secure cache against pollution* option is checked by default in Figure 8-7. It is a good idea to leave this option selected as well because it thwarts DNS spoofing. DNS spoofing is used by intruders or malicious software to attempt to redirect a DNS query to a rogue DNS server.

5. In the *servername* Properties dialog box, click **OK**.

6. Next, you need to check the status of the DNS server. Right-click the DNS server in the tree, point to **All Tasks**, and notice whether Start and Resume are disabled on the menu (see Figure 8-8). When Start is disabled, this means the DNS server is running. When Start or Resume is enabled, the DNS server is stopped or paused. You can restart the DNS server if it has stopped by clicking **Start**; and you can resume a paused DNS server by clicking **Resume**.

Figure 8-8   All Tasks menu

7. Close the DNS Manager window.

Review Questions

1. DNS round robin is used for _____.

2. Your company has one server for research statistics processing on subnet 178.20.15 and another server set up identically on subnet 178.20.16. You want to spread the load between these servers. To accomplish this you enable _____.

3. DNS round robin is enabled through which of the following?

   a. Creating a stub zone

   b. Configuring the properties of a DNS server

   c. Creating a CNAME zone

   d. Configuring the properties of a forward lookup zone

4. When a DNS server is not working properly, an initial troubleshooting step is to determine if the DNS server is _____ or _____.

5. True or False? Most DNS management tasks are performed using the DNS Manager console, which is opened from the Administrative Tools menu or as an MMC snap-in.

Lab 8.4 Troubleshoot a DHCP Server Problem

Objectives

- Use the DHCP console to troubleshoot a DHCP server problem
- Use Server Manager to troubleshoot a DHCP server problem

Materials Required

This lab requires the following:

- Windows Server 2008 Standard or Enterprise Edition, with the DHCP Server and Active Directory Domain Services roles installed

Estimated completion time: 20 minutes

Activity Background

A Windows Server 2008 Dynamic Host Configuration Protocol (DHCP) server detects the presence of a new computer on a network and leases an IP address to that computer. When an IP address lease expires, a new IP address is leased by the DHCP server, as long as the computer is still on the network. In Microsoft Windows, when you configure a computer to obtain an IPv4 or IPv6 address automatically, a DHCP server can provide the computer's IP address. (Refer to Step 8 in Lab 8.1 for an example of how to configure an IPv6 address automatically.)

When a DHCP server is configured and running, there may be times when you have to troubleshoot a problem with it. For example, a DHCP server is able to function only if its underlying DHCP Server service is started. The DHCP Server service is a program that is installed and started when you install the DHCP Server role. If the DHCP Server service is hung, such as might happen after a power glitch, you may have to stop and restart the DHCP Server service. Also, there may be a service on which the DHCP Server service depends that must be restarted before you can get the DHCP Server service started. Another possibility is that the DHCP server is not properly authorized, which means that the DHCP server does not have the necessary security clearance for assigning IP addresses to local network computers. Still another problem may be that the DHCP database is corrupted, such as after an unexpected server shutdown.

In this activity, you use the DHCP console and Server Manager to learn how to troubleshoot problems with a DHCP server. The DHCP Server role should be installed before you begin, as in Chapter 8 of *MCITP Guide to Microsoft Windows Server 2008, Server Administration (Exam #70-646)*.

Activity

1. Click **Start**, point to **Administrative Tools**, and click **DHCP**.

2. In the left pane in the DHCP window, click the **+** plus sign in front of the server name, such as *accounting. jpcomp.com*.

3. Next, you need to determine if the DHCP server is authorized. In the tree in the left pane, right-click the server and notice if the menu has a selection for Authorize (see Figure 8-9), which means that the DHCP server has not been authorized and so is not processing IP leasing requests. If the menu item is Unauthorize, this means the server is authorized and you do not need to take action. If you see *Authorize* in the menu, click this selection to authorize the DHCP server.

4. Open the same menu as in Step 3, if it is closed (right-click the server name in the tree). Point to **All Tasks**. Notice whether Start and Resume are disabled on the menu. When these options are disabled, the DNS server is neither stopped nor paused. If one of these options is enabled, you can restart the DNS server by clicking Start or Restart, and you can resume a paused DNS server by clicking Resume.

5. Click in an empty portion of the DHCP window to close the menu.

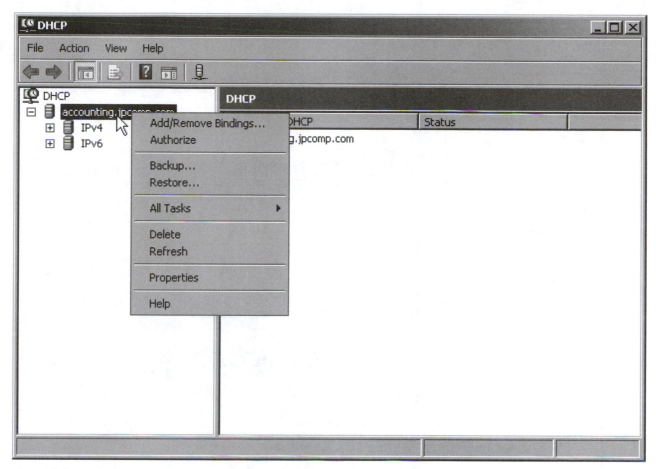

Figure 8-9   Authorize menu item (DHCP server is not authorized)

6. Ensure that the items under the server name in the tree are displayed. (If they are not displayed, click the + plus sign in front of the server name as in Step 2.) Click **IPv4** under the server name in the tree.

7. Right-click a **Scope** folder in the right pane. (There can be multiple scope folders, one for each scope that is configured.) Notice the menu item for Reconcile (which is likely to be grayed out on a newly installed DHCP server without database problems). Do not click this option now, but keep in mind that you can use this option to reconcile scopes in the event that the DHCP server database has become corrupted. If all of your attempts to fix a DHCP server problem do not succeed, try reconciling each scope. However, before you reconcile a scope, first stop the DHCP server (see Step 4). Also, before you reconcile a scope, take the server offline, if possible, by following these steps: click **Start**, click **Network**, click **Network and Sharing Center**, click **Manage network connections**, right-click the connection, and click **Disable**. Remember to give your users ample notice before you take a server offline.

8. Click in a blank area of the DHCP window to close the menu.

9. Close the DHCP window.

10. Open Server Manager, if it is not already open, by following these steps: click **Start**, point to **Administrative Tools**, and click **Server Manager**.

11. In the tree in the left pane, click the + plus sign in front of Roles.

12. In the tree, click **DHCP Server** under Roles.

13. Examine the Events box in the right pane. Any problem events recorded in a log within the last 24 hours for the DHCP server will be reported in this box. An event with a white x within a red circle means there has been a serious problem. If such an event occurs, you can double-click it and read the event description.

14. If necessary, scroll down in the right pane to view the System Services box (see Figure 8-10).

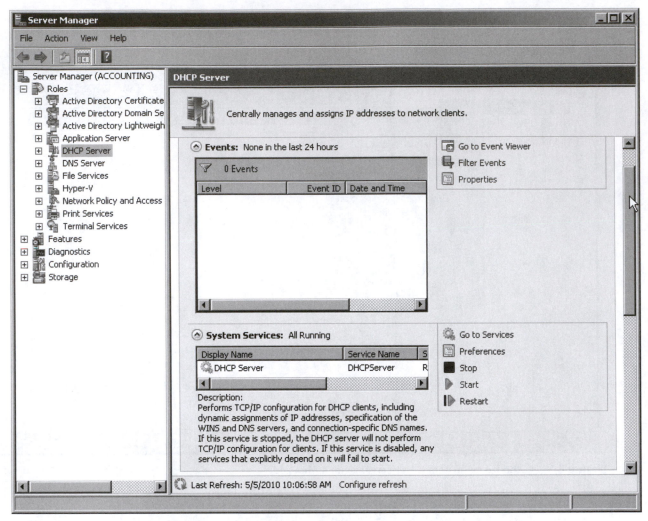

Figure 8-10   Events and System Services boxes in Server Manager

15. In the right pane, verify that you see All Running in the System Services box title (refer to Figure 8-10). You can use the horizontal scroll bar in the box to scroll to view the Status and Startup Type columns, which should have Running for the status and Auto for the Startup Type.

16. To the right of the System Services box in the right pane, notice there are options to Stop, Start, and Restart the DHCP Server service. When the service is started, the Start option should be disabled (in black print).

17. In the right pane, and just to the right of the System Services box, click **Go to Services**.

18. Click the **Standard** tab at the bottom of the middle pane.

19. In the middle pane of Server Manager, double-click **DHCP Server**.

20. Click the **Dependencies** tab. Notice that in order for the DHCP Server service to run, the following services must also be running:

- COM+ Event System
- Remote Procedure Call (RPC)
- Security Accounts Manager
- TCP/IP Protocol Driver
- Windows Event Log

21. Click **Cancel** in the DHCP Server Properties (*servername*) dialog box.

22. In the middle pane of Server Manager, scroll to view each of the services listed in Step 20 and make sure each service is started (look for Started in the Status column). Note that you won't see TCP/IP Protocol Driver listed, but as long as you have the server configured to use TCP/IP and are successfully communicating on the network, this driver is running.

23. Close Server Manager.

Review Questions

1. A DHCP Server _____ IP addresses.

2. You have had an unexpected hardware failure on your DHCP Server and now you suspect that the DHCP database is corrupted. What step can you take to fix the problem?

   a. Pause the DHCP Server and let it automatically rebuild the database.

   b. Use the Database Build tool to fix the database.

   c. Reconcile each DHCP scope.

   d. Use the Windows Server 2008 Fix File utility to rebuild the database.

3. Which of the following services must be running before the DHCP Server service can be started? (Choose all that apply.)

   a. Windows Event Log

   b. SSDP Discovery

   c. Security Accounts Manager

   d. Remote Procedure Call (RPC)

4. When you believe that a server service is hung, _____ and then _____ that service.

5. The _____ tool enables you to view log events related to a DHCP Server service as well as to start or stop the service from the same place.

CHAPTER NINE

DEPLOYING IIS AND ACTIVE DIRECTORY CERTIFICATE SERVICES

Labs included in this chapter:

- Lab 9.1 Manage IIS Application Pools

- Lab 9.2 Install the Certification Authority Web Enrollment Role Service and Learn How to Modify Values for Web Enrollment Pages

- Lab 9.3 Manage a CA Server and Configure CA Auditing

- Lab 9.4 Configure a CRL Publication Interval

Microsoft MCITP Exam #70-646 Objectives

Objective	Lab
Planning for Server Deployment	9.1, 9.2
Planning for Server Management	9.3, 9.4
Monitoring and Maintaining Servers	9.3, 9.4
Planning Application and Data Provisioning	9.1

Lab 9.1 Manage IIS Application Pools

Objectives

- Learn to create and manage IIS application pools
- Discover IIS application development role services that can be installed in conjunction with an application server

Materials Required

This lab requires the following:

- Windows Server 2008 Standard or Enterprise Edition with the IIS Web Server role installed

Estimated completion time: **15 minutes**

Activity Background

When you install IIS Web Services, it is likely you will need to know how to configure application pools in IIS. This is particularly important when you are operating an application server, as described in Chapter 12, "Application and Data Provisioning" of *MCITP Guide to Microsoft Windows Server 2008, Server Administration (Exam #70-646)*. An application server can be installed with the Windows Process Activation Service (WAS), which is used for managing application pools with Web-based applications housed in an application server. To facilitate IIS application management through WAS, Web application developers in your organization might ask you to set up specific application pools.

IIS application pools are used to group similar Web applications into pools or groups for management. One advantage of using application pools is the ability to use common settings for applications. Another advantage is for using common worker processes. A worker process is an ASP.NET process that runs on its own without using the same memory as IIS, and developers use ASP.NET to create Web-based applications. A third advantage is that using application pools provides isolation between applications, so that if one application experiences problems, other running applications are not affected. Application pools make IIS applications more reliable.

In this activity, you create a new application pool and view the management tools for an application pool. Next, you review the application development role services that can be installed with the IIS Web Server role.

For all of the activities in this chapter, you'll need to log onto an account with Administrator privileges. Additionally, most of these activities can be completed on a virtual server or computer, such as in Hyper-V.

Throughout the activities in this book, you may occasionally see the User Account Control box with a message that Windows needs your permission to continue. Whenever you see this box, click Continue. Keep this in mind for all of the activities because any interaction with the User Account Control box is not included in the steps.

Activity

1. Click **Start**, point to **Administrative Tools**, and click **Internet Information Services (IIS) Manager**. (Alternatively, you can use the Internet Information Services (IIS) Manager snap-in.)

2. In the tree in the left pane, click the **+** plus sign in front of the server name.

3. Click **Application Pools** in the tree under the server name.

4. Notice in the middle pane that there is one application pool, called DefaultAppPool, that was created when you installed the IIS Web Server role (see Figure 9-1).

5. In the right pane of Internet Information Services (IIS) Manager, click **Add Application Pool**.

6. In the Add Application Pool dialog box, enter **CustomerApps** plus your initials, such as *CustomerAppsJP*, for the Name of the application pool (see Figure 9-2). Click **OK**.

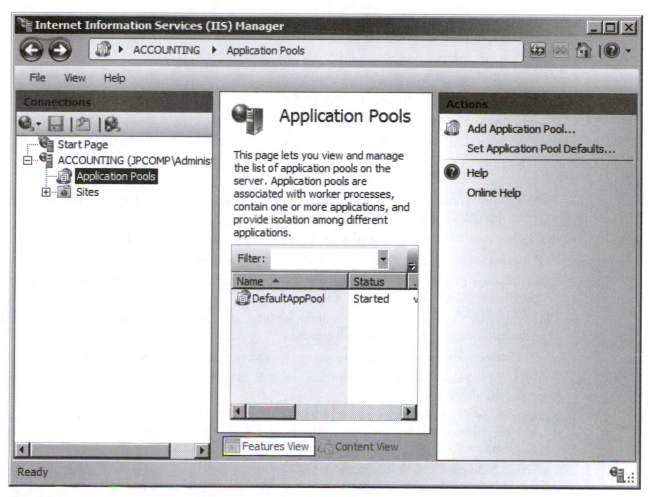

Figure 9-1 Viewing the default application pool

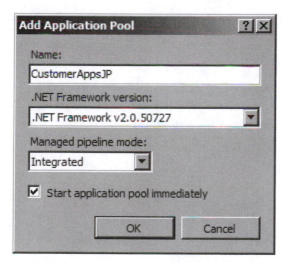

Figure 9-2 Creating a new application pool

7. In the right pane of Internet Information Services (IIS) Manager, notice the management options that are available. For example under Application Pool Tasks, you can start or stop an application pool when you are troubleshooting a problem. The Recycle option enables you to restart worker processes in an application pool, if applications are not responding properly. Under Edit Application Pool you can edit the basic settings or configure advanced settings. The Recycling option enables you to configure the conditions for recycling an application pool. Recycling means that the worker processes are automatically shut down and

restarted for an application. You can also rename or remove an application pool; and you can view the applications within the application pool.

8. Close the Internet Information Services (IIS) Manager window.

9. Open Server Manager, if it is not already open.

10. In the left pane, click the **+** plus sign in front of Roles, if Roles is not expanded.

11. Click **Web Server (IIS)**.

12. In the right pane, scroll to the Role Services section.

13. Notice the role services that can be installed with IIS to support Web applications and application development:

   - *ASP.NET*—programming environment used by developers to create Web-based applications enabling server scripting and other Web-based features
   - *.NET Extensibility*—used to extend Web features programmers can develop
   - *ASP (Active Server Pages)*—supplies an environment for developing scripts used in Web applications
   - *CGI (Common Gateway Interface)*—an interface that provides for scripting, however, many Web developers consider CGI scripts to be a security risk
   - *ISAPI (Internet Server Application Programming Interface) Extensions*—a set of extensions that can contribute to developing dynamic Web content
   - *ISAPI Filters*—files that can be used to change how designated IIS processes are executed
   - *Server Side Includes*—a script language that can be used to affect how HTML pages are created as they are being displayed

14. Consider making a note of these services to build your knowledge of options that can be used for application server deployment and provisioning applications, both of which are important areas to understand for the certification exam.

15. Leave Server Manager open for the next lab.

Review Questions

1. Web applications in application pools have which of the following in common? (Choose all that apply.)
   a. Runtime duration
   b. Common settings
   c. Worker processes
   d. IP addresses

2. Use the _____ tool to create a new application pool on an IIS Web Server.

3. Which of the following tools enables you to install the Application Development role services in an IIS Web Server?
   a. Server Manager
   b. Control Panel Applications applet
   c. Active Directory Web Services tool
   d. IIS Installer

4. ISAPI Filters are files used to _____.

5. Server Side Includes is a _____ language.

Lab 9.2 Install the Certification Authority Web Enrollment Role Service and Learn How to Modify Values for Web Enrollment Pages

Objectives

- Install Certification Authority Web Enrollment for certificate services
- Set up values for Web enrollment pages

Materials Required

This lab requires the following:

- Windows Server 2008 Standard or Enterprise Edition with the Active Directory Certificate Services role installed (but without the Certification Authority Web Enrollment role service installed)
- Active Directory Domain Services role installed

Estimated completion time: **15 minutes**

9

Activity Background

Many organizations enable users to access applications through the Web. Using Web applications can be a security vulnerability, however, because these users are not authorized through a traditional user account within Active Directory. To close this security hole, the Active Directory Certificate Services (ADCS) role comes with an optional role service you can install called Certification Authority Web Enrollment. Certification Authority Web Enrollment enables Internet Explorer (version 6 or higher) to submit a request for a certificate via a Web application. Consequently, Certification Authority Web Enrollment ensures that a Web application user does not bypass the need to obtain a certificate from a Certificate Authority (CA). The certificate tightens security because it offers proof that the user is trustworthy.

To illustrate Certification Authority Web Enrollment, consider a college that is developing a Web-based student services application for students to access information about the classes that they have taken, classes they are enrolled in, grades, and financial information. When a student logs on to access her information, it is important to take steps to make sure the client user account is trustworthy by using certificate services. Installing the Certification Authority Web Enrollment role service provides the extra level of user authentication that is needed to help assure confidential student information is not compromised. Additionally, this step may be required by computer system and financial auditors.

When you use Certification Authority Web Enrollment, you can also set up default values to be used for Web enrollment pages. Web enrollment pages are used to connect to a CA server through a Web browser and request a certificate. Some of the default values that you can set up include:

- Company or organization name
- Department or unit name
- City
- State
- Country
- Number of days during which a client can retrieve a certificate after a request is made

For this activity, you install the Certification Authority Web Enrollment role service and then you edit the certdat.inc file to specify values to be used in Web pages.

Activity

1. Open Server Manager, if it is not already open (click **Start**, point to **Administrative Tools**, and click **Server Manager**).

2. In the tree in the left pane, click the **+** plus sign in front of Roles, if the items under Roles are not displayed.

3. Under Roles in the tree, click **Active Directory Certificate Services**.

4. Scroll the right pane in Server Manager to view Role Services.

5. In the right pane of Server Manager, click **Add Role Services**.

6. In the Select Role Services window, check the **Certification Authority Web Enrollment** check box (see Figure 9-3). (Note: if the Web Server IIS role is not already installed, you'll see the Add Role Services box to install it. Also, if certain Web Server[IIS] roles are not installed, such as the Application Development role service, you'll also see the Add Role Service box to install these role services. Click **Add Required Role Services** if you see this box.)

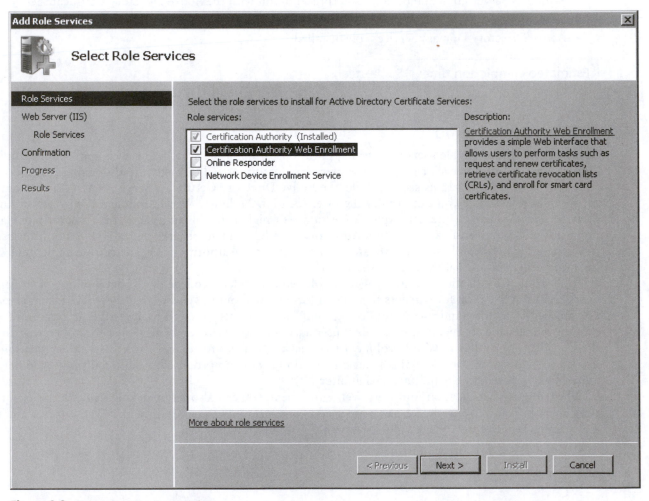

Figure 9-3 Select Role Services window

7. Click **Next** in the Select Role Services window.

8. If you see the Web Server (IIS) window, click **Next**.

9. If you see the Select Role Services window to choose Web Server (IIS) role services, click **Next**.

10. In the Confirm Installation Selections window, click **Install**. The installation may take a few minutes.

11. In the Installation Results window, click **Close**.

12. Close Server Manager.

13. Click **Start** and click **Computer**.

14. Browse to the /Windows/System32/CertSrv folder.

15. Right-click the **certdat.inc** file, point to **Open With**, and click **Notepad**. (If instead of *Open With* you see only *Open*, click this menu item. If you see two instances of *Open* on the menu, click the second instance of *Open*. If none of these approaches open the file, click the **Open** down arrow on the toolbar, click **Choose Default Program**, and click **Notepad**.)

16. Notice the default values for which you can customize information for your organization (see Figure 9-4). For example, you can modify sDefaultCompany="" to sDefaultCompany="*mycompany*" to specify the name of your company or modify sDefaultOrgUnit="" to specify sDefaultOrgUnit="*department*" to specify the name of a department. In addition, you can modify the nPendingTimeoutDays=10 parameter to specify the number of days during which a client can retrieve a certificate after a request is made.

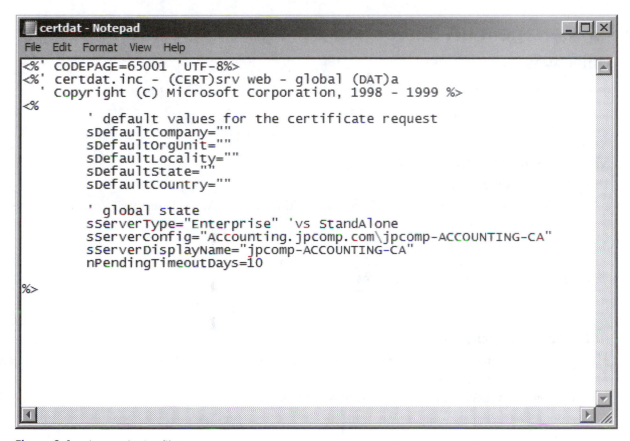

Figure 9-4 The certdat.inc file

17. Close the certdat - Notepad window.

18. Close the CertSrv window.

Review Questions

1. First National Bank offers online banking services for customers. Their Web-based access for online banking should be protected by which of the following CA role services?

   a. Certification Authority Web Enrollment

   b. Certification Authority .NET Security

   c. Certification Authority User Authorization

   d. Certification Authority Online Respond and Security

2. When you install the Certification Authority _____ role service, you also need to have the _____ server role installed.

3. Web enrollment pages are used to _____.

4. Which of the following are default values that you can configure for use in Web enrollment pages? (Choose all that apply.)

   a. Size of the page

   b. Authentication method used for the user to log on

   c. Company name

   d. Number of days a client has to retrieve a certificate after a request is made

5. _____ is the name of the file used to configure the default values that you can configure for use in Web enrollment pages.

Lab 9.3 Manage a CA Server and Configure CA Auditing

Objectives

- Perform management tasks on a CA server, including renewing a CA certificate
- Configure auditing options for a CA server

Materials Required

This lab requires the following:

- Windows Server 2008 Standard or Enterprise Edition with the Active Directory Certificate Services role installed
- Active Directory Domain Services role installed

Estimated completion time: **15 minutes**

Activity Background

After a CA server is installed, there are several options available in the Certification Authority tool for managing the server. For instance, you can:

- Start or stop the Active Directory Certificate Services service
- Submit a new request using a request file
- Back up a certificate authority server
- Restore a certificate authority server
- Renew a CA certificate

Another important management function is to monitor changes made to certificate services. You can monitor changes to certificate services and other certificate services activities by setting up auditing. For example, you might audit changes made to certificate services to track who is making them, in case your server has an intruder problem. You also may want to audit when backups have been done, so that if you have to perform a restore, you have a record of the last backup.

For this activity, you learn how to access CA management options and how to set up auditing.

Activity

1. Click **Start**, point to **Administrative Tools**, and click **Certification Authority**. (You can also open this tool as an MMC snap-in.)

2. In the certsrv – [Certification Authority (Local)] window, right-click the server in the tree, point to **All Tasks**, and notice the menu items for managing the server (see Figure 9-5). Leave the menu open for Step 3.

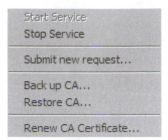

Figure 9-5 Management options

3. Click **Stop Service** to stop the Active Directory Certificate Services service. Plan to stop this service when you need to perform certain tasks, such renewing a CA certificate or backing up the CA server.

4. Right-click the server in the tree, point to **All Tasks**, and click **Renew CA Certificate**. In the Renew CA Certificate dialog box, read the information regarding when you need a new certificate for your CA and when you need a new signing key (see Figure 9-6).

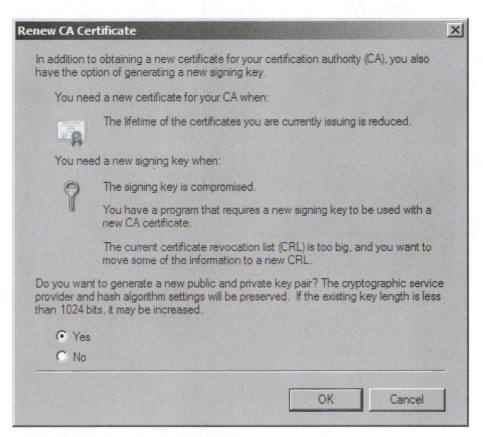

Figure 9-6 Renew CA Certificate dialog box

5. In the Renew CA Certificate dialog box, ensure that **Yes** is selected and click **OK** for a new certificate and new signing key for the CA server.

6. Right-click the server in the tree, point to **All Tasks**, and click **Start Service**.

7. In the certsrv – [Certification Authority (Local)] window, right-click the server in the tree, point to **All Tasks**, and click **Properties**.

8. In the Properties dialog box, click the **Auditing** tab (see Figure 9-7).

9. Check the **Back up and restore the CA database, Change CA configuration,** and **Change CA security settings** check boxes.

10. Click **OK** in the Properties dialog box.

11. Close the certsrv – [Certification Authority (Local)] window.

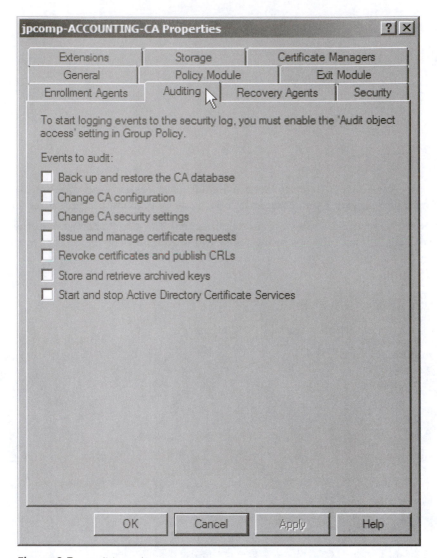

Figure 9-7   Auditing tab

Review Questions

1. Before you can renew a CA certificate you must first _____.

2. You can renew a CA certificate using the _____ tool.

3. When you renew a CA certificate, you can also do which of the following?

   a. Create a new CA rights zone

   b. Issue an e-mail notification to users

   c. Create a new signing key for the CA server

   d. Change the CA encryption method

4. Which of the following are management tasks you can perform on a CA server? (Choose all that apply.)

   a. Back up the CA server

   b. Restore the CA server

   c. Start the Active Directory Certificate Services service

   d. Pause the Active Directory Certificate Services service

5. True or False? You can configure Windows Server 2008 to audit events involving changes to the configuration of a CA server.

Lab 9.4 Configure a CRL Publication Interval

Objectives

- Configure the publication interval for CRLs
- Enable delta CRLs and configure their publication intervals

Materials Required

This lab requires the following:

- Windows Server 2008 Standard or Enterprise Edition with the Active Directory Certificate Services role installed
- Active Directory Domain Services role installed

Estimated completion time: **15 minutes**

Activity Background

There are two methods for determining if a certificate is revoked for a specific user: using certificate revocation lists (CRLs) and using Online Responder Service. Using CRLs is the traditional method and Online Responder Service is a newer more modern approach. In Active Directory Certificate Services, you can use either of the two methods or both. One advantage of Online Responder Service is that it can provide faster determination when a certificate is revoked and it offers additional services not available with CRLs. However, Online Responder Service is not available in Windows Server 2008, Standard Edition. It can, however, be installed in Windows Server 2008, Enterprise and Datacenter Editions. If you are using Standard Edition with Active Directory Certificate Services, you'll need to use CRLs.

Active Directory Certificate Services also offers the use of delta CRLs for faster notification of revoked certificates. A delta CRL provides information only on the certificates revoked after the last full CRL was published.

After you install Active Directory Certificate Services, plan to configure publication intervals for CRLs and delta CRLs. You can customize the publication intervals to meet the needs of your organization.

In this activity, you use the Certification Authority tool to configure the publication intervals of CRLs and delta CRLs.

Activity

1. Click **Start**, point to **Administrative Tools**, and click **Certification Authority**.

2. Click the **+** plus sign in front of the server name in the tree in the left pane, if necessary, to expand the items under the server.

3. Right-click **Revoked Certificates** and click **Properties**. In the Revoked Certificates Properties dialog box, the default CRL publication interval is "1 Weeks" and Publish Delta CRLs is selected by default with a publication interval of "1 Days" (see Figure 9-8).

4. In the Revoked Certificates Properties dialog box, set the CRL publication interval to **5 Days**. Leave Publish Delta CRLs selected and the delta CRL Publication interval at **1 Days**.

5. In the Revoked Certificates Properties dialog box, click the **View CRLs** tab. Notice the CRLs and Delta CRLs shown.

6. On the View CRLs tab, click one of the CRLs to highlight it and click **View CRL**. Use the scroll bar, if necessary, to review the CRL information in the Certificate Revocation List dialog box.

7. Click **OK** in the Certificate Revocation List dialog box.

8. Click **OK** in the Revoked Certificates Properties dialog box.

9. Close the certsrv – [Certification Authority (Local)] window.

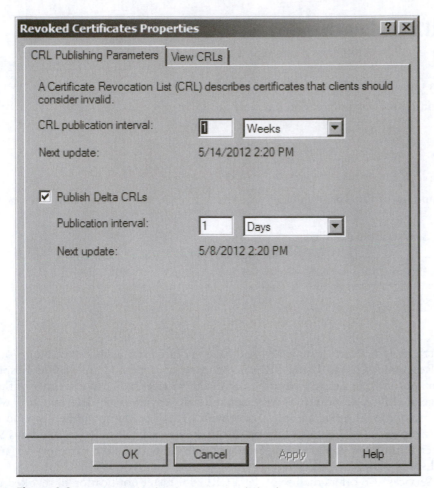

Figure 9-8 Revoked Certificates Properties dialog box

Review Questions

1. For Active Directory Certificate Services, _____ is another method for determining revoked certificates in addition to using CRLs.

2. Which of the following are parameters you can use when configuring a CRL publication interval? (Choose all that apply.)

   a. Years

   b. Months

   c. Weeks

   d. Days

3. You can configure the publication interval of a CRL through which of the following?

   a. Administrative Tools Services tool

   b. Default Domain CRL audit policy

   c. The Certificate Authority tool Issued Certificates properties

   d. The Certificate Authority tool Revoked Certificates properties

4. A delta CRL provides information on _____.

5. True or False? The contents of a CRL cannot be viewed as a security precaution so that intruders cannot change this information.

CONFIGURING REMOTE ACCESS SERVICES

Labs included in this chapter:

- Lab 10.1 Configure Network Address Translation

- Lab 10.2 Troubleshoot a VPN Server Problem

- Lab 10.3 Configure a RADIUS Server

- Lab 10.4 Install the TS Gateway and TS Web Access Role Services

Microsoft MCITP Exam #70-646 Objectives

Objective	Lab
Planning for Server Deployment	10.1, 10.3, 10.4
Planning for Server Management	10.3
Monitoring and Maintaining Servers	10.2, 10.3
Planning Application and Data Provisioning	10.4
Planning for Business Continuity and High Availability	10.2

Lab 10.1 Configure Network Address Translation (NAT)

Objectives

- Understand the purpose of Network Address Translation (NAT) and how to implement it
- Configure Network Address Translation (NAT) on a VPN server

Materials Required

This lab requires the following:

- Windows Server 2008 Standard or Enterprise Edition with the Network Policy and Access Services role installed with the Network Policy Server role service
- A VPN server previously set up through the Routing and Remote Access tool as in Chapter 10, "Configuring Remote Access Services" in *MCITP Guide to Microsoft Windows Server 2008, Server Administration (Exam #70-646)*

Estimated completion time: **15 minutes**

Activity Background

One way to reinforce network protection for clients using a VPN server is to implement Network Address Translation (NAT). When NAT is used, all network addresses on the internal network protected by NAT are hidden from view to outsiders. Outsiders on the external network, such as the Internet, see only one IP address that masquerades the actual IP addresses used on the internal network. On the internal network behind the NAT, the network administrator can use a range of IP addresses for each of the network's VPN clients, such as 192.168.18.1, 192.168.18.2, 192.168.18.3, and so on. The IP address on the NAT device as seen by outsiders might be 129.81.1.1 (a fictional address for this example). When the computer on the internal network, such as one that has the address 192.168.18.15, communicates with a computer on the other side of the NAT device, its address is translated to 129.81.1.1.

There are two important advantages to using NAT. First, addresses on the internal network do not have to be registered on the Internet because they are only seen on the internal network. Second, NAT provides protection from external network and Internet intruders. This protection is good, but it is not invincible. Dedicated attackers can use a technique called "spoofing" to appear as though they are a legitimate computer on the external network with which the NAT device is communicating.

When you use NAT in Windows Server 2008 Routing and Remote Access Services, you can configure it to work through one or more network interfaces, including interfaces attached to a local or wide area network.

In this activity, you configure NAT for a VPN server.

For all of the activities in this chapter, you'll need to log on to an account with Administrator privileges. Additionally, most of these activities can be completed on a virtual server or computer, such as in Hyper-V.

Throughout the activities in this book, you may occasionally see the User Account Control box with a message that Windows needs your permission to continue. Whenever you see this box, click Continue. Keep this in mind for all of the activities because any interaction with the User Account Control box is not included in the steps.

Activity

1. Click **Start**, point to **Administrative Tools**, and click **Routing and Remote Access**.

2. In the tree, if necessary, expand the items under the server name by clicking the **+** plus sign in front of the server.

3. If necessary, in the tree, click the **+** plus sign in front of IPv4.

4. In the tree, right-click **General** under IPv4, click **New Routing Protocol** in the New Routing Protocol dialog box, click **NAT**, if necessary, and click **OK**. (If you already see NAT in the tree under IPv4, you can skip this step).

5. In the tree, right-click **NAT** under IPv4 and click **Properties** (see Figure 10-1).

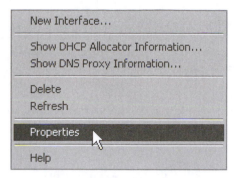

Figure 10-1 Opening the NAT properties

6. In the NAT Properties dialog box, click the **Translation** tab. Note the following parameters that you can configure:

- *Remove TCP mapping after (minutes)*—amount of time the mapped address is kept in the router's translation table (the VPN server can also be configured to provide routing services to route packets to network segments) for a TCP communication

- *Remove UDP mapping after (minutes)*—amount of time the mapped address is kept in the router's translation table for a UDP communication

7. Click the **Address Assignment** tab.

8. In the Address Assignment tab, check the **Automatically assign IP addresses by using the DHCP allocator** check box (see Figure 10-2). Leave the IP address parameter set to 192.168.0.0, which is a standard address range for NAT (192.168.0.0 to 192.168.255.255 for class C networks). Also, leave the Mask at 255.255.255.0.

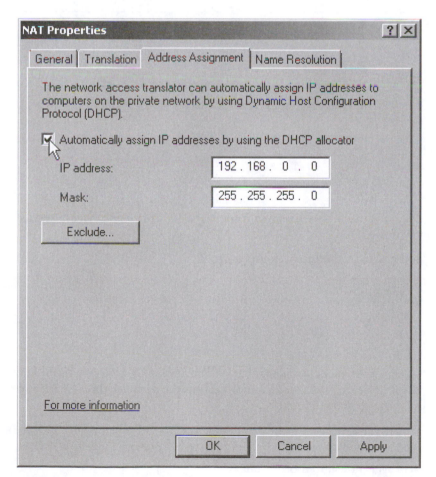

Figure 10-2 Address Assignment tab

9. Click the `Exclude` button.

10. You can use the Exclude Reserved Addresses dialog box to specify addresses that should not be assigned through DHCP. For example, you might exclude the addresses of servers because those addresses are statically assigned. Click `Cancel` in the Exclude Reserved Addresses dialog box.

11. Click the `Name Resolution` tab.

12. Click the `Clients using Domain Name System (DNS)` check box to enable this feature so that IP addresses can be resolved through DNS.

13. Click `OK` in the NAT Properties dialog box.

14. Leave the Routing and Remote Access window open for the next activity.

Review Questions

1. IP addresses configured through NAT can be resolved through _____.

2. Addresses provided through NAT do not have to be _____ through the Internet.

3. Dedicated attackers can penetrate NAT protection through using which of the following techniques?

   a. Drilling down

   b. Spoofing

   c. IP cracking

   d. Worming

4. You can configure NAT for use with a VPN server using the _____ tool.

5. The class C address range of _____ to _____ can be used with NAT.

Lab 10.2 Troubleshoot a VPN Server Problem

Objectives

- Troubleshoot a VPN server to verify that the server is enabled and that the network interface is connected
- Verify that VPN services are started and that the Windows Firewall is configured to allow VPN communications

Materials Required

This lab requires the following:

- Windows Server 2008 Standard or Enterprise Edition with the Network Policy and Access Services role installed with Network Policy Server
- A VPN server set up through the Routing and Remote Access tool

Estimated completion time: **15 minutes**

Activity Background

There can be times when a VPN server experiences problems that you must quickly address. You'll know when there are problems by the calls you receive from users who cannot log into the network through their VPN connections. Four common problems you may encounter are:

- The VPN server is not enabled
- A network interface is not connected or is disabled
- A service related to VPN functions is not started or is hung
- The Windows Firewall has been reconfigured and is blocking VPN communications

For this activity, you practice troubleshooting a VPN server for problems so that you are prepared to quickly resolve them. At the same time, you learn how to do function checks to ensure a VPN server is working normally.

Activity

1. Open the Routing and Remote Access console, if it is not already open.

2. Make sure that the items in the tree in the left pane are displayed under the server name.

3. In the tree, right-click the server name and click **Properties**.

4. On the General tab in the *servername* Properties dialog box, ensure that the check box for **IPv4 Remote access server** has a checkmark (see Figure 10-3). This box enables the VPN server using IPv4. If your network also uses IPv6, be certain the **IPv6 Remote access server** box is checked as well.

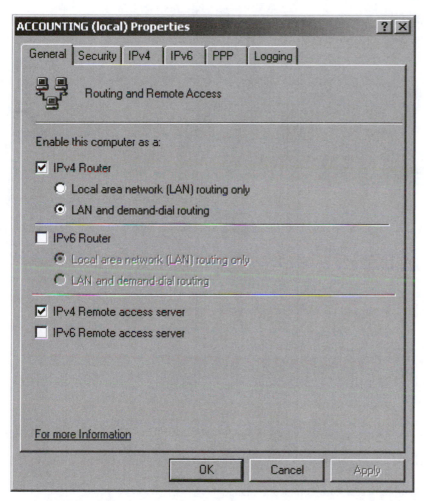

Figure 10-3   General tab

5. Click **OK** in the *servername* Properties dialog box.

6. In the tree under the server, click **Network Interfaces**. (Note that if you are using a virtual server or are set up to use a remote dial-up server instead of a VPN server, then you may not see Network Interfaces. In this case, skip to Step 7.)

7. In the right pane, locate the network interface used by the VPN server, such as Local Area Connection. Check the Status column to be sure the network interface has a status of enabled and connected. Close the Routing and Remote Access window.

8. Click **Start**, point to **Administrative Tools**, and click **Services**. A VPN server requires the following services to be started:
   - Routing and Remote Access
   - Remote Access Auto Connection Manager
   - Remote Access Connection Manager

9. In the Services window, make sure the **Extended** tab is selected at the bottom of the right pane.

10. Scroll to view Remote Access Auto Connection Manager, click it, and view its status, which should be started. If the service is not stared, click **Start** the service in the right pane.

11. Double-click **Remote Access Auto Connection Manager**.

12. Click the **Dependencies** tab. Notice that this service depends on the Remote Access Connection Manager and the Telephony services. Click **Cancel** (see Figure 10-4).

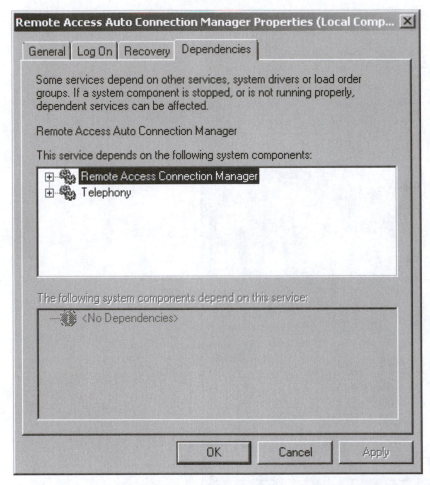

Figure 10-4   Services on which the Remote Access Auto Connection Manager service depends

13. In the Services window, make sure the Remote Access Connection Manager service is started. Next, double-click **Remote Access Connection Manager**.

14. Click the **Dependencies** tab and note that the Remote Access Connection Manager service depends on the Secure Socket Tunneling Protocol Service and Telephony services. Click **Cancel**.

15. In the Services window, ensure that the Routing and Remote Access service is started. Next, double-click **Routing and Remote Access**.

16. Click the **Dependencies** tab. The services on which the Routing and Remote Access service depends are:
    - Base Filtering Engine
    - HTTP
    - NetBIOSGroup
    - Remote Access Connection Manager
    - Remote Procedure Call (RPC)

17. Click **Cancel**.

18. In the right pane of the Services window, make sure that the Telephony, Secure Socket Tunneling Protocol Service, Base Filtering Engine, and Remote Procedure Call services are started (the HTTP and NetBIOS-Group services are not displayed in the Services window).

19. Close the Services window.

20. Click **Start** and click **Control Panel**.

21. Click **Classic View**, if necessary.

22. Double-click **Windows Firewall**.

23. In the left side of the window, click **Allow a program through Windows Firewall**.

24. Make sure the **Exceptions** tab is selected and scroll to find VPN. There should be a checkmark in the VPN check box to enable VPN communications through Windows Firewall. (If your server is configured as a remote dial-up server and not a VPN server, you will not see VPN listed on the Exceptions tab.)

25. Click **Cancel** in the Windows Firewall Settings dialog box.

26. Close the Windows Firewall window.

27. Close Control Panel.

Review Questions

1. You suspect that the network interface used by your VPN server is not connected or is disabled. What step can you take in the Routing and Remote Access tool to check the status of the network interface? (Choose all that apply.)
   a. Click General under IPv4 or IPv6
   b. Click Action in the toolbar and click Status
   c. Click Network Interfaces under the server name
   d. Click IGMP under IPv4 or IPv6

2. True or False? For a VPN server to be working the Routing and Remote Access, Remote Access Auto Connection Manager, and Remote Access Connection Manager services must be started.

3. To enable a VPN server that uses IPv6 communications, which of the following should be configured in the Routing and Remote Access tool?
   a. IPv6 remote procedure call
   b. IPv6 VPN extensions
   c. IPv6 remote security
   d. IPv6 remote access server

4. For successful communications between a VPN server and the network or Internet, VPN must be designated as a(n) _____ in Windows Firewall.

5. True or False? When a VPN server is running live, it is safe to stop the Remote Procedure Call service for maintenance.

Lab 10.3 Configure a RADIUS Server

Objectives

- Configure a RADIUS client
- Configure RADIUS accounting

Materials Required

This lab requires the following:

- Windows Server 2008 Standard or Enterprise Edition with the Network Policy and Access Services role installed with the Network Policy Server role service
- A VPN server already configured

Estimated completion time: **20 minutes**

Activity Background

Many organizations have multiple VPN or dial-up remote access servers. In such situations, it makes sense to configure a Network Policy Server (NPS) to function as a Remote Authentication Dial-In User Service (RADIUS) server. An NPS server configured as a RADIUS server provides the following capabilities:

- A central source for authenticating, through Active Directory, user access requests to RADIUS client servers
- Remote access accounting of user authentication requests so that you can keep track of users who have succeeded or failed in logging on to a VPN or remote dial-up server

When you configure RADIUS, you can configure VPN servers, remote dial-up servers, switches that use 802.1x authentication, and wireless access points as RADIUS clients. When you configure a RADIUS client, it is necessary to provide the friendly name of the client, the client address, the vendor name (such as RADIUS Standard), and the shared secret (a password shared between the client and the RADIUS server).

On medium and large networks that have multiple RADIUS servers, you can also configure an NPS to be a RADIUS proxy. A RADIUS proxy ensures that messages are efficiently routed between RADIUS servers and RADIUS clients. For example, you might use a RADIUS proxy for messages that go between different Active Directory forests. Another reason for a RADIUS proxy server is to help with the load of processing large numbers of authentication requests on an extremely busy network. A third use for a RADIUS proxy is for routing authorization messages that go between different directory services, such as between Windows and Linux.

In this activity, you configure a server running NPS to also function as a RADIUS server. The Network Policy and Access Services role must already be installed with Network Policy Server role services as in Chapter 10, "Configuring Remote Access Services" in *MCITP Guide to Microsoft Windows Server 2008, Server Administration (Exam #70-646)*.

Activity

1. Click **Start**, point to **Administrative Tools**, and click **Network Policy Server**.
2. In the tree in the left pane, click **RADIUS Clients and Servers**, if necessary.
3. In the right pane, click **Configure RADIUS Clients** (see Figure 10-5).

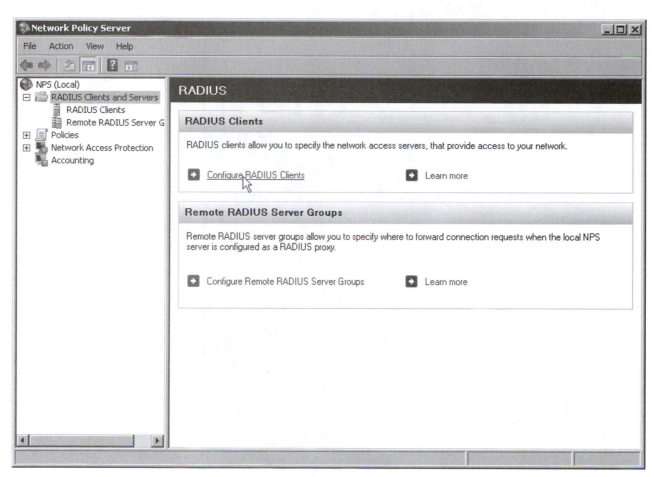

Figure 10-5   Configuring RADIUS clients

4. Click **Action** in the toolbar and click **New RADIUS Client**.

5. In the New RADIUS box, be sure the check box for **Enable this RADIUS client** is checked.

6. In the Friendly name text box, enter the name of your VPN server, such as **accounting.jpcomp.com**.

7. Enter the IP address of your VPN server in the Address (IP or DNS) text box.

8. Click the down arrow for **Vendor name** to review the possible selections. Use the default selection, which is **RADIUS Standard**. (Vendor names are provided in the event that you are using equipment from a vendor that employs proprietary attributes.)

9. Leave **Manual** selected for the Shared Secret.

10. Enter a shared secret (a password used between a RADIUS client and RADIUS server) in the Shared secret text box and reenter it in the Confirm shared secret text box. The New RADIUS Client dialog box should now look similar to Figure 10-6.

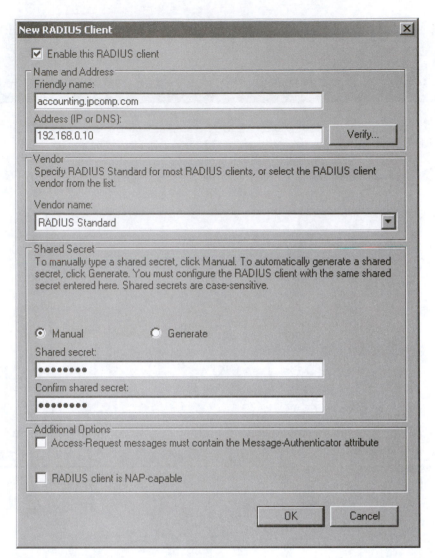

Figure 10-6 New RADIUS Client dialog box

11. Click **OK**.

12. The client you have configured should now appear in the right pane in the Network Policy Server window (see Figure 10-7). Ensure that the Status column shows the server as enabled.

13. In the tree in the left pane, click **Accounting**.

14. In the right pane, click **Configure Local File Logging**.

15. In the Settings tab of the Local file Logging dialog box, ensure the following are selected (see Figure 10-8):

    - **Accounting requests**
    - **Authentication requests**
    - **Periodic accounting status**
    - **Periodic authentication status**

16. Click the **Log File** tab. Note the location of the log files for RADIUS server accounting (\Windows\ system32\LogFiles). If your organization has very active RADIUS clients, the log files can quickly fill up a lot of disk space. In this situation, the best practice is to specify a location that is not on a system partition to avoid taking up disk space needed for other server functions.

17. Click **OK** in the Local File Logging dialog box.

18. Close the Network Policy Server window.

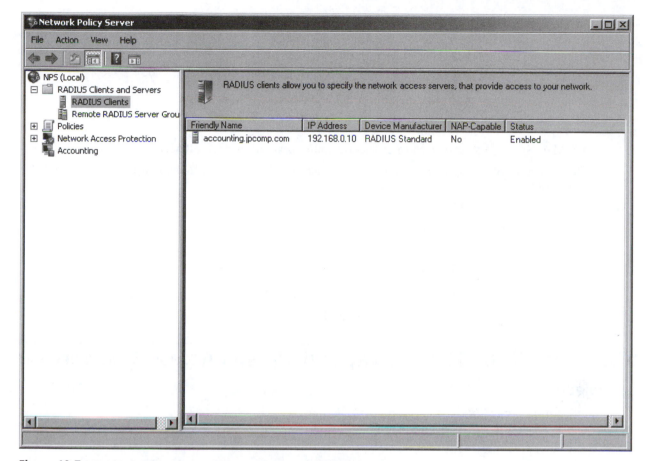

Figure 10-7   Network Policy Server window with the new client listed

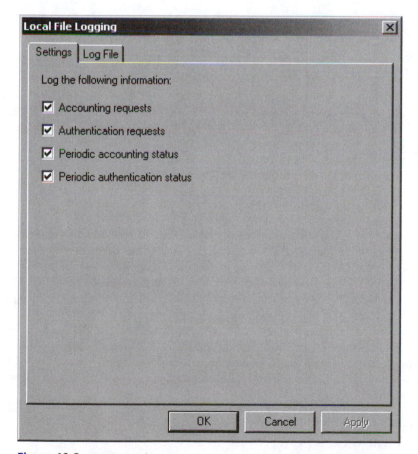

Figure 10-8   Settings tab

Review Questions

1. Which of the following are reasons for using a RADIUS server? (Choose all that apply.)

   a. To avoid having to configure more than one VPN or remote dial-up server on a large network

   b. To provide for accounting statistics

   c. To manage licensing for VPN servers

   d. To provide a central source for authenticating users

2. A RADIUS _____ is used to efficiently route messages between RADIUS servers and RADIUS clients.

3. Which of the following is information you must provide when configuring a RADIUS client? (Choose all that apply.)

   a. Client address

   b. Vendor name

   c. Nearest switch to a client

   d. Number of client accounts

4. A password used between a RADIUS client and RADIUS server is called a(n) _____.

5. Use the _____ tool to configure a RADIUS server.

Lab 10.4 Install the TS Gateway and TS Web Access Role Services

Objectives

- Install the TS Gateway role service for terminal services
- Install the TS Web Access role service for terminal services

Materials Required

This lab requires the following:

- Windows Server 2008 Standard or Enterprise Edition with the Terminal Services role installed, but without the TS Gateway and TS Web Access role services installed
- Web Server (IIS) role installed
- The Network Policy and Access Services role installed with the Network Policy Server role service

Estimated completion time:	**15 minutes**

Activity Background

When you have the Terminal Services role installed, you can also add two useful role services: TS Gateway and TS Web Access. TS Gateway can be an alternative to using a VPN for secure over-the-Internet access to enable a user to run applications on a Windows Server 2008 server. TS Gateway can work through Windows Firewall security and it can work in conjunction with NAT. TS Gateway employs Hypertext Transfer Protocol Secure (HTTPS), which is a form of HTTP that uses Secure Sockets Layer (SSL) for security. SSL is a data encryption technique used between a server and a client, such as between a client's browser and an Internet server.

TS Web Access enables end users to connect to a terminal server and run applications through a Web browser. TS Web Access uses a new feature in Windows Server 2008 called RemoteApp. When the Web browser starts a terminal services session, the terminal server starts the RemoteApp program which provides a list of remote applications the end user can run on the terminal server. Through RemoteApp, an end user can start several programs to run in one session on the terminal server.

(Note that in Windows Server 2008 R2, terminal services were renamed as *remote desktop services*. In addition, TS Gateway was renamed *remote desktop gateway* and TS Web Access was renamed remote desktop Web access.)

For this activity, you install the TS Gateway and TS Web Access role services.

Activity

1. Open Server Manager, if it is not already open.

2. Click the **+** plus sign in front of Roles in the left pane, if necessary.

3. Click **Terminal Services** in the left pane under Roles.

4. Scroll down in the right pane to Role Services.

5. Click **Add Role Services**.

6. In the Select Role Services window, click the check boxes for **TS Gateway** and **TS Web Access**. If you see the Add Role Services dialog box to add the Web Server (IIS) role and role services, click **Add Required Role Services**. You may see this box when you click TS Gateway or when you click TS Web Access. Click **Next**.

7. Ensure that **Choose an existing certificate for SSL encryption (recommended)** is selected (see Figure 10-9) and click **Next**.

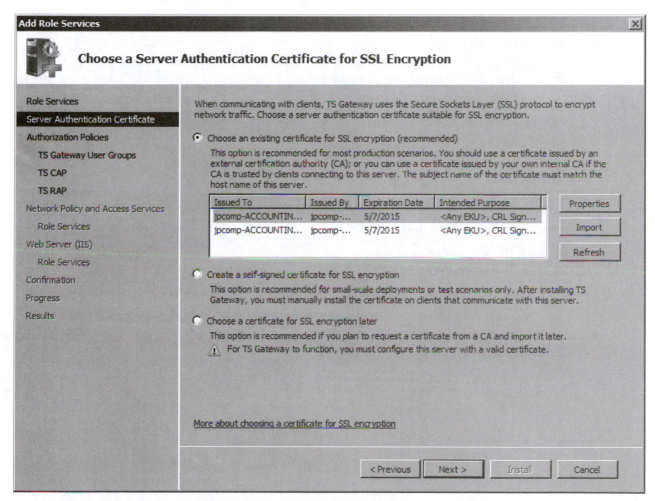

Figure 10-9   Choose a Server Authentication Certificate for SSL Encryption window

8. In the Create Authorization Policies for TS Gateway window, leave **Now** selected and click **Next**.

9. Click **Next** in the Select Groups That Can Connect Through TS Gateway window.

10. Click **Next** In the Create a TS CAP for TS Gateway window.

11. In the Create a TS RAP for TS Gateway window, click **Allow users to connect to any computer on the network** and click **Next**.

12. If you see the Network Policy and Access Services window, click **Next**.

13. If you see the Web Server (IIS) window, click **Next**. Also, if you see the Select Role Services window to specify role services for Web Server (IIS), click **Next**.

14. Click **Install** in the Confirm Installation Selections window.

15. In the Installation Results window, you might see an error about your not having sufficient permissions to select the specified certificate for SSL encryption. In this case, you can use TS Gateway Manager later to select another certificate (when you open TS Gateway Manager, you'll see an error message about the need to select a certificate and an option to select a certificate). Do not worry about this error for this practice installation. Click **Close**.

16. Close Server Manager.

17. Click **Start**, point to **Administrative Tools**, point to **Terminal Services**, and note the TS Gateway Manager and TS Web Access Administration tools that are available for managing TS Gateway and TS Web Access.

18. Click the pointer on the desktop to close the menus.

Review Questions

1. Your IT manager is interested in finding a secure alternative to VPN for enabling users to remotely access a server. Which of the following do you suggest?

    a. TS Gateway

    b. TS Port Access

    c. Web Gateway

    d. RemoteApp Portway

2. HTTPS uses _____ for security.

3. TS Web Access users can run applications on a terminal server through which of the following?

    a. A remote procedure window

    b. A Web browser

    c. The Command Prompt window

    d. The remote desktop simulation window

4. TS Web Access is installed as a(n) _____ that is part of the terminal services role.

5. True or False? One disadvantage of using TS Gateway is that you cannot control access to connect to servers by designating user groups.

WINDOWS SERVER 2008 VIRTUALIZATION

Labs included in this chapter:

- Lab 11.1 Configure Virtual Machine Hardware

- Lab 11.2 Add a Virtual Hard Disk and Edit a Virtual Hard Disk

- Lab 11.3 Manage Hyper-V Settings

- Lab 11.4 Take a Snapshot of a Virtual Machine

Microsoft MCITP Exam #70-646 Objectives

Objective	Lab
Planning for Server Deployment	11.1, 11.2
Planning for Server Management	11.1, 11.2, 11.3
Planning Application and Data Provisioning	11.1, 11.2
Planning for Business Continuity and High Availability	11.3, 11.4

Lab 11.1 Configure Virtual Machine Hardware

Objectives

- Understand Hyper-V hardware configuration options
- Explore Hyper-V hardware configuration options using Hyper-V Manager

Materials Required

This lab requires the following:

- Windows Server 2008 Standard or Enterprise Edition with the Hyper-V role installed
- A virtual machine installed in Hyper-V

Estimated completion time: **15 minutes**

Activity Background

After Hyper-V is installed, you can configure many hardware settings for each virtual machine within a virtual server. These hardware settings include the following:

- Add new hardware, such as a new SCSI Controller or an additional NIC
- Set a start up order for boot devices in the BIOS
- Add or subtract the amount of RAM to allocate for the virtual server
- Specify the number of logical processors to use with the virtual server (on a multi-processor computer)
- Add hard drives to a disk controller
- Configure or remove a NIC
- Configure virtual COM ports
- Set up to use a floppy disk drive

In this activity, you fully explore the hardware configuration options in Hyper-V. Your server should already be set up for the Hyper-V role and have a virtual machine configured, as is done via the activities in Chapter 11, "Windows Server 2008 Virtualization" in *MCITP Guide to Microsoft Windows Server 2008, Server Administration (Exam #70-646)*.

For all of the activities in this chapter, you'll need to log on to an account with Administrator privileges.

Throughout the activities in this book, you may occasionally see the User Account Control box with a message that Windows needs your permission to continue. Whenever you see this box, click Continue. Keep this in mind for all of the activities because any interaction with the User Account Control box is not included in the steps.

Activity

1. Click **Start**, point to **Administrative Tools**, and click **Hyper-V Manager**.

2. Ensure that the virtual machine's state is off. If it is not off, right-click the virtual machine's name under Virtual Machines in the middle pane and click **Shut Down**. If you see the Shut Down Machine dialog box, click **Shut Down**.

3. If necessary, click the virtual machine name under Virtual Machines in the middle pane to highlight it.

4. In the right pane labeled Actions, click **Settings** under the virtual machine's name. (Alternatively, you can highlight the virtual machine name in the middle pane under Virtual Machines, click **Action** in the toolbar, and click **Settings**.)

5. In the Settings for *virtualservername* window, click **Add Hardware** in the left pane (see Figure 11-1). Note that you can use this option to add hardware, such as a SCSI controller from which to add more virtual disks.

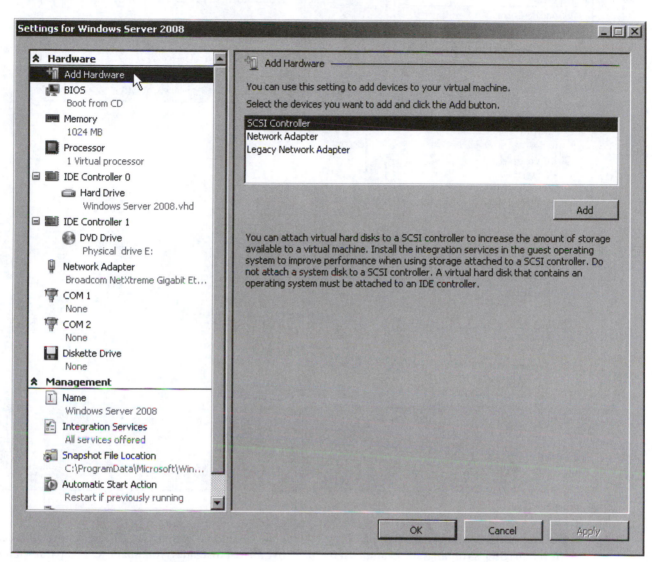

Figure 11-1   Add Hardware option

6. Click **BIOS** in the left pane. You can configure to turn num lock on or off at startup (see Figure 11-2). Also, you can configure a boot order for devices from which to start the operating system. For the boot order it is useful to set it so that CD is first and next is the boot hard drive, such as IDE or SCSI. In this way, when you install an operating system in a virtual machine, the virtual machine automatically tries the CD/DVD drive first so that it can automatically initiate the operating system's set up program.

7. Click **Memory** in the left pane. Note that, depending on the amount of RAM in your computer, you can allocate from 8 MB or more to an operating system in a virtual machine (you need at least 512 MB for Windows Server 2008).

8. Click **Processor**. You can set the number of processors to use with this option (depending on the number of processors in the host computer). The resource control options you can configure are:

- *Virtual machine reserve (percentage)*—sets the CPU percentage allocated to this virtual machine, which is configured on the basis of the number of virtual machines housed in the virtual server; for example, you might set this at about 20 percent when there are five virtual machines

- *Virtual machine limit (percentage)*—sets the maximum CPU percentage that can be used by the virtual machine; for example, if this is set at 100 percent, then when needed, this virtual machine can use up to 100 percent of the CPU resources

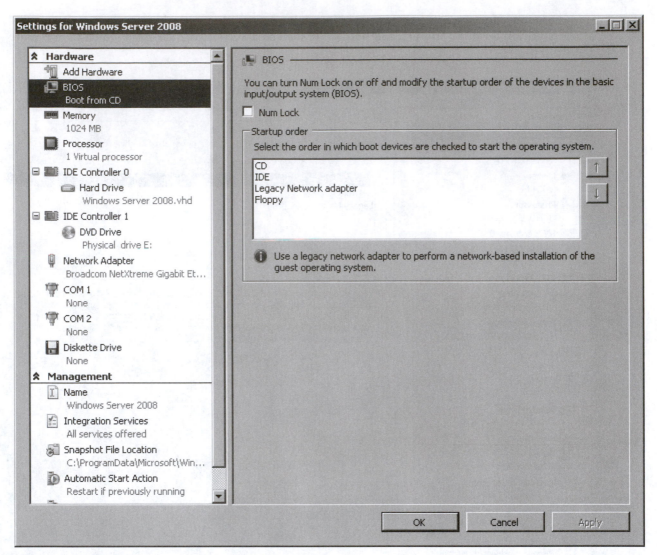

Figure 11-2   BIOS option

- *Relative weight*—sets the amount of CPU resources allocated to the virtual machine relative to all other virtual machines running; for example, if there are five virtual machines, you might set this parameter at 20

9. Click **IDE Controller (0)** or **SCSI Controller** in the left pane, depending on your hardware configuration. Note that you can use this option to add hard and DVD drives to the controller.

10. Click **Network Adapter** in the left pane. This option enables you to configure a network adapter or to remove one. If you are configured to use an external virtual network, you can also select to assign a VLAN ID. A VLAN ID is a unique number that identifies this external virtual network (used by the virtual machine) from other virtual networks configured for other virtual machines. (An external virtual network is one that offers communication between virtual machines and the physical network through a NIC.)

11. Click **COM 1** in the left pane. This option enables you to connect a virtual COM port on the virtual machine to a COM port on the computer by using a named pipe. In Windows, a named pipe is typically a file or process that enables client/server communications between two entities, in this case between a virtual COM port and a physical COM port.

12. Click **Diskette Drive**. If your computer has a floppy disk drive, you can use this option to make it available to the virtual machine.

13. Close the Settings for *virtualservername* window.

Review Questions

1. The BIOS hardware configuration option for a virtual machine in Hyper-V enables you to set up the _____.

2. The COM 1 hardware configuration option enables you to set up communications between a virtual COM port on a virtual machine and the physical COM port on the host computer by using _____.

3. Which of the following are processor options that you can configure in a virtual machine? (Choose all that apply.)

   a. Virtual machine limit

   b. Relative weight

   c. Processor speed

   d. Processor register allocation

4. True or False? Hyper-V does not support the use of legacy floppy disk drives.

5. To use Windows Server 2008 as a guest operating system in a Hyper-V virtual machine, you need to allocate a minimum of _____ in memory to the virtual machine.

Lab 11.2 Add a Virtual Hard Disk and Edit a Virtual Hard Disk

Objectives

- Create a new virtual hard disk
- Edit an existing virtual hard disk

Materials Required

This lab requires the following:

- Windows Server 2008 Standard or Enterprise Edition with the Hyper-V role installed
- A virtual machine installed in Hyper-V

Estimated completion time: **20 minutes**

Activity Background

An ongoing Hyper-V activity on a virtual machine is managing disk space. As you monitor the use of a virtual hard disk on a specific virtual machine, you may decide that you need more disk space or that the disk's performance could use improvement because it seems slow. Hyper-V offers the Edit Virtual Hard Disk Wizard to enable you to reallocate hard disk space for the virtual disk that you select. There are three edit functions that can be performed on an existing virtual hard disk for a virtual machine:

- *Compact*—reduces the size of a virtual disk used for a virtual machine by deleting blank space created when data has been deleted (you might think of this process as similar to defragmenting a disk)

- *Convert*—changes a dynamic virtual hard disk into a fixed virtual hard disk; a dynamic virtual hard disk is the default and can dynamically grow in size to meet growing disk needs, however if the dynamic capability is not needed, it is good practice to convert to a fixed virtual hard disk for better disk performance

- *Expand*—increases the size of the virtual hard disk to accommodate more disk space

Also, when a virtual server experiences heavier use or you want to add new virtual machines, it may be necessary to add a new virtual hard disk. To simplify this task, Hyper-V offers the New Virtual Hard Disk Wizard, which steps you through adding a new hard disk. When you create a new virtual hard disk you can choose to:

- Create a new dynamic virtual hard disk
- Create a new fixed virtual hard disk

- Create a differencing virtual hard disk that enables you to isolate disk changes by creating separate disk files for the main virtual disk and for virtual disks allocated to specific virtual machines. This technique results in a parent–child relationship in which the virtual hard disk is the parent and the disk space used for a specific virtual machine is the child. Isolating changes in this way enables you to undo specific disk changes for a virtual machine without affecting the parent disk. Note that a "differencing" or child disk expands dynamically as needed.

Keep in mind that a dynamic virtual disk can expand up to the maximum size that you have allocated for that dynamic virtual disk. The amount of space occupied by a specific differencing disk, however, can expand beyond the space allocated to the differencing disk to encompass unused space on its parent disk.

For this activity, you learn how to edit a virtual hard disk and how to add a new virtual hard disk to a virtual server.

Activity

1. Open Hyper-V Manager, if the tool is not already open.

2. Ensure that the virtual machine's state is off (the virtual machine is shut down).

3. In the right pane of Hyper-V Manager, click **Edit Disk**.

4. Click **Next** in the Before You Begin window.

5. Click **Browse** in the Locate Virtual Hard Disk window (see Figure 11-3).

6. In the Open window, click the hard disk .vhd file for the virtual machine in your virtual server, such as *Windows Server 2008.vhd*. (If there are multiple files because you have multiple virtual machines, click one of the files or check with your instructor about which file to use.) Click **Open**.

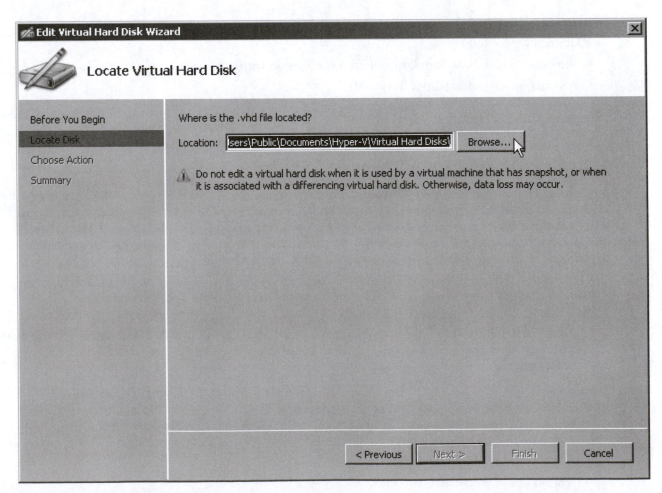

Figure 11-3 Locate Virtual Hard Disk window

7. Click **Next** in the Locate Virtual Hard Disk window.

8. In the Choose Action window, ensure that **Compact** is selected (see Figure 11-4). Click **Next**.

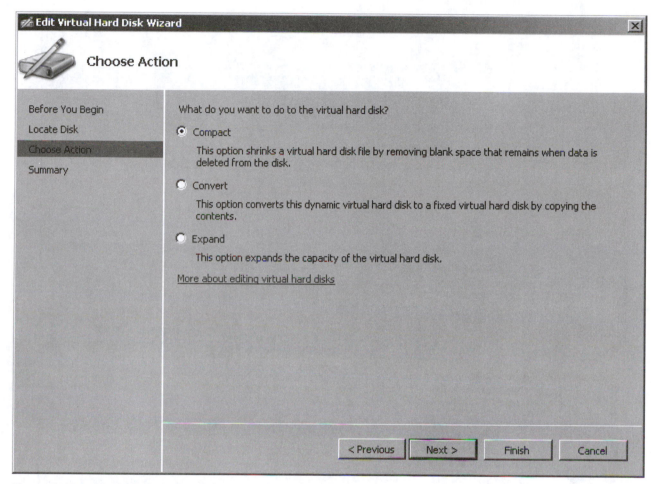

Figure 11-4 Choose Action window

9. Review your selections in the Completing the Edit Virtual Hard Disk Wizard window and click **Finish**. (You'll see a message box showing the programs used by the compact activity. In addition, you may see a popup message that the system is installing a driver.)

10. In the Hyper-V Manager window, click **New** in the right pane and click **Hard Disk**.

11. Click **Next** in the Before You Begin window.

12. In the Choose Disk Type window, make sure that **Dynamically expanding** is selected (see Figure 11-5). Click **Next**.

13. In the Specify Name and Location window, enter the name New Virtual Hard Disk plus your initials and the .vhd extension, as in *New Virtual Hard DiskJP.vhd*. Leave the default location for the virtual hard disk file. Click **Next**.

14. In the Configure Disk window, click **Create a new blank virtual hard disk**, if necessary. Then, enter 15 GB in the Size box (see Figure 11-6). Click **Next**.

15. Review the description of your selections in the Completing the New Virtual Hard Disk Wizard window and click **Finish**.

16. Leave the Hyper-V Manager window open for the next activity.

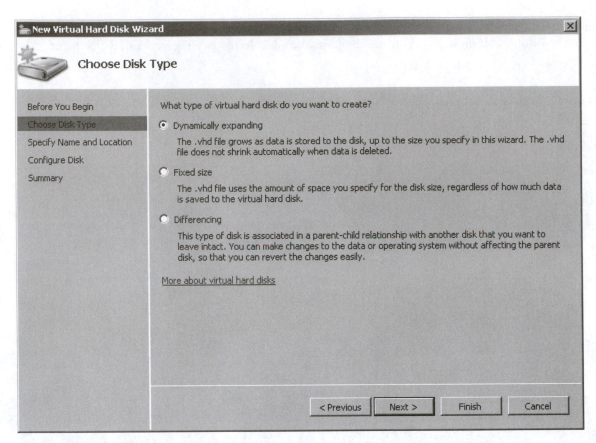

Figure 11-5 Choose Disk Type window

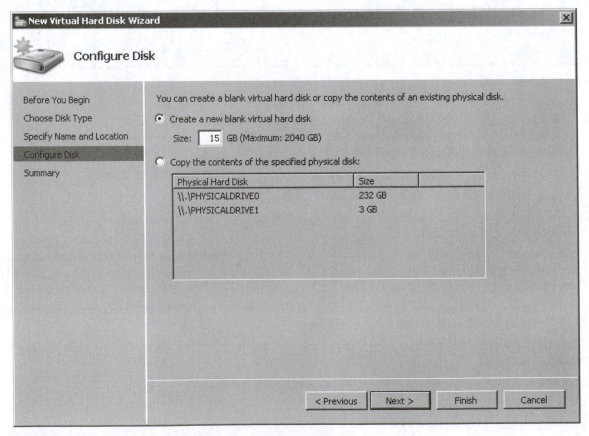

Figure 11-6 Configure Disk window

Review Questions

1. Which of the following describes a dynamic virtual hard disk?

   a. The disk can be shared for use between virtual servers.

   b. The disk can be alternated for use between virtual machines.

   c. The disk can be striped for better performance.

   d. The size of the disk can expand as the data expands on a virtual machine.

2. Use the _____Wizard to create a new virtual hard disk.

3. Your organization uses a virtual machine on which many new files are created and old files deleted. Which of the following processes enables you to recover empty virtual hard disk space after old files have been deleted?

   a. Compact

   b. Refresh

   c. Convert

   d. Extract

4. A Hyper-V virtual machine uses a(n) _____ file type as a virtual hard disk.

5. When you want to create a new virtual hard disk that enables you to periodically undo disk changes, you should configure a(n) _____ virtual hard disk.

Lab 11.3 Manage Hyper-V Settings

Objectives

- Learn how to modify the name of a virtual server
- Select integration services that can be used with a virtual server
- Learn how to designate the location of snapshot files
- Configure a startup action for a virtual server
- Configure a stop action for a virtual server

Materials Required

This lab requires the following:

- Windows Server 2008 Standard or Enterprise Edition with the Hyper-V role installed
- A virtual machine installed in Hyper-V

Estimated completion time: **15 minutes**

Activity Background

Configuring hardware and managing virtual hard disks are not the only management settings associated with a virtual server. For each virtual machine in the virtual server, you can also perform the following:

- Modify a virtual server's name
- Specify the Hyper-V integration services made available to a virtual machine
- Specify where to store snapshot files
- Determine the action a virtual machine takes when you boot its host computer. For example, when you boot the host computer after taking it down to fix hardware, you can have a virtual server automatically start.
- Determine the action taken by a virtual server when Windows Server 2008 is shut down on the host computer, such as shutting down the virtual machine

Configuring the boot and shutdown actions is important because following "best practices" requires that each virtual server be kept in a known state. A known state is either properly started or properly shutdown. Proper startup means that all functions and software on the server are correctly started for users. Proper shutdown involves an orderly process of closing all files and stopping server services and end user programs. As an example of an improper shutdown, you or another server administrator might not remember to turn off or shut down all virtual servers before shutting down the main Windows Server 2008 server. The result could be one or more corrupted files. Likewise, you or someone else might not remember to reboot all virtual servers after restarting the host Windows Server 2008 server. Both of the preceding examples result in having servers in unknown states that risk damage to files or no services to users. However, by configuring the Hyper-V startup and shutdown options, you are assured the virtual servers are kept in a healthy known state.

In this activity, you examine and configure Hyper-V management settings related to a virtual server's name, integration services, the location of snapshot files, and startup and shutdown actions.

Activity

1. Open Hyper-V Manager, if it is not still open.

2. Be sure the virtual machine's state is off. The value in the State column for the virtual machine in the middle pane under Virtual Machines should be "Off."

3. Click to highlight the virtual machine, if it is not highlighted.

4. Right-click the virtual machine in the middle pane under Virtual Machines and click **Settings**.

5. In the Settings for *virtualservername* window, click **Name** in the left pane under Management. In the right pane, note that you can edit the name of the virtual machine and you can record notes about the virtual machine.

6. Click **Integration Services** in the left pane. In the right pane, note the services you can select to use with this virtual machine (see Figure 11-7). Integration services are components and drivers that enable the guest operating system to perform important functions in a secure environment and coordinate those functions with the host operating system. At the time of this writing, the integration services included the following:

   • *Operating system shutdown*—provides a way to safely shut down the guest operating system from Hyper-V. This option enables safe shutdown when you are not directly in the guest operating system window. It also enables the host operating system to send a message to the guest operating system to shut down.

   • *Time synchronization*—enables the time to be synchronized between the guest operating system and the host operating system

   • *Data Exchange*—provides a way to exchange key data values between the guest operating system and the host operating system. An example of exchanged data is the value containing the version of the guest operating system.

   • *Heartbeat*—the host sends periodic heartbeat requests to the guest. The presence or absence of a heartbeat sent back by the guest enables the host operating system to determine if the guest operating system has become unresponsive; when a virtual machine is running, you'll see the heartbeat status in the middle pane of Hyper-V Manager. The status is written as *Heartbeat: OK* (refer to Figure 11-10).

   • *Backup (volume snapshot)*—enables the volume shadow copy service of the host operating system to work with the guest operating system to take volume snapshots of the guest operating system

7. In the left pane, click **Snapshot File Location**. If you have not yet taken a virtual machine snapshot, you can change the location of where snapshots are stored. You learn about snapshots in Lab 11.4.

8. Click **Automatic Start Action** in the left pane of the Settings for *virtualservername* window. In the right pane, this option enables you to specify which action the virtual machine takes when the host computer is booted. Click **Always start this virtual machine automatically**, so that it always starts when the host computer is booted (see Figure 11-8).

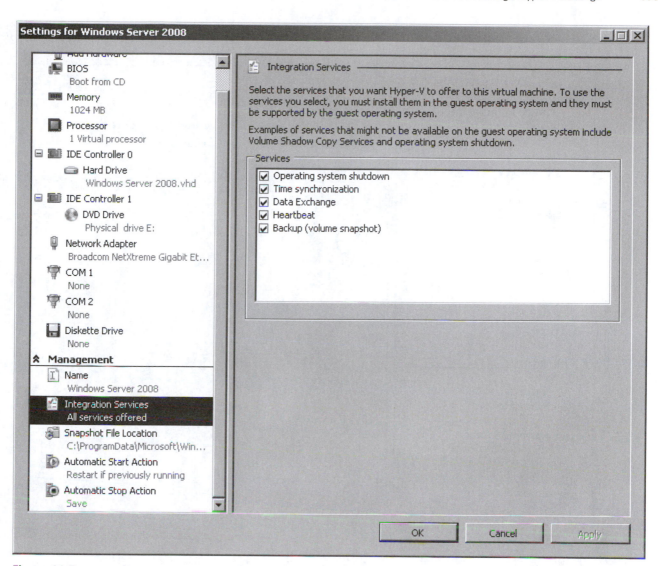

Figure 11-7 Integration Services

9. In the Startup delay box, enter **240** seconds. This is the amount of time Hyper-V will wait after the host computer operating system boots until it starts this virtual machine. If you have multiple virtual machines all set to start automatically, you should space out the time delay for each one. For example, if there are four virtual machines you might set the time delay at 120 seconds for the first virtual machine, 240 seconds for the second one, and so on.

10. Click **Automatic Stop Action** in the left pane. In the right pane you can configure what action the virtual machine takes when the host computer operating system is shut down. The right pane options are as follows:

    - Save the virtual machine state

    - Turn off the virtual machine

    - Shut down the virtual machine

11. Make sure that **Save the virtual machine state** is selected; saving the virtual machine state is the safest option for most host computer shut down situations and is also the default.

12. Click **OK** in the Settings for *virtualservername* window.

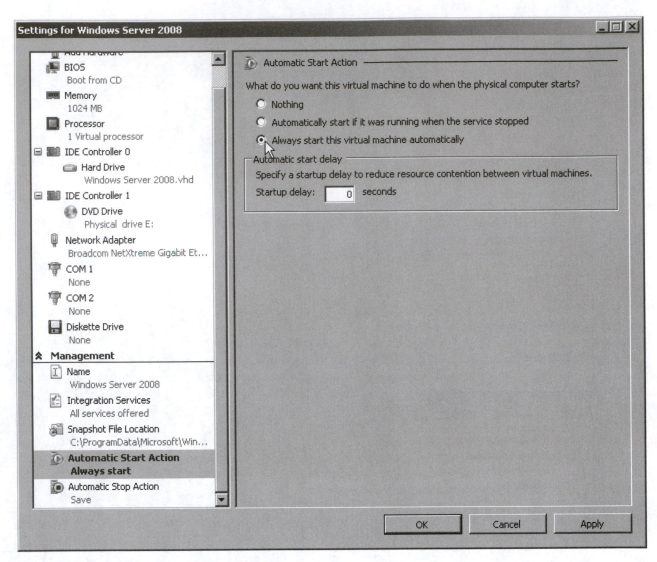

Figure 11-8 Automatic Startup Action options

Review Questions

1. True or False? Hyper-V has a management option that enables you to change the name of a virtual machine even after the operating system has been installed.

2. Time synchronization is a(n) _____ that you can enable for a virtual machine in Hyper-V.

3. Which of the following is an automatic stop action that you can configure for a virtual machine? (Choose all that apply.)

   a. Move unsaved database files to the host machine

   b. Turn off the virtual machine

   c. Shut down the guest operating system

   d. Change the virtual machine state to pause

4. When you configure the automatic start action parameters for a virtual machine, the startup delay is used to _____.

5. True or False? To do "Nothing" is one automatic start action option for a virtual machine.

Lab 11.4 Take a Snapshot of a Virtual Machine

Objectives

- Take a snapshot on a live virtual machine
- Use a snapshot to go back to a previous virtual machine state

Materials Required

This lab requires the following:

- Windows Server 2008 Standard or Enterprise Edition with the Hyper-V role installed
- A virtual machine installed in Hyper-V

Estimated completion time: **15 minutes**

Activity Background

Whenever you make changes to a virtual machine, such as performing an update to the operating system or installing new software, plan to take a snapshot before and after you make the change. A snapshot saves key information about a virtual server such as virtual machine settings and configuration, virtual machine system data, processor state, memory contents, and other information. You can take a snapshot with the virtual machine started or stopped, and the process of taking a snapshot causes only a brief pause in a started virtual machine.

Snapshots are well suited for test or development servers, but they also can provide a measure of safety for live systems when no full backup is available. Snapshots are not a replacement for a full backup, but they do provide you with important settings and data to fall back on when you don't have time or the opportunity to take a full backup before making a system change.

Hyper-V tracks all snapshots by the date and time of each one. When you need to return to a particular state of the virtual machine, you need only select the snapshot you want and use the option to revert back to that snapshot.

For this activity, you take a snapshot of a live system and then you revert back to that snapshot.

Activity

1. Open Hyper-V Manager, if it is not already open.

2. Start the virtual machine in Hyper-V. In the middle pane, right-click the virtual machine shown under Virtual Machines and click **Start**.

3. Wait a few minutes for the virtual machine to start, and be sure that the virtual machine is still highlighted. Right-click the virtual machine and click **Snapshot** (see Figure 11-9). Note that the State column of the virtual machine in the middle pane shows Creating Snapshot. After a few minutes the State column returns to Running.

4. Depending on the speed of your server, it may take a few more minutes for the Snapshots section of the middle pane to update to display the snapshot (see Figure 11-10). You can also click **Refresh** in the right pane, if necessary, to update the Hyper-V Manager window.

5. Right-click the virtual machine in the middle pane and click **Shut Down**.

6. If you see the Shut Down Machine box, click **Shut Down**.

7. Wait a few minutes for the virtual machine's State column to display Off. Right-click the virtual machine in the middle pane and click **Revert**.

8. If you see the Revert Virtual Machine box, click **Revert**. After a few minutes, note that the virtual machine's State column displays Saved.

9. Close the Hyper-V Manager window.

Figure 11-9 Taking a snapshot

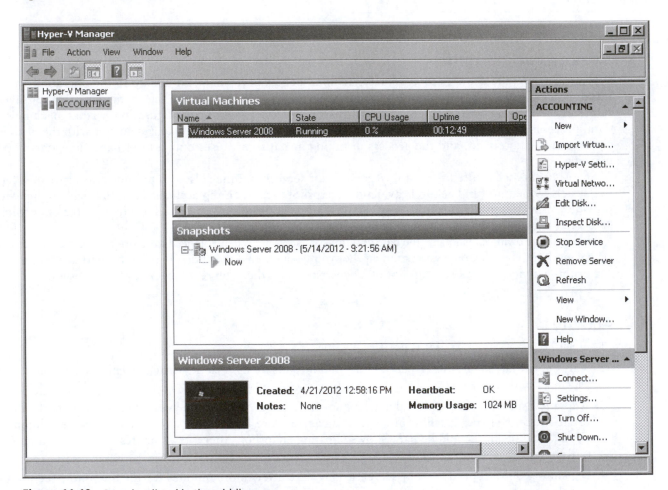

Figure 11-10 Snapshot listed in the middle pane

Review Questions

1. Which of the following is information saved by a Hyper-V snapshot? (Choose all that apply.)

    a. Virtual machine configuration

    b. Virtual machine processor state

    c. Virtual machine memory contents

    d. Virtual machine system data

2. A virtual machine snapshot is not a replacement for _____.

3. True or False? A snapshot cannot be taken while a virtual machine is running.

4. Which of the following is displayed about a specific snapshot in the middle pane of Hyper-V under Snapshots? (Choose all that apply.)

    a. Snapshot size

    b. Snapshot location

    c. Snapshot time

    d. Snapshot date

5. The _____ option is used to apply a snapshot to a virtual machine in order to go back to a previous state.

11

APPLICATION AND DATA PROVISIONING

Labs included in this chapter:

- Lab 12.1 Install the Windows Process Activation Service (WAS) Support Role Service

- Lab 12.2 Configure TS RemoteApp Settings

- Lab 12.3 Configure Programs That Can Be Run Through TS RemoteApp

- Lab 12.4 Enable Offline Files

Microsoft MCITP Exam #70-646 Objectives

Objective	Lab
Planning for Server Deployment	12.1, 12.2, 12.3
Planning Application and Data Provisioning	12.1, 12.2, 12.3, 12.4
Planning for Business Continuity and High Availability	12.4

Lab 12.1 Install the Windows Process Activation Service (WAS) Support Role Service

Objectives

- Understand how the Windows Process Activation Service Support role service is important for supporting Web applications
- Install the Windows Process Activation Service Support role service

Materials Required

This lab requires the following:

- Windows Server 2008 Standard or Enterprise Edition with the Application Server role installed, but with the Web Server (IIS) Support role service and the Windows Process Activation Service Support role service not installed
- Web Server (IIS) role already installed

Estimated completion time: **20 minutes**

Activity Background

The Application Server role can include the installation of the Windows Process Activation Service (WAS) Support role service. WAS enables better integration between applications and an Internet Information Services (IIS) server. If your organization plans to develop or use IIS applications on an internal network or through an external network such as the Internet, plan to install the WAS Support role service.

The WAS Support role service does the following:

- Enables applications built on Windows Communication Foundation (WCF) to use more IIS features
- Provides assistance in creating and managing IIS application pools
- Enables use of the World Wide Web Publishing Service
- Provides a way for applications to start and stop dynamically on the basis of messages transmitted through the network—a capability that results in more efficient use of IIS server services

In this activity, you install the WAS Support role service. Your server should already have the Application Server role installed, but without the WAS Support role service, as is done through the activities in Chapter 12, "Application and Data Provisioning" in *MCITP Guide to Microsoft Windows Server 2008, Server Administration (Exam #70-646)*. In addition, the Web Server (IIS) role should already be installed, as is done in Chapter 9 of the same book.

For all of the activities in this chapter, you'll need to log onto an account with Administrator privileges. Additionally, most of these activities can be completed on a virtual server or computer, such as one running Hyper-V.

Throughout the activities in this book, you may occasionally see the User Account Control box with a message that Windows needs your permission to continue. Whenever you see this box, click Continue. Keep this in mind for all of the activities because any interaction with the User Account Control box is not included in the steps.

Activity

1. Open Server Manager, if it is not opened.
2. Click the **+** plus sign in front of Roles in the left pane.
3. Click **Application Server** under Roles in the left pane.
4. Scroll to the Role Services section in the right pane.

5. Click **Add Role Services** in the right pane.

6. Click the **Windows Process Activation Service Support** check box.

7. You are likely to see the Add Role Services dialog box to install .NET Framework 3.0 features and Message Queuing (see Figure 12-1), click **Add Required Features** (or **Add Required Role Services** depending on what must be added). (If the Web Server [IIS] role is not installed, you'll also see an option to install the Web Server [IIS] role in the Add Role Services dialog box.)

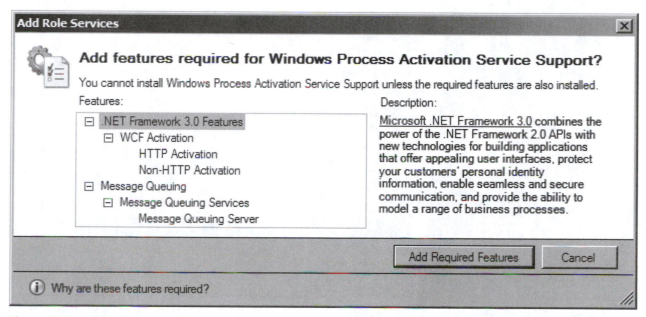

Figure 12-1   Add Role Services dialog box

8. In the Select Role Services window, note the following services that should be automatically selected under Windows Process Activation Service Support:

   - **HTTP Activation**—enables applications to use HTTP activation to start or stop on the basis of messages transmitted through the network

   - **Message Queuing Activation**—enables application processes to activate through message queuing

   - **TCP Activation**—enables application processes to be activated through TCP (using TCP port 808, which is an exception created in Windows Firewall for TCP activation)

   - **Named Pipes Activation**—enables application processes to be activated by named pipes

9. Click **Next** in the Select Role Services window.

10. Review your selections in the Confirm Installation Selections window (see Figure 12-2). Click **Install**.

11. In the Installation Results window, click **Close**.

12. In Server Manager, click the **+** plus sign in front of Configuration in the left pane.

13. In the tree in the left pane, click **Services** under Configuration.

14. In the middle pane, scroll to find and then double-click **Windows Process Activation Service**.

15. In the Windows Process Activation Service Properties (*servername*) dialog box, click the **Dependencies** tab.

16. Note the four services that depend on the Windows Process Activation Service and generally correspond to the services selected in Step 8 (see Figure 12-3).

17. Click **OK** in the Windows Process Activation Service Properties (*servername*) dialog box.

18. Close Server Manager.

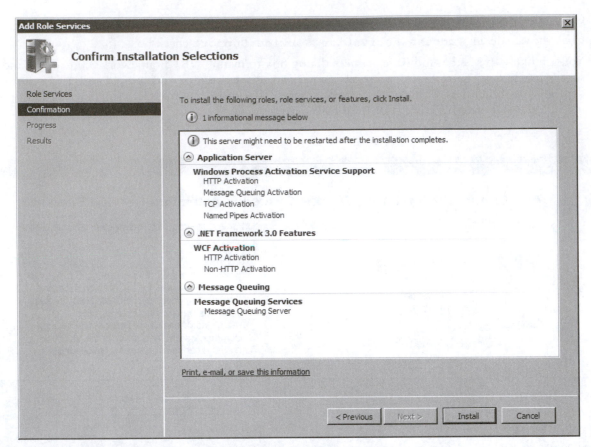

Figure 12-2 Confirm Installation Selections window

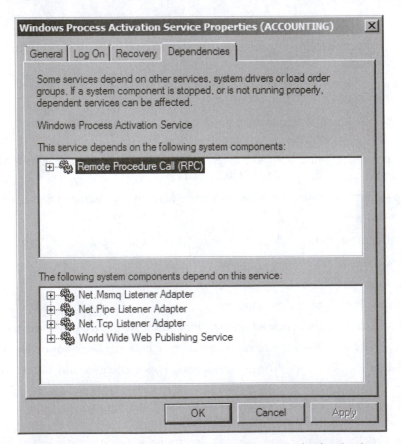

Figure 12-3 Dependencies of the Windows Process Activation Service

Review Questions

1. The Windows Process Activation Service (WAS) enables better integration between _____ and _____.

2. Installing WAS is necessary to use the World Wide Web _____ Service.

3. Which of the following must be installed to also install the Windows Process Activation Service Support role service? (Choose all that apply.)

   a. Web Server (IIS) role

   b. UDP Activation

   c. Message Queuing

   d. .NET Framework 3.0

4. True or False? Enabling Web applications to start and stop dynamically yields more efficient use of Web server services.

5. WAS is valuable for working with IIS _____ pools.

Lab 12.2 Configure TS RemoteApp Settings

Objectives

- Use the System window to configure remote access security
- Use TS Remote Manager to configure RemoteApp settings

Materials Required

This lab requires the following:

- Windows Server 2008 Standard or Enterprise Edition with the Terminal Services role installed
- Completion of Lab 10.4 in this book

Estimated completion time: **15 minutes**

Activity Background

Applications can be made accessible to clients remotely by using TS RemoteApp, which you set up in Lab 10.4 by installing the TS Web Access role service. (Note that in Windows Server 2008 R2 terminal services are renamed "remote desktop services" and TS RemoteApp is simply called "RemoteApp").

A list on a terminal server designates the TS RemoteApp applications that a client can use. The applications run on the terminal server and not on the client's computer. One advantage to this approach is that "thin client" computers can be used to save money that would otherwise be spent on more powerful client computers. Thin clients are computers that have limited memory, CPU, and disk resources. Memory, CPU, and disk resources are instead used on the server to run applications. In addition, application updates are made to the application on the server, which is an advantage for ensuring users experience the application in a standardized way. Using thin clients and performing application updates on the terminal server also makes user support much easier.

When you offer TS RemoteApp applications to clients, an essential first step is to configure the TS Remote-App deployment settings. For this activity, you learn where to configure TS RemoteApp deployment settings.

Activity

1. Click **Start**, type **control system** in the Start Search box, and press **Enter**.

2. In the upper-left side of the System window, click **Remote settings**.

3. On the Remote tab of the System Properties dialog box, you can determine which types of clients can connect to the terminal server. Assume all of the terminal server clients are using Windows XP, Vista, or 7, and

select `Allow connections only from computers running Remote Desktop with Network Level Authentication (more secure)`. Network Level Authentication (NLA) invokes authentication to thwart would-be attackers, particularly those attempting man-in-the-middle (MITM) attacks. Windows Server 2003 and 2008 as well as Windows XP, Vista, and 7 all support NLA.

4. Click `OK` in the System Properties dialog box.

5. Close the System window.

6. Click `Start`, point to `Administrative Tools`, point to `Terminal Services`, and click `TS RemoteApp Manager`.

7. Click `Action` in the toolbar and click `Terminal Server Settings`.

8. In the RemoteApp Deployment Settings dialog box, click the `Terminal Server` tab, if it is not already selected.

9. On the Terminal Server tab, check the `Do not allow users to start unlisted programs on initial connection (Recommended)` check box, if necessary (see Figure 12-4). Microsoft recommends this setting for protection against malicious users, so that potential malware cannot be started as an unlisted program.

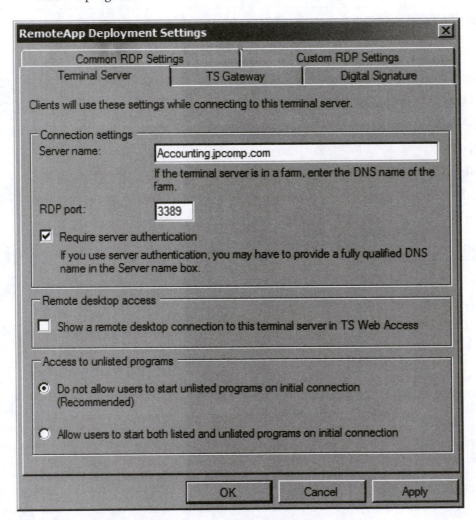

Figure 12-4   Configuring terminal server settings for TS RemoteApp

10. Click the `TS Gateway` tab.

11. Select `Automatically detect TS Gateway server settings`, if it is not already selected. This setting enables the RemoteApp client to use group policy settings that have been configured to manage how the user employs terminal services. This includes group policy security settings that you learn in Chapter 13, "Securing Windows Server 2008" in *MCITP Guide to Microsoft Windows Server 2008, Server Administration (Exam #70-646)*.

12. Click the **Common RDP Settings** tab. Use this tab to configure common Remote Desktop Protocol (RDP) settings, which includes devices and resources that the client is allowed to access. These devices and resources include printers and disk drives (see Figure 12-5).

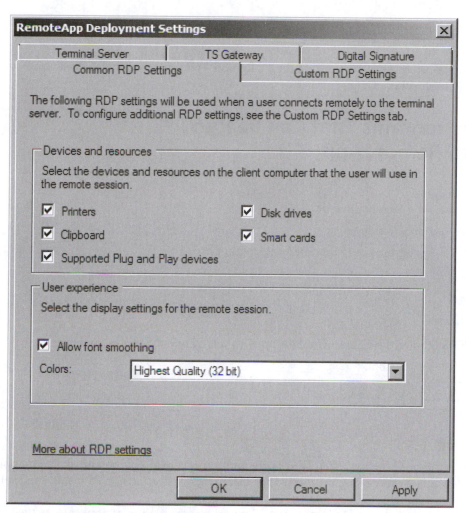

Figure 12-5 Common RDP Settings tab

13. Close the RemoteApp Deployment Settings dialog box.
14. Close the TS RemoteApp Manager window.

Review Questions

1. TS RemoteApp applications run on the _____ and not on the _____.

2. TS RemoteApp is installed when you install the _____ role service in the Terminal Services role.

3. Which of the following clients support the use of Network Level Authentication (NLA)? (Choose all that apply.)

   a. Windows 98

   b. Windows XP

   c. Windows Vista

   d. Windows 7

4. By configuring common RDP settings in TS RemoteApp Manager, you can configure which of the following devices and resources to be accessed by a terminal server client? (Choose all that apply.)

   a. Printers

   b. Clipboard

   c. Disk drives

   d. Supported Plug and Play devices

5. True or False? For best security when configuring the TS RemoteApp settings, enable clients to start unlisted programs on initial connection.

Lab 12.3 Configure Programs That Can Be Run Through TS RemoteApp

Objectives

- Install programs to use via a terminal server
- Configure a RemoteApp program list
- Configure properties for programs on a RemoteApp program list

Materials Required

This lab requires the following:

- Windows Server 2008 Standard or Enterprise Edition with the Terminal Services role installed
- Completion of Lab 10.4 in this book

Estimated completion time: **15 minutes**

Activity Background

After TS RemoteApp is configured, the next step is to make applications available to clients. Each application must be installed in the terminal server using the wizard for installing applications in TS install mode. You can start this wizard from Control Panel.

Once the applications are installed, use TS RemoteApp Manager to create a list of applications the client can access. The application list is displayed for the client when the client accesses the terminal server.

In this activity, you start the wizard for installing applications in TS install mode (but you exit before installing a program). Then you create a list of applications (installed by default for terminal services compatibility) that can be run remotely through RemoteApp.

Activity

1. Click **Start** and click **Control Panel**.

2. Select **Classic View**, if it is not already selected.

3. Double-click the applet for **Install Application on Terminal Server**.

4. In the Install Program From Floppy Disk or CD-ROM dialog box, note that you can insert the media from which to load the program, Click **Next** to continue with the installation. Click **Cancel**.

5. Close Control Panel.

6. Click **Start**, point to **Administrative Tools**, point to **Terminal Services**, and click **TS RemoteApp Manager**.

7. In the TS RemoteApp Manager window, click **Action** in the toolbar and click **Add RemoteApp Programs**.

8. Click **Next** in the RemoteApp Wizard window.

9. In the window to Choose programs to add to the RemoteApp Programs list (see Figure 12-6; the selection list you see may be different depending on what is installed on your server), click the check boxes for the following programs:

   • `Calculator`

   • `Paint`

   • `WordPad`

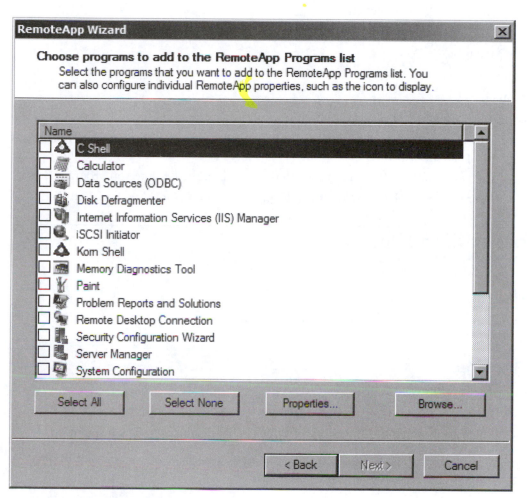

Figure 12-6   RemoteApp Wizard

10. Click `Calculator` in the list of programs and click the `Properties` button. Note that the check box is selected for RemoteApp program is available through TS Web Access. Also, in the RemoteApp program name text box, you can configure the name for this program that users will see in their program selection list. You additionally can configure the path to the program, an alias (Microsoft recommends that you do not change the alias, which is a unique program ID), and whether command-line arguments are allowed. Additionally, there is a button to enable you to configure which icon to use to represent the program in the user's program list. Click `Cancel` in the RemoteApp Properties dialog box.

11. Click `Next` in the Choose programs to add to the RemoteApp Programs list window.

12. In the Review Settings window, click `Finish`.

13. Close the TS RemoteApp Manager window.

14. To verify that these programs are available to users, click `Start`, point to `Administrative Tools`, point to `Terminal Services`, and click `TS Web Access Administration`.

15. If you see the Information Bar box asking whether you noticed the information bar, click `Close`. Also, if you see a security message from Internet Explorer, click `Add` to add this Web location as a permitted site.

16. Click the link for `RemoteApp Programs`. The Calculator, Paint, and WordPad programs should be listed.

17. Close the TS Web Access window. If you see the Internet Explorer dialog box, click `Close Tabs` to close all Internet Explorer tabs.

Review Questions

1. Programs to be made available through RemoteApp can be installed on a terminal server using the Install Application on Terminal Server selection in _____.

    a. the TS Program Installer option on the Administrative Tools Terminal Services menu

    b. Computer Manager

    c. the System window

    d. Control Panel

2. You can use _____ to add a program to the list of programs available through RemoteApp.

3. True or False? When you place a program on the list of programs available through RemoteApp and configure that program's properties, the best practice is to leave the program's alias as the default.

4. By opening _____, you can verify programs you have placed on the RemoteApp programs list.

5. True or False? A maximum of eight programs can be placed on the RemoteApp programs list.

Lab 12.4 Enable Offline Files

Objectives

- Enable offline files on the client computer
- Configure parameters for offline files on the client computer

Materials Required

This lab requires the following:

- Windows Server 2008 Standard or Enterprise Edition
- Offline files should be disabled in Control Panel, which is the default on a new installation

Estimated completion time: **15 minutes**

Activity Background

One of the most common tasks for a server is to offer shared folders for clients to access when the clients are connected to the server through a network. An added feature is that a server and its clients can be configured so that files in a shared folder are available offline when the client is not connected to the network. This is the offline files option in Windows. When a server and its shared folders are set up for the offline files option, files in a shared folder can be cached in the client's computer storage. The client can then access and work on a file while not connected to the server. When the client reconnects to the network, any changes made to an offline file cached on the client can be synchronized with the same file in a shared folder on the network server.

According to Microsoft, offline files are appealing to server clients because they:

- Enable the clients to work faster when working over a slow network connection
- Permit shared files to be accessed when the clients are not connected to the network, such as while on a business trip or working from home
- Enable files cached offline on the clients' computers to be effortlessly synchronized with the same shared files on the server as soon as the clients reconnect to the server
- Offer access to cached versions of shared files when the network or server is down, such as during a power failure or when a hardware failure strikes

To make use of caching files on the client, the server must be configured for file sharing and offline files, as you learned in Chapter 12, "Application and Data Provisioning" in *MCITP Guide to Microsoft Windows Server 2008, Server Administration (Exam #70-646)*. In addition, clients who need the ability to cache files shared from a server, must enable the ability to use offline files in the client operating system. The offline files setting is supported in Windows 7 with the Professional, Enterprise, and Ultimate Editions. It is also supported in the Windows Vista Business, Enterprise, and Ultimate Editions. Early Windows versions, such as Windows XP and 2000 also provide support for the offline files setting, but without some of the improved features introduced with Windows Vista and Windows Server 2008. These features include more efficient file synchronization and four different modes of operation: manual offline, auto offline, online, and slow-link.

For this activity, you learn how to enable the offline files setting at the client. You can use Windows Server 2008 (or you can use Windows 7) to learn how to enable the offline files setting at the client. You will have to reboot the computer after you enable the offline files setting, so save any work before you start this activity.

Activity

1. Click **Start** and click **Control Panel**.

2. Click **Classic View**, if it is not already displayed.

3. Double-click the **Offline Files** applet. (In Windows 7, click **Sync Center** and then click **Manage offline files**.)

4. In the Offline Files dialog box, click **Enable Offline Files**, if offline files is disabled (see Figure 12-7). If Offline files is already enabled, skip to Step 10.

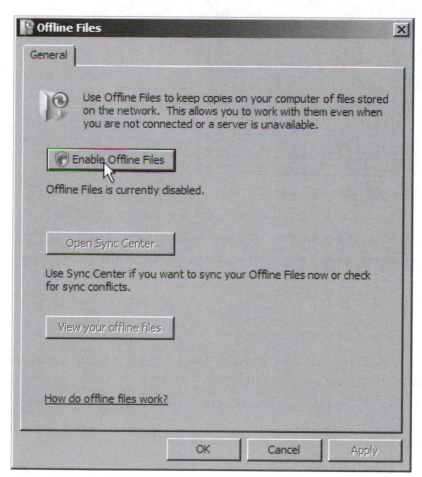

Figure 12-7   Enabling offline files

5. Click **OK**.

6. In the Offline Files dialog box, click **Yes** to restart the computer (save any work first).

7. After the computer reboots, log back in, if necessary.

8. Click **Start** and click **Control Panel**.

9. In Classic View, double-click **Offline Files**. Note that there are three additional tabs, Disk Usage, Encryption, and Network (see Figure 12-8).

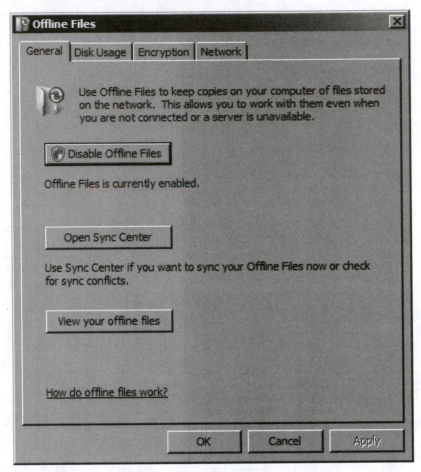

Figure 12-8 Offline Files dialog box after offline files are enabled

10. Click the **Disk Usage** tab, which you can use for allocating space in which to store offline files.

11. Click the **Encryption** tab and note you can use this tab to encrypt offline files.

12. Click the **Network** tab. You can use this tab when you are using a slow network connection to access offline files.

13. Close the Offline Files dialog box and close Control Panel.

Review Questions

1. You can adjust the offline files capability at the client to handle a(n) _____ network connection.

2. True or False? Windows Vista Home Edition can use offline files.

3. True or False? An offline files client can configure the amount of disk space to allocate for offline files at the client computer.

4. Offline files are enabled through which of the following tools on the client?

   a. Control Panel

   b. Computer window

   c. Computer management tool

   d. Map network drive tool

5. When the client with cached offline files reconnects to the server offering shared folders, the client can _____ the cached offline files with the server.

CHAPTER THIRTEEN

SECURING WINDOWS SERVER 2008

Labs included in this chapter:

- Lab 13.1 Configure Default Domain Security Policies
- Lab 13.2 Configure Registry Security
- Lab 13.3 Install Health Registration Authority and Host Credential Authorization
- Lab 13.4 Configure a Health Registration Authority Network Policy

Microsoft MCITP Exam #70-646 Objectives

Objective	Lab
Planning for Server Deployment	13.3, 13.4
Planning for Server Management	13.1
Monitoring and Maintaining Servers	13.1, 13.2, 13.3, 13.4

Lab 13.1 Configure Default Domain Security Policies

Objectives

- Configure default domain security policies for auditing
- Configure default domain security policies for user rights management
- Configure default domain security policies for additional security options

Materials Required

This lab requires the following:

- Windows Server 2008 Standard or Enterprise Edition with the Active Directory Domain Services role installed

> Estimated completion time: **20 minutes**

Activity Background

Group policies are settings that can be used to standardize the working environment of a server and its clients. A server administrator can set hundreds of group policies to manage a server environment. A sampling of server functions and resources that can be managed via group policies includes:

- Server security
- Network encryption and authentication techniques
- Client desktop settings
- Resource access, such as access to shared folders and printers
- Use of scripts
- Software settings and software access
- Active Directory access and activity auditing

The group policies you should address early in the life of a server are those policies that govern security. With an eye on server security, you can set security policies for account authorization, auditing, user rights, network security, and general server activities.

Begin by establishing default domain security policies that are administered through all domain controllers, because default domain security policies apply to all domain end users and resources. Default domain security policies provide an essential level of security, such as logon security, that acts like a safety net to close gaps that might be left by other security measures.

Default domain security policies can be set up using the Group Policy Management snap-in. In Chapter 13, "Securing Windows Server 2008" in *MCITP Guide to Microsoft Windows Server 2008, Server Administration (Exam #70-646)*, you configure several basic security policies, such as policies for user account security and logon event auditing. In this activity, you configure security policies for account management auditing, user rights management, and other security settings.

For all of the activities in this chapter, you need to log on to an account with Administrator privileges. Additionally, most of these activities can be completed on a virtual server or computer, such as in Hyper-V.

Throughout the activities in this book, you may occasionally see the User Account Control box with a message that Windows needs your permission to continue. Whenever you see this box, click Continue. Keep this in mind for all the activities because any interaction with the User Account Control box is not included in the steps.

Activity

1. Click **Start**, type **mmc** in the Start Search box, and press **Enter**.
2. In the Console1 window, click **File** in the toolbar and click **Add/Remove Snap-in**.

3. Click the second **Group Policy Management** selection under Snap-in and click **Add >**.

4. In the Welcome to the Group Policy Wizard, click **Browse**.

5. In the Browse for a Group Policy Object dialog box, click **Default Domain Policy** and click **OK**.

6. Click **Finish** in the Welcome to the Group Policy Wizard window.

7. Click **OK** in the Add or Remove Snap-ins dialog box.

8. Click **Default Domain Policy** in the tree in the left pane.

9. Click the + plus sign for **Computer Configuration** in the tree, if necessary.

10. Click the + plus sign for **Policies** in the tree.

11. Click the + plus sign for **Windows Settings** in the tree.

12. Click **Security Settings** in the tree.

13. Double-click **Local Policies** in the middle pane.

14. Double-click **Audit Policy** in the middle pane (see Figure 13-1).

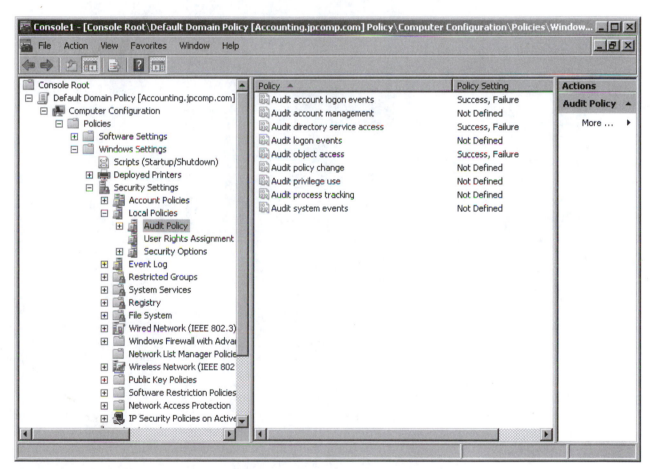

Figure 13-1 Audit Policy options

15. Double-click **Audit account management** in the middle pane.

16. Click the check box for **Define these policy settings** in the Audit account management Properties dialog box. Click the check box for **Success** (see Figure 13-2) so that there is an audit trail in the Security event log of successful changes to user accounts and groups. Click **OK**.

17. Click **User Rights Assignment** in the tree.

18. Double-click **Manage auditing and security log** in the middle pane.

19. In the Manage auditing and security log Properties dialog box, click the check box for **Define these policy settings**. Click the **Add User or Group** button.

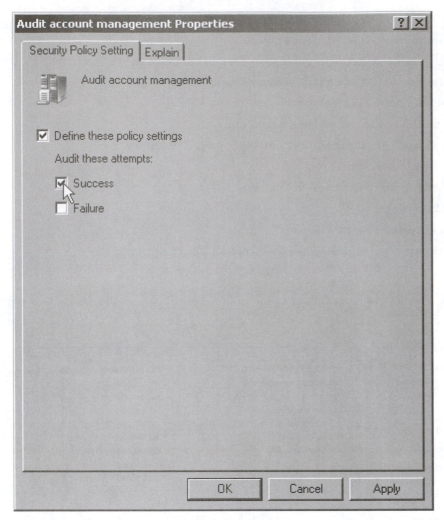

Figure 13-2   Auditing successful account management activities

20. In the Add User or Group dialog box, click **Browse**.

21. In the Select Users, Computers, or Groups dialog box, click the **Advanced** button.

22. Click the **Find Now** button.

23. Under Search results, double-click **Administrators** and click **OK** in the Select Users, Computers, or Groups dialog box.

24. Click **OK** in the Add User or Group dialog box.

25. Click **OK** in the Manage auditing and security log Properties dialog box. In the Policy Setting column in the middle pane, you should now see Administrators for Manage auditing and security log (see Figure 13-3). This setting enables you to secure who can manage information related to auditing, which can be a requirement made by financial and computer system auditors.

26. Click **Security Options** in the tree.

27. In the middle pane, double-click **Interactive logon: Do not display last user name**.

28. In the Interactive logon: Do not display last user name Properties dialog box, click **Define this policy setting**. Ensure that **Enabled** is selected and click **OK**. This option can provide a further level of security, including at the server console, so that an intruder who has physical access to a computer has less information to go on when trying to maliciously access a user's account. In the middle pane, double-click **Interactive logon: Prompt user to change password**.

29. In the Interactive logon: Prompt user to change password Properties dialog box, click **Define this policy setting**. Enter **10** days, so that users start receiving messages about password expiration starting at 10 days before the password expires. Click **OK**.

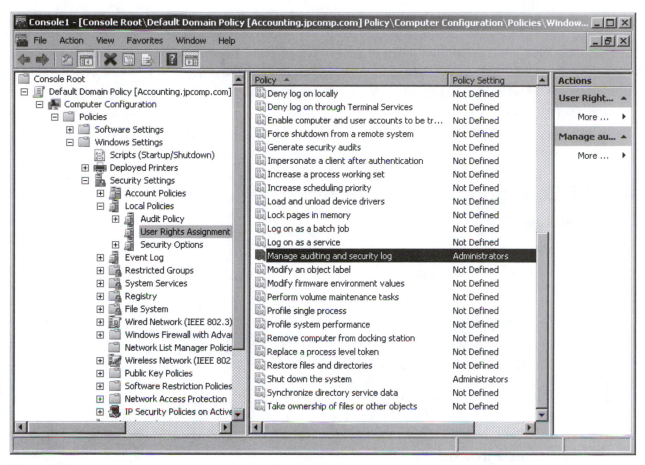

Figure 13-3   Administrators in the Policy Setting column

30. In the middle pane, double-click **Microsoft network server: Disconnect clients when logon hours expire**.

31. In the Microsoft network server: Disconnect clients when logon hours expire Properties dialog box, click **Define this policy setting**. Ensure that **Enabled** is selected. This policy ensures that client computers are not left logged on and unattended when users are not at work, such as over night or on weekends. For this to work effectively, the Logon Hours option on the Account tab in the properties of each user account need to be defined, such as 6:00 A.M. to 7:00 P.M. weekdays and no access on weekends. Click **OK**.

32. Close the console window. Click **No** so that you do not save the console settings.

Review Questions

1. You have defined logon hours for each account in your company, but many users defeat this security measure by leaving their computers logged on after they leave work. To remedy this problem you can _____.

2. Setting _____ security policies is a way to deploy security measures to apply to all computers in a domain.

3. Which of the following are general categories of security policies that you can configure within Local Policies for a domain? (Choose all that apply.)

   a. Security Options

   b. Machine Options

   c. User Rights Assignment

   d. Private Key Assignment

4. True or False? The financial auditors for your bank want you as the server administrator to keep audit records showing when user accounts have been created or deleted, or when account properties have been modified. You know you can do this by creating a security policy to audit account management.

13

5. The passwords for user accounts in your company are set to expire every 60 days. Many users travel extensively and complain that they would like 20 days advance notification so that they are better prepared to plan for a new password. Which of the following is your response?

   a. Password expiration notification is hard coded into Windows Server 2008 and cannot be changed.

   b. The maximum password expiration notification is 10 days prior to when a password expires.

   c. The maximum password expiration notification is 14 days prior to when a password expires.

   d. You have the ability to set password expiration notification to start at 20 days prior to when the password expires.

Lab 13.2 Configure Registry Security

Objectives

- Configure Registry security for a root key
- Examine all root key security settings

Materials Required

This lab requires the following:

- Windows Server 2008 Standard or Enterprise Edition

Estimated completion time: **15 minutes**

Activity Background

The Windows Registry is a complex database that contains vital information about all aspects of Windows Server 2008. For instance, it contains information about hardware components including the CPU, disks and disk drivers, NICs, and other hardware. Additionally, the Registry holds information about installed services, user profiles, software configuration, and a range of other information.

   Protecting the Registry is a first line of defense for securing a server because a poorly conceived change to the Registry, a poorly executed entry by a software program, or an intrusion by an attacker can each spell disaster, such as preventing a server from booting. Considering the importance of the Registry, it is surprising that some server administrators neglect to control who has access to make changes to it.

   The Registry consists of five root keys:

- HKEY_LOCAL_MACHINE
- HKEY_CURRENT_USER
- HKEY_USERS
- HKEY_CLASSES_ROOT
- HKEY_CURRENT_CONFIG

For each root key, you can configure permissions to control who has access to make changes. In this activity, you use the Registry editor to configure permissions for the Registry.

Activity

1. Click **Start**, type **regedit** in the Start Search box, and press **Enter**.

2. Right-click **HKEY_CLASSES_ROOT** in the tree in the left pane and click **Permissions** (see Figure 13-4).

3. In the Permissions for HKEY_CLASSES_ROOT dialog box, click **Administrators (*domainname\ Administrators*)** and note the default permissions for this group, which are Full Control and Read.

4. Click **Users (*domainname\Users*)** and note that this group has Read permissions.

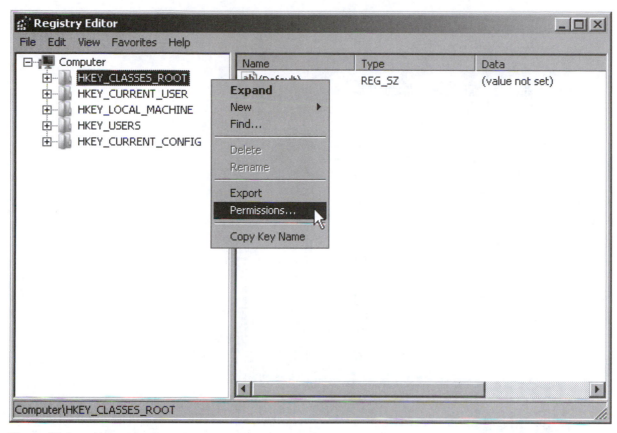

Figure 13-4   Configuring permissions

5. For the purposes of this lab, assume that members of the Server Operators group need to periodically modify certain Registry values as part of their jobs. To enable the Server Operators group to modify Registry values, you need to give this group permissions to make limited Registry changes. Click the **Add** button.

6. In the Select Users, Computers, or Groups dialog box, click **Advanced**.

7. Click the **Find Now** button.

8. Under Search results, click **Server Operators** and click **OK**.

9. Click **OK** in the Select Users, Computers, or Groups dialog box.

10. Ensure that **Server Operators** is selected in the Permissions for HKEY_CLASSES_ROOT dialog box. Note that Server Operators is given Special permissions by default. Click the **Advanced** button, click **Server Operators (servername\Server Operators)** in the Advanced Security Settings for HKEY_CLASSES_ROOT dialog box, and click **Edit**.

11. Click the **Allow** check boxes for Query Value, Set Value, Enumerate Subkeys, and Notify, and leave **Allow** selected for Read Control (see Figure 13-5).

12. Click the check box for **Apply these permissions to objects and/or containers within this container only** and click **OK**.

13. Click the **Auditing** tab in the Advanced Security Settings for HKEY_CLASSES_ROOT dialog box.

14. Click **Add**. Click **Advanced**, click **Find Now**, double-click **Server Operators**, and click **OK**. Click the **Successful** and **Failed** check boxes for Query Value and Set Value. These settings allow you to track this group's activities through the Security event log. Click **OK** in the Auditing Entry for HKEY_CLASSES_ROOT dialog box.

15. Click **OK** in the Advanced Security Settings for HKEY_CLASSES_ROOT dialog box.

16. Click **OK** in the Permissions for HKEY_CLASSES_ROOT dialog box.

17. Examine the permissions associated with the other root keys listed in the left pane of the Registry Editor.

18. Close the Registry editor.

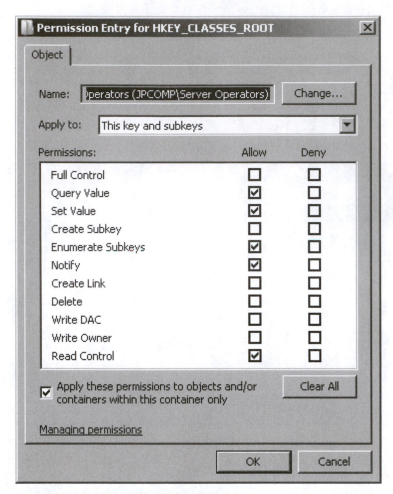

Figure 13-5   Configuring special permissions

Review Questions

1. The standard permissions for the Registry root keys include which of the following? (Choose all that apply.)

   a. Full Control

   b. Read

   c. Delete

   d. Create

2. The Users (*domainname*\Users) group has _____ permissions to a root key by default.

3. True or False? You cannot audit changes made to the Registry.

4. Permissions for root keys in the Registry are configured using the _____.

5. True or False? Special permissions can be set up for access to the Registry.

Lab 13.3 Install Health Registration Authority and Host Credential Authorization

Objectives

- Understand Health Registration Authority and Host Credential Authorization
- Install the Health Registration Authority role service
- Install the Host Credential Authorization role service
- Create a health policy

Materials Required

This lab requires the following:

- Windows Server 2008 Standard or Enterprise Edition with the Network Policy and Access Services role installed with the Network Policy Server role service
- Health Registration Authority and Host Credential Authorization role services not previously installed
- Web Server (IIS) role installed
- Active Directory Certificate Services role installed

Estimated completion time: **20 minutes**

Activity Background

A network is only as secure as its weakest point. One component that can become a "weakest point" is an "unhealthy" client. An unhealthy client is a client that is not current on updates, that does not have a virus and malware scanner, that does not use a firewall, or that is infected with a virus. If this type of client accesses a network, it can be a network-wide gateway to an intruder, or it can spread a virus or malware to the server or to other server clients.

When you deploy a network, you can install a Health Registration Authority (HRA) server to validate each client's Statement of Health (SoH). A SoH is a certificate issued by a Certificate Authority (CA) server on the basis of a predefined health policy, and the certificate provides information about a client's security status and recent updates. If the client is not sufficiently protected, the HRA server can deny network access or grant limited access. In Windows Server 2008, a Network Policy Server also functions as the HRA server when the Health Registration Authority role service is installed.

If an organization uses Cisco networking devices and Cisco Network Admission Control, then consider installing the Host Credential Authorization Protocol (HCAP) role service with a Network Policy Server. HCAP enables you to interface Windows Server 2008 Network Access Policy with Cisco Network Admission Control. When you combine these capabilities, the end result is threefold:

- The Windows Server 2008 Network Policy Server authorizes clients by using the 802.1X authentication (for wired or wireless connections) as described in Chapter 13 in *MCITP Guide to Microsoft Windows Server 2008, Server Administration (Exam #70-646)*. A Network Policy Server can also authorize clients by acting as an HRA server that examines SoH certificates and sets the network health policy.
- A Cisco authentication, authorization, and accounting (AAA) server additionally authenticates clients against its Cisco Network Admission Control policy, which can include examining SoH certificates.
- The Windows Server 2008 Network Policy Server and the Cisco AAA server coordinate their separate security activities through HCAP (both the Network Policy Server and the Cisco AAA server must be configured to use HCAP).

In very general terms, here is how a client gains authorization to connect to the network:

- The client requests a connection through a Cisco network device, such as a router or switch, using 802.1X authentication
- The Cisco network device sends the request to the Cisco AAA server
- The Cisco AAA server verifies the client's SoH against the Cisco Network Admission Control policy
- The Cisco AAA server forwards the SoH to the Windows Server 2008 Network Policy Server by using the Host Credential Authorization Protocol (HCAP)
- The Windows Server 2008 Network Policy Server evaluates the client's SoH and sends its result back to the Cisco AAA server through HCAP
- The Cisco AAA server evaluates its SoH determination and that of the Network Policy Server and either allows access to the client, requires the client to contact a remediation server for updates, or denies access

There is not room in this book to fully explain a Cisco AAA server or Cisco Network Admission Control policy. As you prepare for certification, keep your focus on understanding that HCAP can be installed as a role service of the Network Policy and Access Services role. Additionally, HCAP is a protocol used to transport SoH information between a Cisco AAA server and a Windows Server 2008 Network Policy Server. The bottom line

13

is to determine if a client meets the security and health policy requirements of the Cisco AAA server and the Network Policy Server.

For this activity, you install the Health Registration Authority and Host Credential Authorization role services. A Network Policy Server should already be installed as in Chapter 10, "Configuring Remote Access Services" in *MCITP Guide to Microsoft Windows Server 2008, Server Administration (Exam #70-646)*, and a RADIUS server should be configured as described in Lab 10.3 in this book. Also, the Web Server (IIS) role and the Active Directory Certificate Services roles should be installed as in Chapter 9, "Deploying IIS and Active Directory Certificate Services" in *MCITP Guide to Microsoft Windows Server 2008, Server Administration (Exam #70-646)*.

Activity

1. Click **Start**, point to **Administrative Tools**, and click **Server Manager**.

2. In the tree in the left pane, click the **+** plus sign in front of Roles.

3. Click **Network Policy and Access Services**.

4. Scroll the right pane to the Role Services section and click **Add Role Services**.

5. Click the check box for **Health Registration Authority**. If you see the Add Role Services dialog box to add management role services for Web Server (IIS), click **Add Required Role Services**.

6. Click the check box for **Host Credential Authorization Protocol**. If you see the Add Role Services dialog box to add security role services for Web Server (IIS), click **Add Required Role Services**.

7. Click **Next** in the Select Role Services window.

8. In the Choose the Certification Authority to use with the Health Registration Authority window, click **Use the local CA to issue health certificates for this HRA server** (see Figure 13-6) or check with your instructor about which option to use for a CA. Click **Next**.

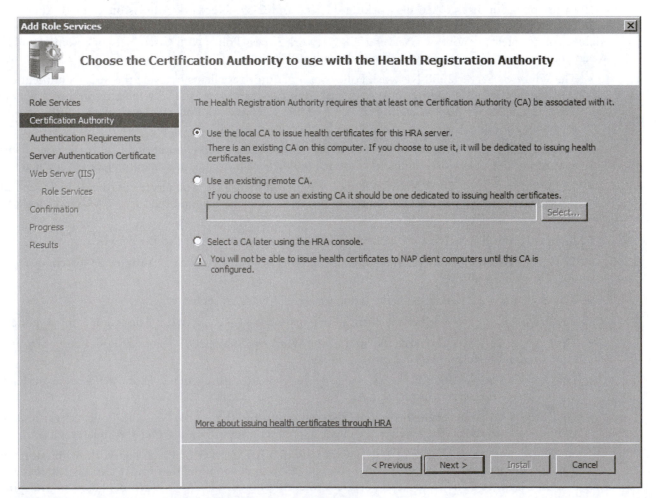

Figure 13-6   Choose a certification authority

9. In the Choose Authentication Requirements for the Health Registration Authority window, ensure that **Yes, require requestors to be authenticated as members of a domain. (recommended)** is selected. Click **Next**.

10. If you see the Choose a Server Authentication Certificate for SSL Encryption window, select **Choose an existing certificate for SSL encryption (recommended)** and select a certificate; or check with your instructor about which option to use. Click **Next**.

11. If you see the Web Server (IIS) window, click **Next**. Also, if you see the Select Role Services window for Web Server (IIS), click **Next**.

12. In the Confirm Installation Selections window, click **Install**.

13. Click **Close** in the Installation Results window.

14. Close Server Manager.

15. Click **Start**, point to **Administrative Tools**, and click **Network Policy Server**.

16. If necessary, expand the tree in the left pane to view the items under Policies.

17. Right-click **Health Policies** in the tree and click **New** to create a new health policy.

18. In the Create New Health Policy dialog box, enter **Health Policy** plus your initials, such as *Health PolicyJP* in the Policy name text box.

19. Click the down arrow in the **Client SHV (SHV is Security Health Validator) checks** text box and review the selections. Be sure that **Client passes all SHV checks** is selected. This means that the client must pass all requirements in the security health policy.

20. Click the check box for **Windows Security Health Validator** (see Figure 13-7).

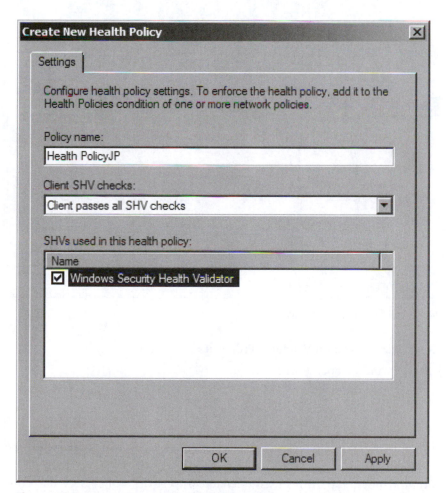

Figure 13-7   Create New Health Policy dialog box

21. Click **OK** in the Create New Health Policy dialog box.

22. In the left pane of the Network Policy Server, click the + plus sign in front of **Network Access Protection**, if necessary to view the items under it.

23. Click **System Health Validators** in the left pane under Network Access Protection.

24. Right-click **Windows Security Health Validator** under Name in the right pane and click **Properties**.

25. Click the **Configure** button in the Windows Security Health Validator Properties dialog box.

26. In the Windows Security Validator dialog box, review the health requirements selected by default for Windows Vista clients (see Figure 13-8). You can configure health requirements for Windows Vista and Windows XP to match the needs of your organization. (In Windows Server 2008 Release 2, you can also configure health requirements for Windows 7 clients.) Click **Cancel**.

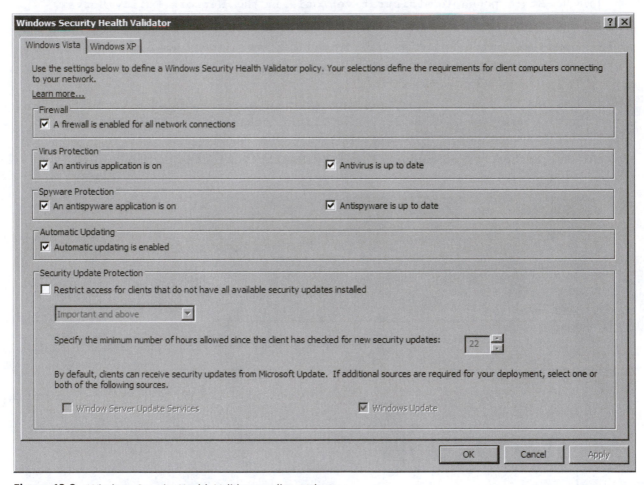

Figure 13-8   Windows Security Health Validator policy settings

27. Click **Cancel** in the Windows Security Health Validator Properties dialog box.

28. Leave the Network Policy Server window open for the next activity.

Review Questions

1. A(n) _____ server in Windows Server 2008 is a Network Policy Server on which the Health Registration Authority role service is installed.

2. Host Credential Authorization Protocol (HCAP) is used to enable a Network Policy Server to coordinate a client's network access request with a(n) _____ server.

3. A(n) _____ is a certificate that shows the health of a client.

4. A new health policy is created in which of the following?

   a. Control Panel Network Policy applet

   b. Network Policy Server

   c. HCAP server

   d. Network and Sharing Center

5. True or False? When you install the Health Registration Authority role services, you must also choose a Certification Authority.

Lab 13.4 Configure a Health Registration Authority Network Policy

Objectives

- Learn the parameters that can be set in a network policy
- Configure a Health Registration Authority network policy

Materials Required

This lab requires the following:

- Windows Server 2008 Standard or Enterprise Edition
- Network Policy and Access Services role installed with the Network Policy Server, Health Registration Authority, and Host Credential Authorization role services installed
- Active Directory Domain Services role installed
- Web Server (IIS) role installed
- Active Directory Certificate Services role installed

Estimated completion time: **20 minutes**

13

Activity Background

Now that you have created an HRA server, the next step is to configure a network policy that applies to clients accessing the network through that HRA server. In this activity, you create a network access policy for the HRA server you have configured in Lab 13.3. As you progress through this activity, you also learn the steps for configuring any network policy and the parameters that you can use in a policy.

Activity

1. Open the Network Policy Server window, if it is not open.

2. Expand Policies in the left pane to view the items under it, if necessary.

3. Right-click **Network Policies** and click **New**.

4. In the Specify Network Policy Name and Connection Type window, enter **HRA**, a space, and your initials, such as *HRA JP*.

5. Select **Type of network access server**, if this option is not selected.

6. Click the **Type of network access server** down arrow and review the possible selections so that you know you can create a policy for any of these types of access, which include:

   - Unspecified
   - Terminal Server Gateway
   - Remote Access Server (VPN-Dial up)
   - DHCP Server

- Health Registration Authority
- HCAP Server

7. Select **Health Registration Authority** (see Figure 13-9). Click **Next**.

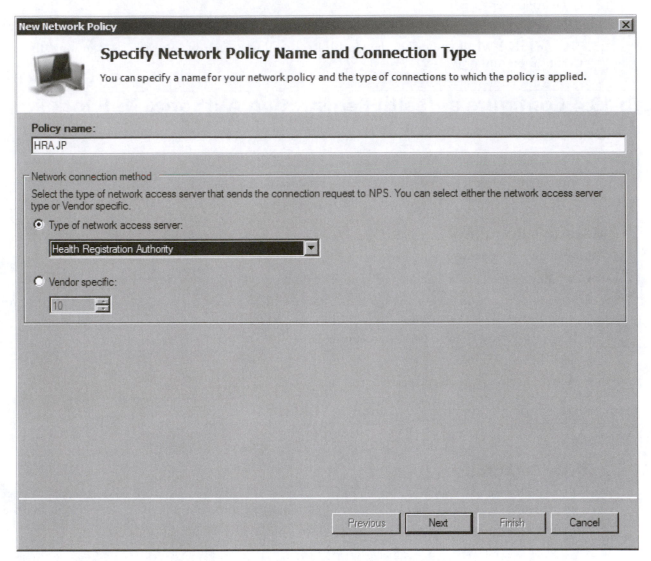

Figure 13-9   Specify Network Policy Name and Connection Type window

8. In the Specify Conditions window, click the **Add** button.

9. In the Select condition window, review the range of conditions that you can add and then click **Windows Groups**. Click the **Add** button.

10. In the Windows Groups box, click **Add Groups**.

11. Click the **Advanced** button in the Select Group box.

12. Click the **Find Now** button.

13. Under Search results, click **Domain Guests** (for the sake of practice) and click **OK**.

14. Click **OK** in the Select Group dialog box.

15. Click **OK** in the Windows Groups dialog box.

16. Click **Next** in the Specify Conditions window.

17. In the Specify Access Permission window, be sure that **Access granted** is selected and click **Next**.

18. In the Configure Authentication Methods window, review the types of authentication methods. Leave the defaults already selected, but click the **Add** button for EAP Types. In the Add EAP dialog box, click **Microsoft: Protected EAP (PEAP)** and click **OK**.

19. Click **Next** in the Configure Authentication Methods window.

20. In the Configure Constraints window (see Figure 13-10), click each of the parameters in the left pane to view the options that can be set in the right pane.

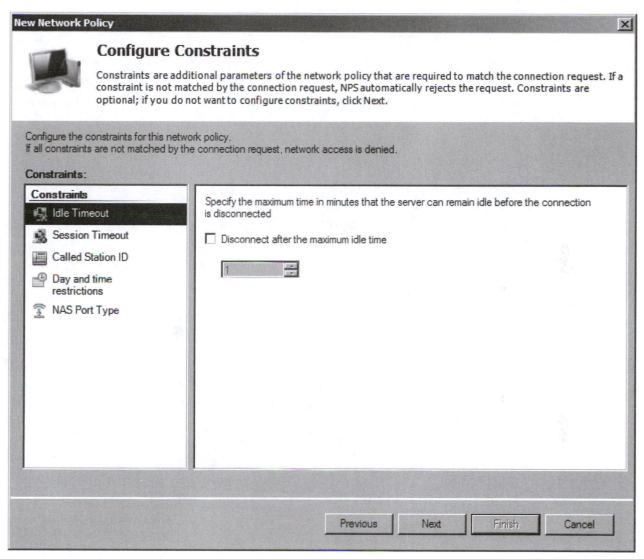

Figure 13-10   Configure Constraints window

21. Click **Day and time restrictions** in the left pane.

22. In the right pane, click **Allow access only on these days and at these times** and click **Edit**.

23. In the Day and time restrictions dialog box, drag the cursor across **Sunday** to select all of the time slots and then click **Denied** so this area appears in white. Select all of the **Saturday** time slots and click **Denied**. Click **OK**.

24. Click **Next** in the Configure Constraints window.

25. In the Configure Settings window, click each of the options in the left pane to view the parameters you can configure.

26. Click **NAP Enforcement** in the left pane and notice that **Allow full network access** is selected by default.

27. Click **Next** in the Configure Settings window.

28. In the Completing New Network Policy window, review your settings. Click **Finish**.

29. Click **Network Policies** in the left pane under Policies in the Network Policy Server window.

30. In the right pane of the Network Policy Server window look for your new policy under Policy Name. Right-click the policy and click **Properties**. You can use the tabs in the Properties dialog box to modify the policy whenever necessary. Click **Cancel**.

31. Close the Network Policy Server window.

Review Questions

1. True or False? A network policy can only be configured to apply to a particular user group.

2. Which of the following are types of network access servers that can be defined for a network policy? (Choose all that apply.)

   a. Terminal Server Gateway

   b. Web server

   c. DHCP server

   d. Shared Files Server

3. True or False? Microsoft's Protected EAP (PEAP) is an authentication method available for a Health Registration Authority server.

4. Which of the following are time restrictions that can be set up for a network policy? (Choose all that apply.)

   a. Day of the month

   b. Day of the week

   c. Month in the year

   d. Time of day

5. The Computer Security committee for your company wants users who are logged on to the network but idle for over 1 hour to be logged off automatically. Which of the following network policy constraints can you set to accomplish this request?

   a. Time restriction

   b. NAS restriction

   c. Idle timeout

   d. Port type disconnect

SERVER AND NETWORK MONITORING

Labs included in this chapter:

- Lab 14.1 Use Task Manager to Monitor a Server

- Lab 14.2 Use Resource Monitor

- Lab 14.3 Use Performance Monitor to Evaluate Paging File and Memory Performance

- Lab 14.4 Use Performance Monitor to Evaluate Disk Performance

Microsoft MCITP Exam #70-646 Objectives

Objective	Lab
Monitoring and Maintaining Servers	14.1, 14.2, 14.3, 14.4

Lab 14.1 Use Task Manager to Monitor a Server

Objectives

- Monitor a server using Task Manager
- Determine which applications, processes, and services are running
- Determine the CPU and memory resources used by a server
- Monitor network utilization at a NIC
- Monitor users on a network

Materials Required

This lab requires the following:

- Windows Server 2008 Standard or Enterprise Edition

Estimated completion time: **20 minutes**

Activity Background

Task Manager is a useful monitoring tool for getting a quick picture of a server. The more you use Task Manager, the more you will get from using it. For instance, you'll start to know at a glance what is normal for a particular server and what is not normal. Such expertise will help you determine, for example, which services should be running and the typical performance of the CPU.

The Task Manager tabs for monitoring information are:

- *Applications*—displays currently running applications
- *Processes*—lists running processes, such as explorer.exe (Windows Explorer) and dns.exe (for DNS Server)
- *Services*—lists services and their status, running, stopped, or paused
- *Performance*—displays real-time CPU and memory performance at a glance
- *Networking*—shows real-time network performance in terms of network utilization at all server NICs
- *User*—lists users connected to the server and provides tools to log off or disconnect users, as well as to send users a message

Two advantages of Task Manager are that you can start it quickly and it typically requires fewer server resources than many other monitoring tools. You might think of it as the Swiss Army knife of your monitoring tools because it has a little bit of everything and it is easy to keep handy.

In this activity, you use the features in Task Manager to monitor activity on a server.

For all the activities in this chapter, you'll need to log on to an account with Administrator privileges. Additionally, most of these activities can be completed on a virtual server or computer, such as in Hyper-V.

Throughout the activities in this book, you may occasionally see the User Account Control box with a message that Windows needs your permission to continue. Whenever you see this box, click Continue. Keep this in mind for all the activities because any interaction with the User Account Control box is not included in the steps.

Activity

1. Right-click the **taskbar** in a blank area and click **Task Manager**.

2. Click the **Applications** tab, if it is not displayed.

3. Start the Notepad application by clicking **Start**, pointing to **All Programs**, clicking **Accessories**, and clicking **Notepad**.

4. In Task Manager, click **Untitled - Notepad** and click **End Task** to terminate this program (which you might do for a hung program, for example).

5. Click the **Processes** tab in Task Manager.

6. Adjust the columns, if necessary, so that you can view the User Name of the user running the process, the CPU utilization for the process, and the Memory used. To adjust the width of a column, move the pointer over the column's boundary line until you see a crosshair and then drag the boundary line.

7. Use the scroll bar to view the CPU utilization and memory used for each process and determine which process is currently using the most CPU resources and which is using the most memory.

8. Assume for a moment that you want to verify the location of an executable file used by a process, such as the explorer.exe process that runs Windows Explorer. You might verify the location as one way to be sure the version of Windows Explorer is the same version that came with Windows and is not a malware version running from an unauthorized location. Right-click **explorer.exe** and click **Open File Location**.

9. Minimize Task Manager, if necessary, to view the window showing the file location, which should be in the Windows folder. Close the file location window.

10. Maximize Task Manager, if needed.

11. In Task Manager, right-click another process and notice whether the menu has a Set Affinity option. The Set Affinity option is available on a multiple processor server. If you have this option, click it and note that you can select on which CPU (or on multiple CPUs) to run the process (see Figure 14-1). Click **Cancel** in the Processor Affinity dialog box.

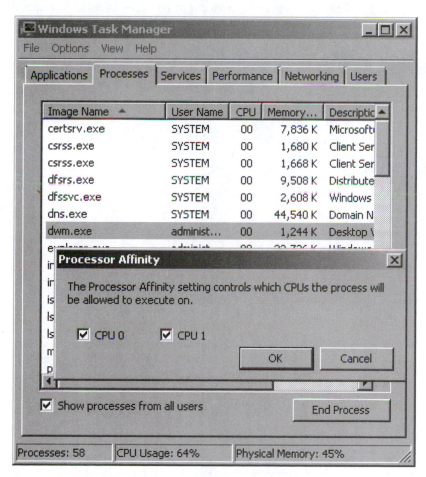

Figure 14-1   Processor Affinity dialog box

12. Click the **Services** tab.

13. Use the scroll bar to survey which services are running.

14. Right-click a service and note there are options to Stop Service, Start Service, and to Go to Process to determine which process is used by a service. Move the pointer away from the menu and click to close the menu.

15. Click the **Services** button to open the Services console from which to manage a service. Close the Services console.

16. Click the **Performance** tab in Task Manager.

17. Spend a few minutes monitoring the CPU and memory graphs. On many servers, the CPU Usage will periodically go up to 100%. This can be normal and often shows that processes are effectively using the CPU resources. However, if the CPU Usage always stays at 90–100%, this can be an indication that the server needs more CPU resources, such as another CPU. It can also mean that the server is running one or more inefficient programs. During these times, you can go back to the Processes tab to see exactly what processes are running to try to track down an inefficient program.

18. Click the **Networking** tab. Monitor the network activity shown in the network graph or graphs (depending on how many NICs are active in the server) for a few minutes. Note the bottom portion of the tab lists the network adaptors and the network utilization, link speed, and state of each adaptor. If you think an adapter is experiencing a problem, is overloaded, or is disconnected, you can get quick information on this tab.

19. Click the **Users** tab. This tab lists the users connected to the computer. When you highlight a particular user, you can click the Disconnect or Logoff buttons to release that user's connection. You can also send a message to a user.

20. In this step you practice logging off your account. Before you log off your account, close any active programs and save any work, if necessary. Right-click your account. Note that there are options to Send a Message, Connect, Disconnect, Log Off, and for Remote Control of an account (options that do not apply to your account because you are the active account are deactivated). Click **Log Off** (see Figure 14-2).

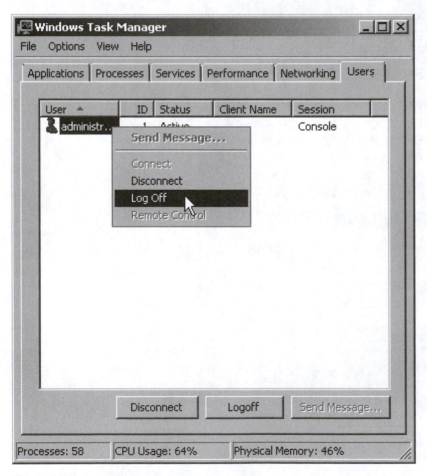

Figure 14-2 Log off your account

21. In the Windows Task Manager box, click **Log off user** to confirm you want to proceed. Note that your account is logged off.

22. Log back on.

Review Questions

1. Your server has two NICs, but you are not certain that one of the NICs is properly connected to the network. The Task Manager _____ tab enables you to verify a NIC's connection.

2. The Task Manager _____ tab provides information about CPU usage in real-time.

3. Which of the following options is accessible from the Task Manager Processes tab and enables you to specify a processor on which to run a specific process?

   a. Set Properties

   b. Set Priority

   c. Set Affinity

   d. Set Processor

4. True or False? You have been running a spreadsheet program on the server, but the program is not responding and seems to be slowing down the server's responsiveness. You can terminate this program from the Task Manager Monitor Programs tab.

5. You suspect there is an intruder logged onto your server. You can log off or disconnect this intruder using the _____ tab in Task Manager.

Lab 14.2 Use Resource Monitor

Objectives

- Employ Resource Monitor to monitor the use of server resources
- Examine resource use graphs and statistics

Materials Required

This lab requires the following:

- Windows Server 2008 Standard or Enterprise Edition

Estimated completion time:	**15 minutes**

Activity Background

Resource Monitor offers a more in-depth picture of resource use than is available through Task Manager. Resource Monitor provides immediate resource data about a server's processors, disks, network activity, and memory. An important advantage of Resource Monitor is that data is presented both in graphs and statistics. If you need to view which process or program is using more resources, Resource Monitor presents the information from highest to lowest use.

You can start Resource Monitor from Reliability and Performance Monitor, the Task Manager Performance tab, Server Manager, and the Computer Management tool. Resource Monitor is simple to use and is a fast source of resource information.

In this activity, you explore the information available in Resource Monitor.

Activity

1. Click **Start**, point to **Administrative Tools**, and click **Reliability and Performance Monitor**. (You can also open Reliability and Performance monitor as an MMC snap-in).

2. Ensure that **Reliability and Performance** is selected in the tree in the left pane (see Figure 14-3).

3. Note there are four graphs: CPU, Disk, Network, and Memory. Each graph shows the real-time activity for the resource it is measuring. Click the **CPU** down arrow.

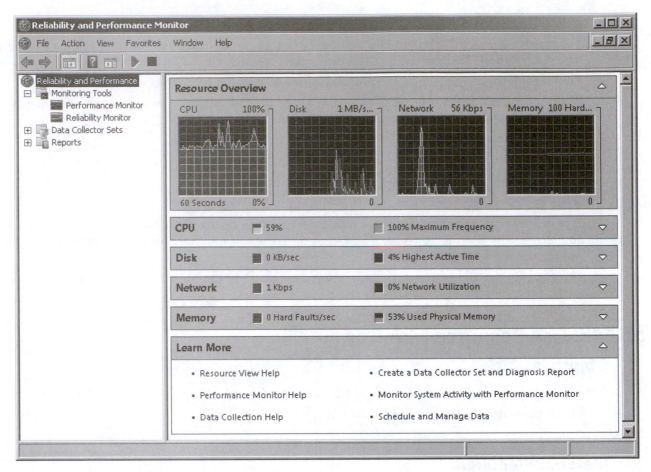

Figure 14-3   Resource Monitor

4. The display under CPU shows current resource activity for the CPU or CPUs in the server (see Figure 14-4). Note which process is using the largest percentage of CPU resources. Additionally, note which processes are in second and third place.

5. Close CPU information by clicking its up arrow.

6. Click the **Disk** down arrow.

7. Note which processes are creating the most disk activity. Compare the read to the write activity for each process.

8. Close the Disk activity information by clicking its up arrow.

9. Click the **Network** down arrow.

10. Note which processes are creating network activity as shown in terms of send, receive, and total transmission activity. The address column provides information about whether the activity is initiated from the server or from an external network source, such as a network device or computer.

11. Close the display of Network activity statistics.

12. Click the **Memory** down arrow.

13. Note which processes are using the most memory, as ranked from first to last in the statistics display. The columns of memory-related statistics for a specific process include:

   - *Commit (KB)*—amount of virtual memory (from the paging file) that is allocated to the process
   - *Working Set (KB)*—total amount of RAM currently in use by the process
   - *Shareable (KB)*—amount of shared memory (RAM and virtual memory that can be shared with other processes) that is allocated for use by the process
   - *Private (KB)*—amount of nonshareable memory (RAM and virtual memory that cannot be shared with other processes) that is allocated for use by the process

14. Leave the Reliability and Performance Monitor window open for the next activity.

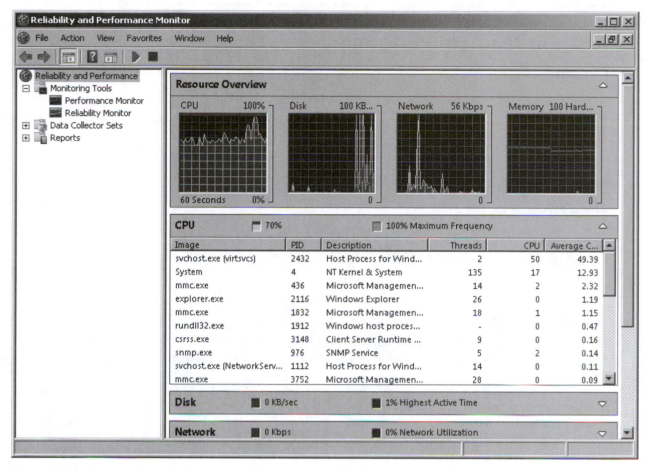

Figure 14-4 CPU activity statistics

Review Questions

1. True or False? Performance Monitor enables you to track the real-time refresh rate of a display monitor.

2. Which of the following is a method for opening Resource Monitor? (Choose all that apply.)

   a. Right-click the taskbar and click Resource Monitor

   b. Click Start, right-click Computer, and click Resource Monitor

   c. Right-click Start and click Resource Monitor

   d. Click Start, point to Administrative Tools, and click Reliability and Performance Monitor

3. Which of the following information is displayed in Resource Monitor for disk activity? (Choose all that apply.)

   a. Disk reads

   b. Disk writes

   c. Page faults

   d. Disk errors

4. In Resource Monitor, network transmission activity is measured in terms of _____, _____, and _____ bytes per minute.

5. True or False? When you use Resource Monitor to monitor CPU activity, you can view the average CPU use as well the current CPU use, so that you can compare the two figures.

Lab 14.3 Use Performance Monitor to Evaluate Paging File and Memory Performance

Objectives

- Use paging file and memory counters in Performance Monitor
- Understand how to monitor memory and paging file activities to diagnose performance bottlenecks and address them

Materials Required

This lab requires the following:

- Windows Server 2008 Standard or Enterprise Edition

Estimated completion time: **20 minutes**

Activity Background

Performance Monitor enables you to monitor a wide range of activities on a server. One very important application of this tool is to monitor paging file and memory use. In combination, these two elements play a significant role in the performance of a server.

Performance Monitor offers several objects and counters that you can use for monitoring paging file and memory performance. An object is an entity such as memory or the paging file. A counter is a measurement technique for an object. For example, the Paging File object has a % Usage counter for measuring the percentage of the paging file that is currently in use. Another Paging File counter is % Usage Peak that shows the highest amount of paging file space used while monitoring.

Consider a situation in which you periodically monitored (over the course of a few days) the Paging File counters % Usage and % Usage Peak and found that % Usage was almost always over 90% and % Usage Peak often went up to 100%. In addition, you monitored the Page Faults/sec counter for the Memory object and continued checking the results. Then, a hard page fault occurred when a program did not have enough physical memory to execute a given function. If there were frequently over five hard page faults per second, this would be a strong indication of a memory bottleneck. In this situation, the combination of results indicates the need to add memory to the server.

Another example of a situation resulting in a page fault is when two processes share the same block of paged data. One process may read the block from disk into memory, just before the other process is about to do the same. The second process is unable to access the paged block, because the paged block is in use. Page faults also occur when there is not enough RAM to be shared by virtual memory and caching.

All the page fault problems discussed thus far can be monitored by using Memory as the object and Page Faults/sec as the counter. In addition, increasing RAM reduces page faults and improves performance. Memory performance is especially important if database systems such as Microsoft SQL Server or Oracle are installed; these database systems are designed to share memory blocks when there is limited RAM.

Table 14-1 provides a summary of tips for monitoring and tuning memory and paging.

For this activity, you monitor a server to evaluate paging and memory performance. You use five counters, Memory: Page Faults/sec, Memory: Pages Input/sec, Memory: Pages Output/sec, Paging File: % Usage, and Paging File: % Usage Peak.

Activity

1. Open Reliability and Performance Monitor, if it is not still open.

2. Click **Performance Monitor** under Monitoring Tools in the tree in the left pane.

3. If there are any counters currently running, as listed at the bottom of the right pane, click them one at a time and click the **Delete** button (the X) in the button bar in the top of the right pane to delete each one.

4. Click the **Add** button (a green plus sign) in the button bar in the right pane.

Table 14-1   Using Memory and Paging File Objects for Monitoring Performance

Object: Counter	Explanation
Memory: Cache Faults/sec	Measures the number of times the paging file is called from disk or relocated in memory. Higher values indicate potential performance problems. (Higher values will be about double or more that of baseline values on a lightly loaded system.) You can remedy this by adding more memory or use a processor with more cache.
Memory: Page Faults/sec	Returns a count of the average number of page faults per second for the current processor. Page faults occur whenever memory pages must be called from disk; the presence of page faults explains how memory overload can manifest as excessive disk activity. If the value is frequently over 5 or more, consider adding more RAM.
Memory: Pages Input/sec Memory: Pages Output/sec	These counters measure the number of virtual memory pages read into (Input/sec) and out of (Output/sec) memory per second. If their total is frequently over 20, this shows a need to add RAM. By using both counters you can assess demands on memory and paging at once. Pages Input/sec translates into page faults. Pages Output/sec shows demand on memory and when this value is frequently over 15–20, you need to add RAM.
Memory: Pages/sec	Tracks the number of pages written to or read from disk plus paging traffic for the system cache. If this value is typically over 20, you need additional RAM.
Paging File: % Usage Paging File: % Usage Peak	Both show how much of the paging file is currently occupied. Neither object/counter should frequently exceed 99%. Look at this information in relation to the Memory counters: Pages Input/sec, Pages Output/sec, and Available Bytes. If the values are frequently over 99%, increase the paging file size.
Server: Pool Paged Peak	Shows the most that the server has used in terms of virtual memory. This should be at least 1.5 times the size of RAM in the server.

5. In the Add Counters dialog box, ensure that `<Local computer>` is selected in the text box for Select counters from computer.

6. Scroll the box under the computer that is selected and click the + plus sign for Memory to view the counters for the Memory object.

7. Click `Page Faults/sec` under Memory and click the `Add >>` button.

8. Click `Pages Input/sec` and click the `Add >>` button.

9. Click `Pages Output/sec` and click the `Add >>` button.

10. Scroll to find the `Paging File` object and click the + plus sign to the right.

11. Click `% Usage` under Paging File and click the `Add >>` button.

12. Click `% Usage Peak` and click the `Add >>` button. The Add Counters dialog box should now look similar to Figure 14-5.

13. Click **OK** in the Add Counters dialog box. You'll see the counters you selected listed in the bottom of the right pane. You may have to scroll to view all the counters. Each counter is identified by a different color so that it can be distinguished in the graph as Performance Monitor continues to run (see Figure 14-6).

14. At the bottom of the right pane, click `Page Faults/sec` to highlight it (but do not click the check box). Note the statistics under the graph for Page Faults/sec, which include Last, Average, Maximum, Minimum, and Duration.

15. Click `Pages Input/sec` at the bottom of the right pane and note its statistics.

16. Click each of `Pages Output/sec`, `% Usage`, and `% Usage Peak` to view statistics for each of these counters.

17. While you are monitoring, open and then close four or five programs or open and then close several items on the Administrative tools menu. Continue monitoring for several minutes.

18. When you are finished monitoring click each of the counters at the bottom of the page one at a time and click the `Delete` button to delete the counter.

19. Leave the Reliability and Performance Monitor window open for the next activity.

14

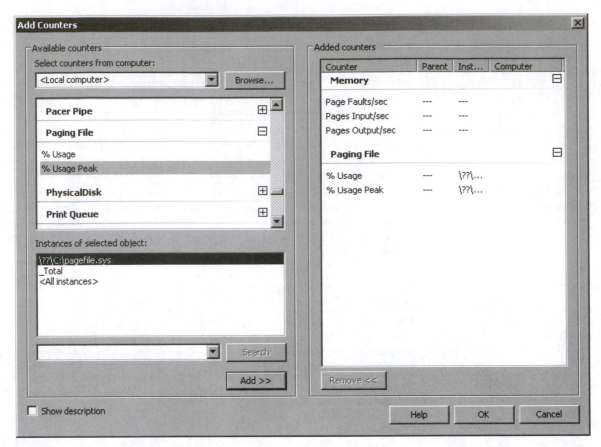

Figure 14-5 Add Counters dialog box

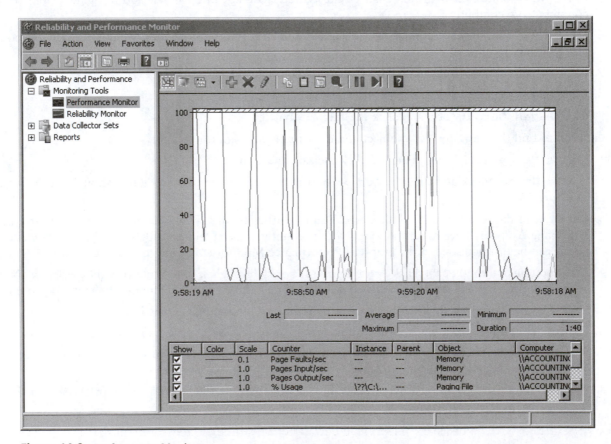

Figure 14-6 Performance Monitor

Review Questions

1. The object/counter Server: Pool Paged Peak shows the maximum amount of _____ the server has used.

2. True or False? If there are frequently over five hard page faults per second, this is an indication there is a memory bottleneck.

3. The _____ object/counter shows the average number of page faults per second.

4. Which of the following are Paging File counters? (Choose all that apply.)

   a. % Copy Read Hits

   b. % Usage Peak

   c. % Flush

   d. % Usage

5. Which of the following are objects you can monitor in Performance Monitor? (Choose all that apply.)

   a. Memory

   b. Keyboard

   c. Network Mask

   d. Server

Lab 14.4 Use Performance Monitor to Evaluate Disk Performance

Objectives

- Use Performance Monitor to monitor disk performance
- Understand how to use disk objects and counters to diagnose specific types of performance issues

Materials Required

This lab requires the following:

- Windows Server 2008 Standard or Enterprise Edition

Estimated completion time: **20 minutes**

14

Activity Background

The amount of activity on specific hard disks can be related to server performance problems. For example, if you have multiple disks and one of the disks holds a majority of the server's most frequently accessed large files, that disk can be a bottleneck. The solution is to redistribute the frequently accessed large files across the disks.

The two primary disk objects used by Performance Monitor are LogicalDisk and PhysicalDisk. Use LogicalDisk to observe activity on a set of disks, such as a striped volume. Use PhysicalDisk if you want to monitor a specific disk, such as disk 0 in a set of five disks. Watch at least two counters, % Disk Time and Current Disk Queue Length. The first counter shows the amount of activity on a disk and the second shows the number of waiting requests to access the disk. If one disk frequently is busy at the 100% level, information on the number of waiting requests helps to diagnose the problem. If there are 0 to 1 requests normally in the queue, the disk load is acceptable. If the queue generally has 2 or more requests, it is time to move some files from the overloaded disk to one less busy.

The best way to determine which files to move is to understand what applications and data are on the server and how they are used. If all the server disks are constantly busy, it may be necessary to purchase disks with more spindles or to add additional data paths.

If you have configured RAID-5 volumes, a bottleneck may be linked to more active disk writing than you initially estimated. RAID-5 disks are able to read data faster than they can write it because they must take time to calculate and write parity and fault tolerance data with each write operation. You can compare read to write activity by using the following Performance Monitor measures:

- For read activity, monitor the LogicalDisk and PhysicalDisk counters Avg. Disk Bytes/Read and Avg. Disk sec/Read.
- For write activity, monitor the LogicalDisk and PhysicalDisk counters Avg. Disk Bytes/Write and Avg. Disk sec/Write.

The Avg. Disk Bytes/Read or Write counter measures the average number of bytes transferred to or from the disk per each read or write activity. The Avg. Disk sec/Read or Write counter shows the average number of seconds it takes to perform the disk read or write activity. If the disk write activity is much more frequent than read activity and the users report delays in their work, consider using disk mirroring or duplexing instead of stripe sets with parity or RAID-5 volumes. Table 14-2 shows how to use several important objects and counters for disk monitoring.

Table 14-2 Using Objects and Counters to Monitor Disk Performance

Object: Counter	Explanation
LogicalDisk: % Disk Time	Measures the percentage of time that a disk is busy with Read or Write requests. If this level is sustained at 80% or greater, redistribute files to spread the load across multiple logical drives. Also check the corresponding PhysicalDisk counter.
LogicalDisk: Avg. Disk Bytes Read LogicalDisk: Avg. Disk Bytes Write	Used together, these provide a way to compare disk read to disk write activity, as a way to determine if you need to modify a currently established fault tolerance method or add disk spindles.
LogicalDisk: Avg. Disk Bytes/ Transfer	Measures the average number of bytes transferred between memory and disk during Read and Write operations. If the value is at or near 4 KB, this might mean excessive paging activity on that drive. A larger number indicates more efficient transfers than a smaller one, so watch for declines from the baseline as well.
LogicalDisk: Avg. Disk Queue Length LogicalDisk: Current Disk Queue Length	These objects/counters indicate how many system requests are waiting for disk access. If the queue length is greater than 2 for any logical drive, consider redistributing the load across multiple logical disks or, if this is not possible, upgrade the disk subsystem. Also check the corresponding PhysicalDisk counters. Monitor these counters with Avg. Disk Read Queue Length and Avg. Disk Write Queue Length for more detailed statistics.
PhysicalDisk: Avg. Disk Queue Length PhysicalDisk: Current Disk Queue Length	These objects/counters track activity per hard disk, but provide much of the same kind of information that the logical disk counters do. However, the problem threshold for physical disks is different than for logical ones. For physical disks, the threshold is between 1.5 and 2 times the number of spindles on the hard drive. For ordinary drives, this is the same as for logical disks. However, for RAID arrays, the number is equal to 1.5 to 2 times the number of drives in the array. Monitor these counters with Avg. Disk Read Queue Length and Avg. Disk Write Queue Length for more detailed statistics.
PhysicalDisk: % Disk Time	Measures the percentage of time that a hard drive is kept busy handling Read or Write requests. The sustained average should not exceed 90%, but even if sustained averages are high, this value is not worrisome unless the corresponding queue length numbers are in the danger zone as well.
PhysicalDisk: Avg. Disk Bytes Read PhysicalDisk: Avg. Disk Bytes Write	Used together, these provide a way to compare disk read to disk write activity, as a way to determine if you need to modify a currently established fault tolerance method or add disk spindles.
PhysicalDisk: Avg. Disk Bytes/ Transfer	Measures the average number of bytes transferred by Read or Write requests between the drive and memory. Here, smaller values are more worrisome than larger ones because they can indicate inefficient use of drives and drive space. If a small value is caused by inefficient applications, try increasing file sizes. If it is caused by paging activity, an increase in RAM is a good idea.
PhysicalDisk: Disk Bytes/sec	Tracks the number of bytes read from and written to disk each second. Use this object/counter combination to study the transfer rate of a disk to determine if you need to purchase a faster disk drive.

In this activity, you use the following disk counters to monitor disk performance: LogicalDisk: % Disk Time, PhysicalDisk: % Disk Time, LogicalDisk: Current Disk Queue Length, PhysicalDisk: Current Disk Queue Length, LogicalDisk: Disk Bytes/sec, and PhysicalDisk: Disk Bytes/sec.

Activity

1. Open Reliability and Performance Monitor, if necessary.

2. Delete any counters that are still running.

3. Click the **Add** button (green plus sign) in the button bar to open the Add Counters dialog box.

4. In the Add Counters dialog box, click the **+** plus sign for LogicalDisk to view its counters.

5. Click % Disk Time.

6. Hold down the Ctrl key and click Current Disk Queue Length and Disk Bytes/sec.

7. Leave **_Total** selected under Instances of selected object.

8. Click **Add >>**.

9. Scroll to and click the **+** plus sign for PhysicalDisk.

10. Click **% Disk Time**.

11. Hold down the **Ctrl** key and click **Current Disk Queue Length**, and **Disk Bytes/sec**.

12. Ensure that **_Total** is selected under Instances of selected object.

13. Click **Add >>**. Your selections should look similar to Figure 14-7.

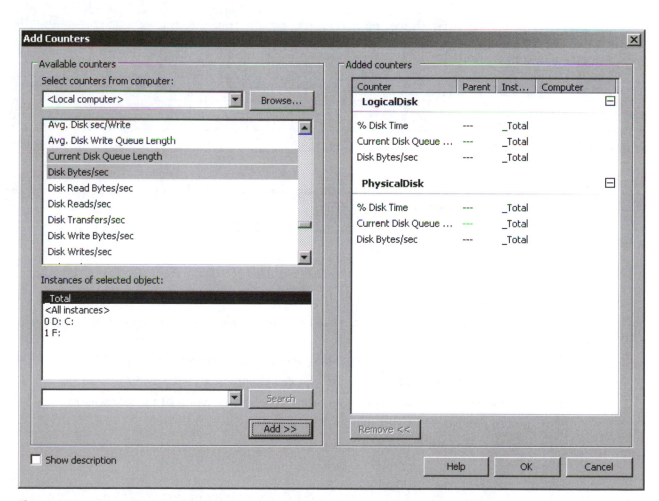

Figure 14-7   Add Counters dialog box

14. Click **OK** in the Add Counters dialog box.

15. Open and close four or five programs or selections from the Administrative Tools menu to see how your server responds (see Figure 14-8).

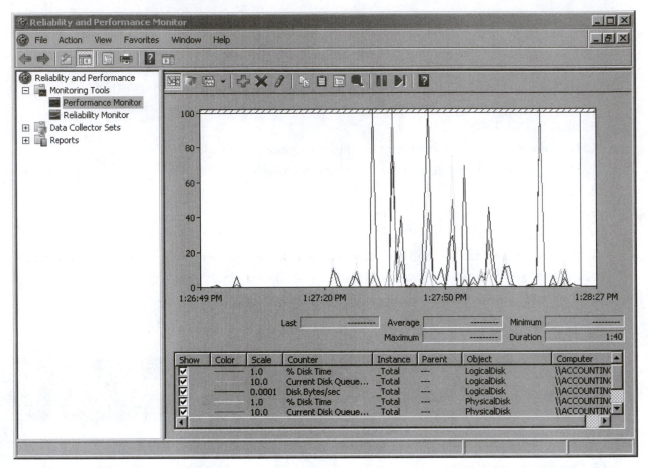

Figure 14-8   Monitoring disk activity

16. For practice, click the down arrow for the **Change graph type** button on the button bar in the right pane and click **Histogram bar**.

17. Monitor the disk activity for a few minutes and then delete all the counters you have started.

18. Close Reliability and Performance Monitor.

Review Questions

1. When using Performance Monitor, you can change from a line graph to a histogram bar graph by using the button bar's _____ button.

2. The LogicalDisk and PhysicalDisk Current Disk Queue Length counters show _____.

3. True or False? Disk monitoring cannot be used for disks configured as RAID-5.

4. The PhysicalDisk: Disk Bytes/sec counter can help you determine which of the following?

   a. If you need to purchase a faster disk drive.

   b. If you need to rewind the spindles on a disk drive.

   c. If the disk read speed is faster than the disk write speed.

   d. If the disk controller handles data faster than the physical hard disk.

5. Typically, you would use the _____ object to monitor a striped volume consisting of a set of disks.

MANAGING SYSTEM RELIABILITY AND AVAILABILITY

Labs included in this chapter:

- Lab 15.1 Use the Enable Boot Logging Option
- Lab 15.2 Change the DSRM Password and Access DSRM
- Lab 15.3 Configure Shadow Copies
- Lab 15.4 Use Network and Sharing Center to Diagnose a Connection Problem

Microsoft MCITP Exam #70-646 Objectives

Objective	Lab
Planning for Server Deployment	15.3
Planning for Business Continuity and High Availability	15.1, 15.2, 15.3, 15.4

Lab 15.1 Use the Enable Boot Logging Option

Objectives

- Boot using the Enable Boot Logging option
- Determine which system and driver files are loaded when Windows Server 2008 boots

Materials Required

This lab requires the following:

- Windows Server 2008 Standard or Enterprise Edition with Active Directory installed

Estimated completion time: **20 minutes**

Activity Background

There are times when a server has trouble booting, such as when a device driver is corrupted or is not loading properly. This might happen when you try to reboot a server following a system crash or after installing some new hardware. When you reboot, the system starts booting, but then has trouble during the boot process. These troubles might include taking a long time to boot, displaying an error message, placing an error message in an event log, or crashing.

One critical file that may have problems is the hal.dll (hardware abstraction layer) file, which contains a set of program routines used to control different hardware elements in a computer, including the use of device registers, PCI bus functions, input/output ports, and multiple processors. Another critical file, ntoskrnl.exe, is the kernel image file for Windows Server 2008. If ntoskrnl.exe does not load, it could be as simple as a problem keyboard that can be fixed by attaching a different keyboard. Another possibility is a damaged hard drive. If the ntoskrnl.exe file is corrupted, you can replace it through restoring the system state files.

A first step in locating a boot problem is to identify which file is not loading properly when Windows Server 2008 boots. You can determine this by using the Enable Boot Logging option on the Advanced Boot Options menu. The Advanced Boot Options menu is accessed by quickly pressing F8 when you first turn on the server and just after the BIOS activities and power-on self test complete. The Enable Boot Logging option creates the ntbtlog.txt file, which is a text file that shows the boot files and device drivers that are loaded when Windows Server 2008 is booted. The boot process loads many driver files, any one of which can result in boot problems. If there is a problem with a file, the log records a message such as "Did not load driver\SystemRoot\System32\Drivers*filename*."

For this activity, you boot into the Advanced Boot Options menu and use the Enable Boot Logging option to create the ntbtlog.txt file. After the computer boots, you examine the ntbtlog.txt file to determine whether any device driver files did not load.

For all the activities in this chapter, you'll need to log on to an account with Administrator privileges. Additionally, most of these activities can be completed on a virtual server or computer, such as in Hyper-V.

Throughout the activities in this book, you may occasionally see the User Account Control box with a message that Windows needs your permission to continue. Whenever you see this box, click Continue. Keep this in mind for all the activities because any interaction with the User Account Control box is not included in the steps.

Activity

1. Ensure all users are logged off Windows Server 2008.

2. Shut down and reboot the computer (click **Start**, point to the **right-pointing arrow** at the bottom of the Start menu, click **Restart**, select the appropriate option in the Shut Down Windows dialog box, and click **OK**; or shut down the server, turn off the power, and reboot).

3. Press **F8** just after the BIOS activities and power-on self test (POST) complete after the computer turns on. You may need to press F8 several times, depending on your computer. Also, on some computers and in virtual machines, the BIOS activities and POST occur very quickly, which means you need to press F8 immediately after the computer or virtual machine is restarted.

4. In the Advanced Boot Options menu, use the down arrow to highlight **Enable Boot Logging**. Press **Enter**.

5. Wait for the server to boot normally.

6. Log on to Windows Server 2008.

7. Click **Start** and click **Computer**.

8. Browse to the **Windows** folder.

9. Double-click the **Windows** folder to open it.

10. Scroll to find the **ntbtlog** file (or ntbtlog.txt file depending on your folder display settings) and double-click the file to open it into Notepad (or WordPad, if your server is configured to use WordPad for .txt files) as shown in Figure 15-1.

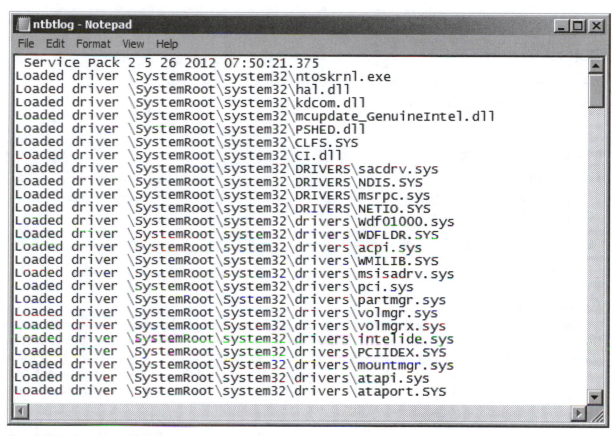

```
ntbtlog - Notepad

File   Edit   Format   View   Help
 Service Pack 2 5 26 2012 07:50:21.375
Loaded driver \SystemRoot\system32\ntoskrnl.exe
Loaded driver \SystemRoot\system32\hal.dll
Loaded driver \SystemRoot\system32\kdcom.dll
Loaded driver \SystemRoot\system32\mcupdate_GenuineIntel.dll
Loaded driver \SystemRoot\system32\PSHED.dll
Loaded driver \SystemRoot\system32\CLFS.SYS
Loaded driver \SystemRoot\system32\CI.dll
Loaded driver \SystemRoot\system32\DRIVERS\sacdrv.sys
Loaded driver \SystemRoot\system32\DRIVERS\NDIS.SYS
Loaded driver \SystemRoot\system32\DRIVERS\msrpc.sys
Loaded driver \SystemRoot\system32\DRIVERS\NETIO.SYS
Loaded driver \SystemRoot\system32\drivers\wdf01000.sys
Loaded driver \SystemRoot\system32\drivers\WDFLDR.SYS
Loaded driver \SystemRoot\system32\drivers\acpi.sys
Loaded driver \SystemRoot\system32\drivers\WMILIB.SYS
Loaded driver \SystemRoot\system32\drivers\msisadrv.sys
Loaded driver \SystemRoot\system32\drivers\pci.sys
Loaded driver \SystemRoot\System32\drivers\partmgr.sys
Loaded driver \SystemRoot\system32\drivers\volmgr.sys
Loaded driver \SystemRoot\System32\drivers\volmgrx.sys
Loaded driver \SystemRoot\system32\drivers\intelide.sys
Loaded driver \SystemRoot\system32\drivers\PCIIDEX.SYS
Loaded driver \SystemRoot\System32\drivers\mountmgr.sys
Loaded driver \SystemRoot\system32\drivers\atapi.sys
Loaded driver \SystemRoot\system32\drivers\ataport.SYS
```

Figure 15-1   ntbtlog file contents

11. Note that ntoskrnl.exe and hal.dll are listed as loading first. (If you are using a virtual machine, you may see the ntkmlpa.exe file instead.)

12. Scroll through the list to determine if any drivers did not load. Sometimes drivers do not load but are also not needed for the computer to run normally, so you may have to do some research about why a specific driver does not load. A good practice is to create and print the ntbtlog.txt file when you first successfully install a server and also create and print the file after you install new software. Sometimes the installation of new software can cause problems with an existing driver, so if you have a before and after printout of drivers that are loaded when the server boots, you can determine which driver is causing a problem.

13. Close the ntbtlog - Notepad window.

Review Questions

1. The ntoskrnl.exe file is the _____ file for Windows Server 2008.

2. To access the Advanced Boot Options menu, press _____ after the server turns on and the BIOS activities and POST are completed.

3. Which of the following is the log file created by the Enable Boot Logging option for booting a server?

   a. sys.log

   b. security.log

   c. boot.txt

   d. ntbtlog.txt

4. True or False? One of the files loaded early in the boot process of Windows Server 2008 is the hal.dll file, which contains program routines used to control specific hardware elements.

5. Many of the files that are loaded when Windows Server 2008 boots are _____ files.

Lab 15.2 Change the DSRM Password and Access DSRM

Objectives

- Use ntdsutil to change the Directory Services Restore Mode password
- Boot into the Directory Services Restore Mode

Materials Required

This lab requires the following:

- Windows Server 2008 Standard or Enterprise Edition with the Active Directory Domain Services role installed

Estimated completion time: **20 minutes**

Activity Background

If there is a problem with Active Directory Domain Services (AD DS), you have the option to restore it using the Directory Services Restore Mode (or DSRM) option on the Advanced Boot Options menu. To access DSRM, you must provide the same password for working on AD DS as you entered when you installed this role. For some administrators, it may be months or even years since they created the password and they have no record of it. There is nothing as frustrating as requiring immediate access to an important server or program function, but to be thwarted at the start because you don't remember the password.

Fortunately, there is a way to reset the password before accessing the DSRM option. You can reset the password by using the ntdsutil command from the Command Prompt window. The ntdsutil command offers maintenance tools for Active Directory. In Windows Server 2008 and Windows Server 2008 R2, ntdsutil is installed when you install the AD DS or the Active Directory Lightweight Directory Services (AD LDS) role. ntdsutil is used to:

- Perform authoritative restores to restore specific AD DS/LDS objects
- Configure AD DS/LDS
- Manage the AD DS/LDS database files
- Evaluate security IDs for users and groups
- Perform many other tasks including resetting the DSRM password

You can run ntdsutil only by using administrator privileges. Also, be sure you fully understand any ntdsutil command before you use it, because a mistake with this tool can alter AD DS/LDS and result in the need to restore the entire AD DS/LDS server role and database.

In this activity, you change the DSRM password and then you access the DSRM safe mode for practice without performing an actual restore. Ensure that you are using a domain controller for the activity.

Activity

1. Click **Start**, point to **All Programs**, click **Accessories**, right-click **Command Prompt**, and click **Run as administrator**.

2. At the command prompt, type **ntdsutil** and press **Enter**.

3. At the ntdsutil: command prompt type **set dsrm password** and press **Enter**.

4. At the Reset DSRM Administrator Password: prompt type **reset password on server null** and press **Enter**.

5. Type your new password and press **Enter** (you must follow the default domain account password policy requirements for password complexity, such as using a password over 8 characters that contains small and capital letters, numbers, and characters such as & or %).

6. Retype the new password to confirm it and press **Enter**.

7. Type **quit** at the Reset DSRM Administrator Password: prompt and press **Enter**.

8. Type **quit** at the ntdsutil: prompt and press **Enter** (see Figure 15-2).

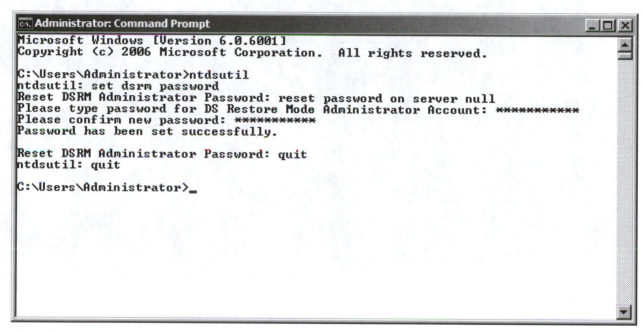

Figure 15-2   Resetting the DSRM password

9. Close the Command Prompt window.

10. Save any work and make sure there are no users connected to the server.

11. Shut down and reboot the server.

12. Press **F8** just after the BIOS activities and POST complete.

13. On the Advanced Boot Options menu, select **Directory Services Restore Mode** and press **Enter**.

14. You'll see the list of drivers loading and then the system will display a message that it is checking the system files.

15. Press **CTRL + ALT + DELETE** to log on.

16. Enter **administrator** for the account name and enter the new DSRM password that you configured.

17. Windows Server 2008 enters the safe mode for DSRM (see Figure 15-3). In this mode you can perform a directory restore.

18. Restart Windows Server 2008 and log on normally.

Figure 15-3 Safe mode for DSRM

Review Questions

1. True or False? The ntdsutil tool is installed when either of the AD DS or AD LDS roles is installed.

2. Which of the following are capabilities of ntdsutil? (Choose all that apply.)

   a. Evaluates security IDs for groups

   b. Manages AD DS database files

   c. Configures AD DS

   d. Performs an authoritative restore

3. DSRM is accessed from the _____ menu.

4. A DSRM password must follow the domain account password policy requirements for _____.

5. ntdsutil is used from the _____ window.

Lab 15.3 Configure Shadow Copies

Objectives

- Enable shadow copies on a volume
- Create a schedule for automated shadow copies

Materials Required

This lab requires the following:

- Windows Server 2008 Standard or Enterprise Edition with file sharing enabled

Estimated completion time: **15 minutes**

Activity Background

An effective way to provide system availability is to enable shadow copies on a server that is used to make shared folders available to users. A shadow copy ensures availability by providing the following:

- Ability to quickly restore a shared folder containing files that have been deleted
- Option to go back to a previous version of a file or to multiple earlier versions of that file
- Ability to manually or automatically save shared folders and files
- Option to save shared folders and files on a regular schedule

Shadow copies enable you to restore a shared folder without having to load special media or use special file restore software. The process is timely and convenient. Any organization that makes shared folders and files available should plan to implement shadow copies. However, it should be remembered that shadow copies are not a replacement for regular Windows Server 2008 backups and should not be considered as formal document versioning software. Shadow copies are meant to supplement these functions and can in some situations offer the best or even only way to recover the contents of a shared file after changes have been made or the file has been deleted.

For this activity, you enable shadow copies and configure a schedule for shadow copies.

Activity

1. Click **Start**, point to **Administrative Tools**, and click **Computer Management**. (You can also configure shadow copies using the Share and Storage Management tool which is an MMC snap-in or can be started from the Administrative Tools menu).

2. In the left pane in the tree, right-click **Shared Folders**, point to **All Tasks**, and click **Configure Shadow Copies**.

3. Click the volume, if necessary, on which to enable shadow copies, such as C:\. (Note that if you use the same volume that holds the system files, you cannot use the revert option to restore shared folders. To use shadow copies, the volume you select for shared folders and shadow copies should not contain the system files. However, if the server you are using for practice has only one volume, such as C:\, you can use it for this activity to learn about configuring shadow files.)

4. Click the **Enable** button (see Figure 15-4).

5. If you see the Enable Shadow Copies dialog box, click **Yes**.

6. Click the **Settings** button in the Shadow Copies dialog box.

7. In the Settings dialog box, note that you can configure the maximum amount of space that shadow copies can occupy on the volume. Also, note that there must be at least 300 MB of space allocated for shadow copies. Ensure that **Use limit** is selected and enter **310 MB**. Click the **Schedule** button.

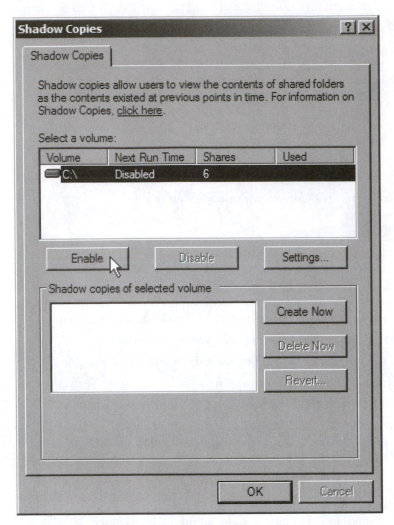

Figure 15-4 Enabling shadow copies

8. In the *drive*:\ dialog box, click the down arrow for Schedule Task and note that you can schedule shadow copies to occur:

- Daily
- Weekly
- Monthly
- Once
- At System Startup
- At Logon
- When idle

Click **Daily**.

9. Set the Start time at **6:00 PM**.

10. Set Schedule Task Daily to Every **4** days (see Figure 15-5).

11. Click **OK** in the *drive*:\ dialog box.

12. Click **OK** in the Settings dialog box.

13. In the Shadow Copies dialog box, click **Create Now** to create a shadow copy. Wait a few moments and note that a shadow copy is created and listed by date and time under Shadow copies of selected volume.

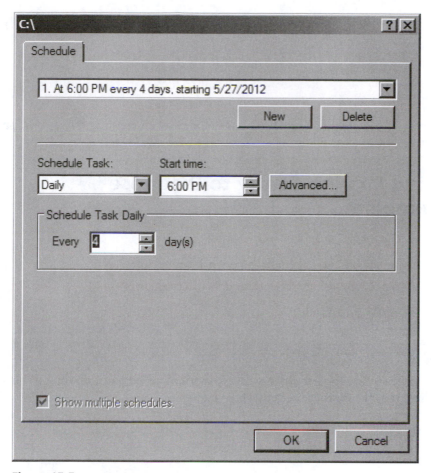

Figure 15-5   Configuring the shadow copies schedule

14. Click **OK** in the Shadow Copies dialog box.

15. Close the Computer Management window.

Review Questions

1. What is the minimum amount of disk space needed for shadow copies?

   a. 1 GB

   b. 750 MB

   c. 500 MB

   d. 300 MB

2. True or False? The volume containing system files is the one most recommended by Microsoft for shadow copies.

3. Which of the following tools can be used to configure shadow copies? (Choose all that apply.)

   a. Computer Management

   b. Group Policy Management

   c. Component Services

   d. Share and Storage Management

4. You can configure shadow copies to be made at which of the following intervals? (Choose all that apply.)

a. Hourly

b. Daily

c. Weekly

d. Monthly

5. True or False? Using shadow copies enables a company to save money by eliminating the need to purchase document versioning software.

Lab 15.4 Use Network and Sharing Center to Diagnose a Connection Problem

Objectives

- Use Network and Sharing Center to disable and enable a network connection
- Diagnose a network connection problem using Network and Sharing Center

Materials Required

This lab requires the following:

- Windows Server 2008 Standard or Enterprise Edition with Network included as an option on the Start menu (as is typically the default in the taskbar properties)

Estimated completion time: **15 minutes**

Activity Background

Network and Sharing Center provides a solid place to start when you are diagnosing a network connection problem at a server or need to disconnect a server from the network for maintenance. Network and Sharing Center is a one-stop network management tool for the following tasks:

- Verifying a network connection
- Viewing computers and devices connected to the network
- Setting up a new network connection
- Managing a network connection
- Diagnosing and repairing a network connection
- Enabling network discovery, file sharing, public folder sharing, and printer sharing

By offering these capabilities all in one place, Network and Sharing Center is often the fastest way to diagnose a network connection problem in Windows Server 2008. Microsoft offers a comprehensive network connection troubleshooting guide based on Network and Sharing Center, which you can access at *technet.microsoft.com/ en-us/library/cc732068(WS.10).aspx*.

In this activity, you use Network and Sharing Center to verify a server's network connection, disable the connection, enable the connection, and diagnose a network connection problem.

Activity

1. Click **Start** and click **Network**.

2. Click **Network and Sharing Center** in the Network window.

3. In the Network and Sharing Center window, view the simple network map to verify that the computer is connected to the network (and the Internet, if applicable).

4. Click **Manage network connections** on the left side of the window.

5. In the Network Connections window, right-click the network connection, such as *Local Area Connection*, and click **Status**.

6. In the Status dialog box, verify that the Media State is Enabled.

7. Ensure there are no users connected to the server (use Task Manager as in Lab 14.1) and then click the **Disable** button in the Status dialog box.

8. In the Network Connections window, the connection is shown as Disabled. Right-click the network connection and click **Diagnose** (see Figure 15-6).

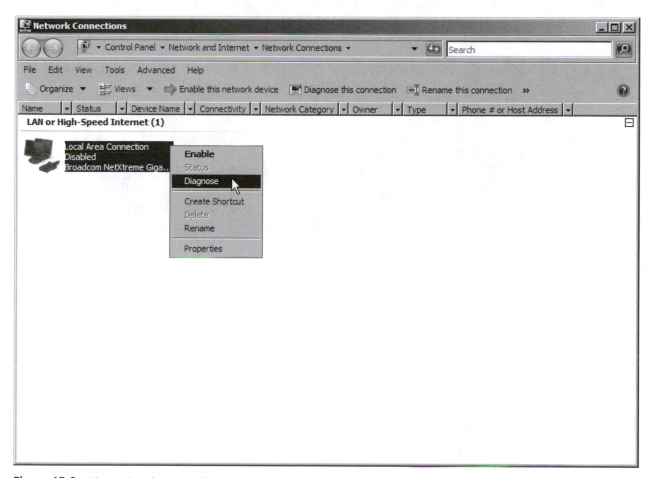

Figure 15-6   Diagnosing the network connection

9. You'll see the Windows Network Diagnostics dialog box, which reports that the connection is disabled (see Figure 15-7). Click **Cancel**.

10. In the Network Connections window, right-click the network connection and click **Enable.**

11. Close the Network Connections dialog box.

12. If you are working in a virtual server environment or using an internal wireless NIC, skip to Step 18.

13. Unplug your network connection, such as the network cable, or safely remove an external wireless network adapter. Note that the simple network map in the Network and Sharing Center window shows a red X to signify the computer is not connected to a network.

14. Click **Diagnose and repair** in the Network and Sharing Center window.

15. Note that the Windows Network Diagnostics dialog box reports that the connection is unplugged (for a cabled connection; see Figure 15-8). Click **Cancel**.

16. Plug in or reattach the network connection.

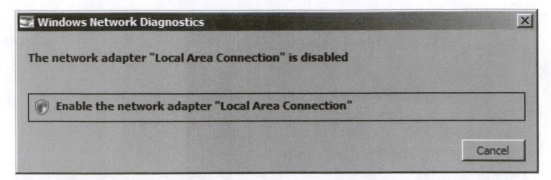

Figure 15-7   Windows Network Diagnostics dialog box

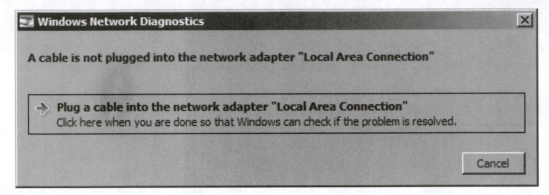

Figure 15-8   Unplugged network connection

17. Wait a few minutes and verify the network connection in the Network and Sharing Center window. If the connection information does not change, click **Diagnose and repair** and then click **Cancel** in the Windows Network Diagnostics dialog box.

18. Close the Network and Sharing Center window.

19. Close the Network window.

Review Questions

1. True or False? A limitation of Network and Sharing Center is that it does not offer a way to set up a new network connection.

2. Your company's server is not accessible to users. When you open Network and Sharing Center to determine the problem, you can use the _____ option to display an analysis of the problem in the Windows Network Diagnostics dialog box.

3. True or False? The Status dialog box can be accessed through the Network Connections window to verify a network connection.

4. Network and Sharing Center provides information about which of the following? (Choose all that apply.)

   a. Number of routers on the network

   b. Whether file sharing is enabled

   c. The status of network discovery

   d. Number of hops to the next server

5. Network and Sharing Center can be opened from the _____ window.

Index

A

activation, of server, 21–24
Active Directory
    audit policy, configuring, 51–54
    management tools, 45–50
    objects, 42–45
Active Directory Certificate Services (ADCS)
    role, 121–124, 127
Active Directory Domain Services (AD DS), 204
Active Directory Domains and Trusts
    snap-in, 46, 47
Active Directory Lightweight Directory
    Services (AD LDS), 204
Active Directory Sites and Services snap-in,
    46, 47–48
Active Directory Users and Computers
    snap-in, 42–45, 55–56
Add or Remove Snap-ins window, 46–47
Add Role Services dialog box, 161–162
Address Resolution Protocol (ARP), 12
Administrative Tools menu, accessing, 7–10
ADSI Edit snap-in, 46, 48–49
Advanced Boot Options menu, 202–203
application pools, 118–120
Application Server role, 160
ASP.NET, 118
auditing
    Certificate Authority (CA), 124–126
    configuring audit policy, 51–54

B

Background Intelligent Transfer Service, 28
backups
    performance optimization, 98–100
    scheduling, 98–100
    volume snapshots, 152
Boot tab, System Configuration tool, 25
booting, Enable Boot Logging option,
    202–204
Builtin folder, 42

C

CA server, 124–126
certificate revocation lists (CRLs), publication
    intervals, 127–128
certificate services, 124–126
Certification Authority tool, 124–126
Certification Authority Web Enrollment,
    121–124, 179–180
Cisco AAA server, 179–180
Cisco Network Admission Control, 179
clients, unhealthy, 179
Command Prompt window, 12–13
Computer Management tool, 8
configuration
    Active Directory audit policy, 51–54
    Hyper-V hardware, 144–147
    IPv6, 102–105
    Network Address Translation (NAT),
        130–132

network interface card (NIC), 36–39
network services, 109–111
RADIUS server, 136–140
Registry security, 176–178
remote access services, 129–142
shadow copies, 207–210
taskbar, 31–33
TS RemoteApp, 163–166
Windows Server 2008 services, 28–30
Conflict/Sharing information, 4
connection problems, 210–212
CPU resources, monitoring, 190, 191–193
Create Quota dialog box, 64–65

D

data exchange, 152
default domain security policies, 172–176
deployment planning
    configuring accessibility options, 18–21
    determining features to be installed, 16–18
    networking capabilities for, 5–7
    system information for, 2–5
device drivers, updates, 33–39
DHCP servers, 112–115
Diagnostic Service Host, 28
Directory Services Restore Mode (DSRM)
    booting into, 204–206
    changing password, 204–206
Disk Management tool, 93–96
disk performance, 197–200
disk properties, viewing, 90–93
disk quotas, 63–66
disk space, 90, 93, 147
disks
    add and edit virtual hard disk, 147–151
    rescan, 93–96
    shrinking, 93–96
Distributed File System (DFS), 60, 62
DNS forwarder, 106–109
DNS queries, 106
DNS root hint, 106–109
DNS round robin, 109–111
DNS servers, 106–111
DNS stub zone, 106–109
Domain Properties window, 47
domain security policies, 172–176
driver updates
    configuring, 33–36
    NIC, 37–39
drives, shared, 66–70
duplex mode, 36
Dynamic Host Configuration Protocol
    (DHCP) servers, 112–115

E

Ease of Access Center options, 18–21
Enable Boot Logging option, 202–204
Event Viewer window, 8
Extensible Authentication Protocol Service,
    29–30

F

features, determining for installation, 16–18
Fiber Channel, 96
file screening management, 63–66
File Server Resource Manager, 60–66
File Services role, installation, 60–63
file sharing, 11
file storage reports, 63–66
files
    offline, 168–170
    shared, 66–70
folders, shared, 66–70, 168–170
ForeignSecurityPrinciples folder, 44
fsmgmt.msc command, 67
full duplex mode, 36

G

getmac utility, 12–13
group policies, 172
Group Policy Management Editor window,
    51–52
Group Policy Management snap-in, 46,
    49–50, 172–176

H

hal.dll file, 202
half duplex mode, 36
Health Registration Authority (HRA)
    configure network policy, 183–186
    installation, 178–183
heartbeat, 152
Host Credential Authorization Protocol
    (HCAP), 178–183
Hyper-V management
    configuring, 144–147
    managing settings, 151–154
    shutdown options, 152–153
    take snapshot of virtual machine,
        155–157
Hypertext Transfer Protocol Secure
    (HTTPS), 140

I

IIS application pools, 118–120
IIS Web Services, 118
Initial Configuration Tasks tool, 16–18
installation
    Certification Authority Web Enrollment,
        121–124
    File Services role, 60–63
    LPR Port Monitor, 76–78
    shared printer, 79–81
    Storage Manager for SANs, 96–98
    Subsystem for UNIX-based Applications,
        71–74
    troubleshooting, 24–26
    of updates, 21–24
    WAS Support role service, 160–163
    Windows Server 2008, 15–26

integration services, 152, 153
Internet Assigned Numbers Authority
     (IANA), 106
Internet Information Services (IIS) Manager, 119
Internet root servers, 106
Internet Small Computer System Interface
     (iSCSI), 96
ipconfig utility, 12–13
IPv4, 102
IPv6, configuring, 102–105

K

known state, Hyper-V startup and shutdown
     options, 152

L

Line Printer Daemon (LPD), 76
Linux operating system, 71
load balancing, 109–110
logical unit numbers (LUNs), 96
LogicalDisk, 197–200
LPR Port Monitor, 76–78

M

MAC address, obtaining, 12–14
Magnifier dialog box, Ease of Access Center,
     19–20
memory resources, monitoring, 190–197
Microsoft SDK for UNIX-based Applications,
     71–74
monitoring
     disk performance, 197–200
     Performance Monitor, 194–200
     Resource Monitor, 191–193
     server, using Task Manager, 188–191

N

Narrator dialog box, Ease of Access
     Center, 20
.NET Framework 3.0, 16
netmask ordering, 109–111
network activity, monitoring, 190, 191–193
Network Address Translation (NAT),
     130–132
Network and Sharing Center, 10–11, 210–212
network connection problems, 210–212
network discovery, turning on, 10–11
network interface card (NIC)
     configuring, 36–39
     MAC address of, 12
network interfaces, 12
network policy, 183–186
Network Policy Server (NPS), 136, 179–180
network services
     configuring, 109–111
     configuring IPv6, 102–105
     DHCP servers, 112–115
     DNS servers, 106–109
networking capabilities, 5–7, 10
New Object – Computer dialog box, add a
     computer to a domain, 44
New Printer Filter Wizard, 82–83
New Virtual Hard Disk Wizard, 147–151
NIC Properties dialog box, 37
ntbtlog file, 203
ntoskrnl.exe file, 202

O

objects, Active Directory, 42–45
offline files, 168–170
Online Responder Service, 127
On-Screen Keyboard, Ease of Access
     Center, 20
operating system shutdown, 152

P

paging file use, monitoring, 194–197
passwords
     Directory Services Restore Mode
          (DSRM), 204–206
     resetting, 54, 55–56
Performance Monitor
     evaluating disk performance,
          197–200
     evaluating paging file and memory
          performance, 194–197
permissions, configuring, 176–178
PhysicalDisk, 197–200
Print Management tool, 77–84
print queues, 82–84
Print Spooler service, 85–87
printer sharing, 11
printers
     create printer filter, 82–84
     installing shared printer, 79–81
     installing UNIX/Linux printing
          capability, 76–78
     troubleshooting print spooler, 85–87
processes, monitoring, 189, 191–193
Programs and Features tool, 34, 35
Properties dialog box, 90

Q

Quick Launch toolbar, 32
quota template, 63–64

R

RADIUS client, configuring, 136–140
RADIUS server, 136–140
RAID-5 disks, 197–198
Registry security, 176–178
Remote Access Auto Connection
     Manager, 134
remote access services
     configuring, 129–142
     configuring RADIUS server, 136–140
     Network Address Translation (NAT),
          130–132
     terminal services, 140–142
     troubleshooting VPN server, 132–135
     TS RemoteApp, 163–166
Remote Authentication Dial-In User Service
     (RADIUS) server, 136–140
Remote Procedure Call (RPC), 86
RemoteApp, 140
     configuring, 163–166
     configuring programs that can run on,
          166–168
rescanning disks, 93–96
Resource Monitor, 191–193
role services, 60, 61, 121–124, 140–142
root hints, 106–109
root key security settings, 176–178

S

Secure Sockets Layer (SSL), 140
security
     Health Registration Authority,
          178–186
     Host Credential Authorization, 178–183
     Registry, 176–178
security groups, 43–45, 54, 55
security policies, default domain, configuring,
     172–176
Select Features window, 17
Server Manager, 9
server monitoring
     Resource Monitor, 191–193
     using Task Manager, 188–191
server roles, 16
services
     configuration, 28–30
     monitoring, 189–190
shadow copies, 207–210
shared folders, 168–170
Shared Folders snap-in, 66–70
shared printer, 79–81
shrinking disks, 93–96
snapshots, of virtual machine, 155–157
spoofing, 130
Start menu, customizing, 31–33
Statement of Health (SoH), 179
Storage Area Network (SAN), 96–98
Storage Manager for SANs, 96–98
stub zones, 106–109
Subsystem for UNIX-based Applications,
     71–74
system availability, 207–210
System Configuration tool, 24–26
     General tab, 25
     Services tab, 25
     Startup tab, 26
     Tools tab, 26
System Information tool, 2–5, 24–26
System Properties dialog box, 34
system reliability, 201–212
System window, 22

T

Task Manager, server monitoring using,
     188–191
taskbar, configuration, 31–33
Taskbar and Start Menu Properties dialog
     box, 32
terminal server, 163–168
terminal services, 140–142
thin clients, 163
time synchronization, 152
troubleshooting
     connection problems, 210–212
     DHCP servers, 112–115
     DNS servers, 109–111
     installation, 24–26
     print spooler, 85–87
     VPN servers, 132–135
TS Gateway role service, 140–142
TS RemoteApp, 140
     configuring, 163–166
     configuring programs that can run on,
          166–168
TS Web Access role service, 140–142, 163

U

unhealthy clients, 179
uninstall programs, 34, 35
UNIX-based applications, 71–74
UNIX/Linux printing, 76–78
updates
    checking for installed, 34–36
    driver, 33–36
    installing, 21–24
User Account Control box, 2, 28
user accounts
    creating, 55
    managing security issues,
        54–57
    resetting passwords, 54, 55–56
    unlocking, 54, 55
Users folder, 42, 44

V

virtualization
    add and edit virtual hard disk, 147–151
    configure virtual machine hardware,
        144–147
    manage Hyper-V settings, 151–154
    take a snapshot of a virtual machine,
        155–157
volume snapshots, 152
VPN servers, 132–135

W

Web enrollment pages, 121–124
Windows Help and Support window, 5–6
Windows Process Activation Service (WAS),
    118
Windows Process Activation Service (WAS)
    Support role service, 160–163
Windows Search Service, 60–63
Windows Server 2008
    activating, 21–24
    configuration, 27–39
    Ease of Access options, configuring, 18–21
    installation, 15–26
    network services, 101–115
    networking capabilities, 5–7
    printer configuration, 75–88
    security, 171–186
    services, 28–30
    updating, 21–24
    virtualization, 143–157
Windows Server Backup tool, 98–100
Windows Update, 22–24, 33–36